SHOTGUNS *and* STAGECOACHES

SHOTGUNS *and* STAGECOACHES

The Brave Men Who Rode for
Wells Fargo in the Wild West

JOHN BOESSENECKER

THOMAS DUNNE BOOKS
St. Martin's Press
New York

Library of Congress Cataloging-in-Publication Data

Names: Boessenecker, John, 1953– author
Title: Shotguns and stagecoaches : the brave men who rode for Wells Fargo in the Wild West /
  John Boessenecker.
Other titles: Brave men who rode for Wells Fargo in the Wild West
Description: New York : Thomas Dunne Books ; St. Martin's Press, [2018] | Includes
  bibliographical references and index.
Identifiers: LCCN 2018019773| ISBN 9781250184887 (hardcover) | ISBN 9781250184900 (ebook)
Subjects: LCSH: Wells, Fargo & Company—Employees—Biography. | Stagecoaches—West
  (U.S.)—History. | Coaching (Transportation)—West (U.S.)—History. | Stagecoach robberies—
  West (U.S.)—History—19th century. | West (U.S.)—Biography.
Classification: LCC HE5903.W5 B64 2018 | DDC 388.3/41092278—dc23
LC record available at https://lccn.loc.gov/2018019773

For Dr. Robert J. Chandler,
historian extraordinaire

CONTENTS

INTRODUCTION

In all of recorded history, mankind has needed to transfer money and goods from one place to another. The enduring difficulty has been finding a safe way to do it. From marauding brigands attacking desert caravans, to pirates on the high seas, to robbers of Wells Fargo stagecoaches, and to modern hackers stealing identities on the Internet, security has remained one of our greatest challenges. For the simple truth is this: As soon as someone gets legitimate wealth, there is always a crook figuring out how to steal it. And with every new secure method to transfer money, criminals are quick to catch up.

This book focuses on a time in American history when the safety and security in the eastern states was not enjoyed by those living in the wild lands of the West. How to connect the civilization of the East Coast to the rugged frontier, how to cement continental commerce, and how to form a bicoastal nation were mammoth tests for American enterprise. This challenge could not have been met without the efforts of Wells Fargo & Company's Express. And Wells Fargo's mission would not have been possible without the valiant shotgun messengers and detectives who protected its treasure, its stagecoaches, and its railroad express cars.

Wells Fargo sprang to life during the California Gold Rush and came to the forefront of every successive American frontier that followed. As soon as a new mining camp or cattle town burst forth, Wells Fargo was there. The company provided both express and banking services, taking in gold and silver and shipping it out of the mining regions. Wells Fargo followed the money, and robbers followed Wells Fargo. The connection between commerce and crime was never more evident than in the story of Wells Fargo. America's frontier regions were violent and lawless in the extreme; study after modern study has shown that to be true. As a result, Wells Fargo and the Wild West became synonymous.

To this day, the name Wells Fargo conjures up vivid images of brave shotgun guards riding atop Concord stagecoaches, battling highway robbers and mounted Indian warriors. It also brings to mind the Broadway musical and 1962 film *The Music Man*, and the unforgettable lyric, "O-ho, the Wells Fargo wagon is a-comin' down the street / Oh please let it be for me!" In a few brief scenes, the iconic Wells Fargo wagon, a familiar sight to generations of Americans, came back to life. From 1852 to 1918, Wells Fargo & Company's Express was an integral part of American society. It was the perfect equivalent of today's Federal Express: Wells Fargo delivered packages to customers throughout the country and was faster and safer than the U.S. mail. The company's agents, messengers, helpers, drivers, and porters lifted, loaded, hauled, and shipped everything from small money packages to crates of fruit, poultry, merchandise, and machinery to destinations near and far. When merchants hung "call cards" in shop windows, Wells Fargo messengers, with their ubiquitous blue caps and black sleeve garters, stopped by in horse-drawn wagons to pick up packages for shipping. Of course, there was nothing dramatic or exciting about that. Ninety-nine percent of Wells Fargo's express service was the routine delivery work so artfully re-created in *The Music Man*.

It was that other 1 percent that made Wells Fargo stand out from every business enterprise in American history: the company's relentless battle against thieves, highwaymen, and train robbers. Wells Fargo hired tough men who were good with guns to protect its express shipments; it employed crack detectives to unravel robberies and track down bandits. Some of the fabled characters of the Old West acted as Wells Fargo messengers, guards, or special officers: Wyatt and Morgan Earp, Bob Paul, Jeff Milton, Jim Hume, Fred Dodge, Harry Morse, and even the poet Bret Harte. But the stories of most of the company's expressmen have been long lost in the shadows of the past. Since the 1930s, many volumes have been published about Wells Fargo, but no book has ever been written about its express guards and sleuths.[1] In the pages that follow are the true stories of twenty of the company's most valiant shotgun messengers and detectives of the Old West.

Wells Fargo's story began with the discovery of gold in the foothills of the Sierra Nevada in January 1848. The news did not reach the East Coast for ten months, and when it did, all hell broke loose. Gold fever swept America and then the world as one of mankind's greatest mass migrations erupted. The gold seekers were overwhelmingly young and male, far from the settling influences of home and family. Once in California's mining region—known as the Mother Lode—young men behaved in ways they would never have dreamed of in front of their mothers, sisters, and sweethearts. They drank, gambled, whored, and brawled. With little or no law enforcement, every man was responsible for his own safety. Thus forty-niners carried bowie knives and the newly invented Colt revolver. This mixture of testosterone, alcohol, and blue steel was a deadly brew, resulting in extremely high rates of violence. The pattern set in the gold camps of California, replete with saloons, gambling halls, brothels, weak police forces, and active vigilance committees, would be followed in every successive boom frontier for the rest of the century: from the Comstock Lode in Nevada, to the gold fields of Idaho, Montana, and Colorado, to the cattle towns of Kansas, to the silver camps of Arizona, and finally to the gold mines of the Klondike.

In New York, financiers Henry Wells and William G. Fargo, two of the owners of the American Express Company, recognized that huge profits could be made in California. Their principal competitor, Adams & Co. Express, began operating on the West Coast in 1849. On

March 18, 1852, they organized Wells Fargo & Company in New York, and three months later opened an office in San Francisco. Because local mail delivery was all but unknown during the Gold Rush, letters and shipments were carried by private express companies. Wells Fargo bought out these smaller concerns and rapidly expanded. By 1866, the company had 146 offices and carried express on four thousand miles of stagecoach lines. Ten years later, it had 438 offices throughout the West, operating on six thousand miles of stage lines and three thousand miles of railroad lines. As railroads expanded, so did Wells Fargo, which grew exponentially: 2,654 offices in 1890, 5,643 offices in 1910, and 10,000 offices throughout the United States in 1918. By that time, it was one of the country's largest business enterprises, with 35,000 employees. However, wartime emergency in 1918 resulted in the federal government's merging all express companies into a single entity, American Railway Express. Although Wells Fargo's lucrative banking business was unaffected, its colorful history as a pioneer express company abruptly ended.[2]

In the popular imagination, Wells Fargo is inextricably linked to stagecoaching. Although Wells Fargo owned and operated stage lines in various places in the West, it was an express company, not a transportation business. It carried letters, packages, and valuables, not passengers. For the most part, Wells Fargo paid local stage lines to carry its green strongboxes. However, in 1866, Wells Fargo began running overland stages, and it acquired ownership interests in numerous local stage lines. After the completion of the transcontinental railroad in 1869, Wells Fargo increasingly transported shipments aboard trains. During the 1870s, as railroads expanded throughout the West, Wells Fargo express cars, usually coupled behind the tender and in front of the baggage car, became a common sight.

Wells Fargo's first messengers, during the California Gold Rush, carried letters by horseback to and from the mining camps; soon they began transporting treasure from the mines on riverboats to San Francisco. They carried guns to ward off highway robbers. In the 1850s, if a stagecoach had a large shipment of gold on board, the local Wells

Fargo agent would guard the treasure. Wells Fargo agents, contrary to popular belief, were not secret agents or detectives. They were typically merchants who owned the Wells Fargo franchise for a town and operated a Wells Fargo office inside their general stores. Their principal duty was to send and receive letters and packages; Wells Fargo agents also acted as bankers by buying gold dust.

During the late 1850s, as stagecoach holdups became increasingly common in California, Wells Fargo authorized its local agents to hire armed guards, later called "shotgun messengers," to accompany treasure shipments. As early as September 1856, newspapers reported an armed Wells Fargo messenger aboard a stage in Shasta County. Years later, friends of Samuel P. Dorsey, Wells Fargo's agent in Grass Valley, claimed that he "introduced the famous shotgun messenger service" about 1857. Allen Kelly, a noted journalist, wrote in 1906 that the credit belonged to James Gannon, a San Francisco politician and police detective who acted as a Wells Fargo special officer in Nevada's Comstock Lode in 1865. However, in England as early as the 1780s, armed "mail guards" rode on stagecoaches, so the tradition had been established long before the Gold Rush. The term *shotgun messenger* did not come into

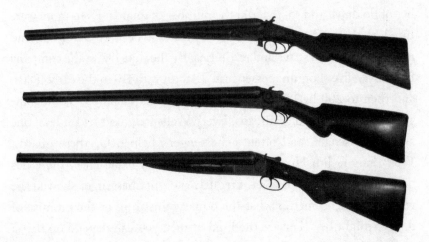

Wells Fargo shotguns changed little over the years. At top is a Parker, made in 1879; center is a Remington, made in 1893; at bottom an Ithaca, made in 1917. [*Author's collection*]

popular use in the West until the 1870s. Such terms as *shotgun rider* and *riding shotgun* were coined by twentieth-century fiction writers and were unknown in the Old West.[3]

Wells Fargo messengers on stagecoaches and trains carried sawed-off double-barreled shotguns, and occasionally a revolver. During the 1860s and early 1870s, the company's shotguns were muzzle-loading percussion guns, purchased by Wells Fargo from San Francisco firearms dealers. Percussion firearms were difficult to reload and became obsolete after the early 1870s as metallic cartridge firearms came on the market. In 1874, E. Remington & Sons began making affordable breech-loading shotguns. They were quickly loaded by snapping open the barrels and inserting a pair of brass shells filled with buckshot. Wells Fargo first used Remington shotguns, and then, in the 1880s, those of other makers, including Parker Brothers and L. C. Smith, all twelve-gauge double-barreled hammer guns. They were known as "messenger's guns" or "cut-off shotguns."[4]

Wells Fargo's shotgun messengers did not guard stages; they protected the company's express boxes. Most coaches did not carry shotgun messengers; a guard was on board only if there was a large express shipment of gold or coin. By 1861, Wells Fargo employed sixteen shotgun messengers. As Wells Fargo's business expanded, so did the number of holdups, and so, too, did the number of guards. Even more were hired as Wells Fargo expanded its operations beyond California and into other western states and territories. By the mid-1870s, the company had thirty-five shotgun messengers. That grew to 110 in the early 1880s, and then to 200 by 1885. By 1918, the company employed 3,000 shotgun guards, mostly on railroads. Every Wells Fargo car had at least one armed messenger, and often a messenger's helper. Of these guards, Wells Fargo's Jim Hume explained, "In all my experience, there has never been an occasion when a regular shotgun messenger showed the white feather no matter what the odds against him or the promise of danger might be. They are the kind of men you can depend on if you get in a fix, with the certainty that they will pull you through or stay by you to the last."[5]

Shotgun messengers on stages occasionally rode inside the coach with the passengers, but their usual seat was next to the driver, on his left. The driver, known as a "whip" or a "jehu"—the Biblical king of Israel famed as a charioteer—worked the reins, or ribbons, for four- and six-horse teams. The typical overland stage was pulled by six horses, consisting of three pairs of animals. The wheel horses, or "wheelers," were the largest and were hitched closest to the coach. Next were the center, or "swing," horses. In front were the leaders, the smallest horses. The animals on the driver's right were the "off" horses, those on his left the "near" horses. Each rein controlled one horse, and it took extraordinary skill to handle a six-horse rig. The driver used his whip not to flay the horses (which he counted as his closest friends), but instead to crack it in the air above the animals' heads to urge them forward. However, in case of emergency, such as a holdup, a driver might lay the lash down on his team.

The major stage lines used the ornate but rugged coaches made by the Abbot-Downing Company of Concord, New Hampshire. A Concord stagecoach could carry up to eighteen passengers, ten inside and eight on top, including the driver and the shotgun messenger. The front seat, also called the "driver's box," was located in the front boot, and just behind it was a front dickey seat, which faced forward and held three passengers. At the back of the stage, also on top, was the rear dickey seat, which faced backward. Behind the stage was a leather rear boot, which held luggage and mail. Concord coaches were drawn by six-horse teams and traveled night and day, with the teams changed every twelve to twenty miles at stage depots along the road. Many stagecoaches on the frontier were uncomfortable and inexpensive "mud wagons," built by local wagon makers and used on short stage routes. Only about one-fourth of all western stages were Concord coaches; the balance were mud wagons.[6]

Stage robbery, like horse and cattle theft, is a crime that has long been identified with Wells Fargo and the western frontier. In California, holdups of Concord coaches and mud wagons first occurred during the Gold Rush, especially in the Mother Lode country, where bandits preyed on shipments of gold from the mines. Stage holdups became increasingly frequent during the 1860s, and between 1870 and 1884, there were 347 actual and attempted robberies of Wells Fargo express shipments aboard stagecoaches, in which six guards and drivers were killed and ten wounded. One persistent myth, kept alive by repetition, insists that stage robberies all but vanished by 1890. The truth is that stagecoach holdups were almost as numerous during the late 1880s and the 1890s. Wells Fargo detective John N. Thacker reported that between 1886 and 1892 the express company was the victim of seventy-four stage robberies in California. Dozens of additional stage holdups took place later in the 1890s and in the early 1900s. The last holdup of a horse-drawn stage in the West took place near Jarbidge, Nevada, in 1916.[7]

Unlike the typical stage robbery portrayed in film and television, bandits did not gallop after the coach across open prairie, riding at breakneck speed and exchanging gunfire with the guard and the passengers. The method real highwaymen used was less dramatic and far more effective. The bandits, or road agents, would simply post themselves on a steep grade where the driver was forced to walk his team. While one robber stepped in front of the coach and seized the lead horses, a second would cover the driver and give the time-honored command "Throw down the box!"

Shootouts rarely occurred, for most coaches did not carry armed guards, and those passengers who carried firearms were often loath to risk their lives to save their own pocketbooks or Wells Fargo's treasure. But if the stagecoach carried a large bullion shipment or a payroll, a Wells Fargo guard was sure to be on board. The highwaymen who preyed on stages were a mixed bag of ex-convicts, loafers, professional thieves, and luckless miners and laborers. Some, like Charles E. Boles (better known as "Black Bart") and Bill Miner (depicted in the 1982 film *The Grey Fox*), had lengthy criminal careers and robbed stagecoaches as a vocation, rarely giving a thought to honest work. Their target was the Wells Fargo treasure box, built of pine, strapped with iron, and painted green. These were carried in the front boot, under the driver's seat. Beginning in the early 1860s, some coaches carried an iron box, known as a "pony safe" because of its small size, bolted to the floor under an inside passenger seat.

With the rapid growth of railroads throughout the West, bandits turned their attention to train robbery. The first western train holdup took place on the newly finished transcontinental railroad near Verdi, Nevada, in 1870. Nonetheless, train holdups in the far west were quite rare at first. Nevada saw two in 1870, California one in 1881 and another in 1888, Utah one in 1883, and New Mexico two in 1883 and 1884. During the late 1880s, train holdups became increasingly common and violent, reaching epidemic proportions in the 1890s. Between 1890 and 1903, there were 341 actual and attempted train robberies in the United States, which resulted in the killing of ninety-nine persons. And just as in the stagecoach era, Wells Fargo's shotgun messengers and detectives led the way in fighting the new terror.[8]

Their stories have been mostly lost in the dustbin of history. That is an injustice that must be corrected. This, then, is the saga of the fighting men who rode for Wells Fargo.

PART ONE

THE GOLD RUSH ERA

WELLS FARGO'S PIONEER MESSENGER

Pilsbury "Chips" Hodgkins

One spring evening in 1851, twenty-six-year-old "Chips" Hodgkins spurred his mule into the California gold-mining camp of Jacksonville. His appearance was much like that of any forty-niner: his dark, wavy hair set off by a full beard and covered by a slouch felt hat, finished off with a red miner's overshirt, canvas trousers, and knee-high boots. And his personality matched that of any other gold seeker: loud, funny, flamboyant, ever ready for a new adventure, but simultaneously kind and gentle. Like most men in the Mother Lode, he had not struck it rich. He gave up his miner's pick and gold pan to become an express rider, one of the first in the far west.

Jacksonville was like many towns in the Gold Rush: at least 98 percent male. Its 250 inhabitants lived in canvas tents and log cabins clustered in a deep canyon along the Tuolumne River. They were unwashed, were heavily whiskered, and longed for female company. Men would gather by the dozens, hats doffed in admiration and respect, just to catch sight of a woman. They would pay exorbitant prices to eat a meal prepared by anyone of the opposite sex. The miners spent their days in backbreaking work, digging along the river and shoveling sand and gravel into long wood sluice boxes in an effort to separate the tiny flakes of gold. Companies of miners exhausted themselves erecting dams and canals in efforts to change the Tuolumne River's course so that they could mine the dry streambed, but winter floods would inevitably wash away their labors. Far from their homes on the East Coast or in Europe, Australia, and South America, and starved for newspapers and letters from loved ones, they looked forward to the arrival of any mounted express messenger.

Chips's distinctive white mule, Polly, pulled up almost by habit at the town's sole restaurant. A small throng gathered as he hitched her to the front porch. His saddlebags held a fortune: two thousand troy ounces of gold nuggets, weighing about 137 pounds, plus something just as valuable: the latest newspapers from the East Coast. Dust-covered and exhausted after his long ride, Chips stepped inside for a hot meal. There he was the center of attention, for he was their link to the outside world. As was customary for an express rider, he had the camp's stagecoach hostler guard his horse and treasure. When he finished eating supper, he stepped outside and checked on his mount and his saddlebags. Two men—he later called them "notorious ruffians"—approached, and one said, "Hello, Chips. Where are you heading tonight?"

Hodgkins was too smart and too suspicious to fall for a ruse like that, so he replied, "Big Oak Flat." That was a remote mining camp atop nearby Priest Grade, which was, and still is, a steep, winding journey into the Sierra Nevada.

One of the outlaws remarked, "You have a big hill to climb."

"I guess I could do it," responded Chips. Then he mounted his horse and started on the trail that led to a ferry across the Tuolumne River to Priest Grade. As soon as he rounded the first bend, he spurred his animal up a side ravine and hid in the brush. A few minutes later, he heard the approaching clatter of horses' hooves, then the voices of the two men. One said, "Hurry on or we won't catch him before he crosses the river."

The second rider responded with an oath: "The odds are we'll catch him going up the hill."

The desperadoes rode on. Then Hodgkins mounted his horse and galloped to his actual destination, Sonora. An important mining center, the town got its name from the first Mexican gold hunters to settle there, and was widely known as the Queen of the Southern Mines. Chips later learned that the two highwaymen had ridden fifteen miles to Big Oak Flat, only to learn he was not there. Several days later, Chips ran into the pair in Sonora. They were with a group of men discussing business, mining, and travel. Hodgkins joined the discussion and at one point commented, "When I have any work to do I always start in and do the best I can."

At that, one of the would-be robbers grinned widely and said, "Yes, and you know your business too."[1]

The career of Chips Hodgkins *was* the early history of Wells Fargo. During the initial years of the California Gold Rush, he worked for its predecessors, and when those small local express firms were absorbed by Wells Fargo, he served the new company faithfully for decades. For forty years, from 1851 to 1891, Chips was the best-known express messenger on the West Coast, transporting tens of millions of dollars in gold, first by horseback, then by stagecoach, and finally by steamship and railroad. He was so scrupulously honest that it was commonly said of him, "No man in the United States ever actually handled more money than he did, but not a nickel of it ever stuck to his fingers."[2]

He was born Pilsbury Hodgkins in Nobleboro, Maine, on February 17, 1825. His parents died during his boyhood, and he was left in the charge of a tyrannical elder brother. At age sixteen, he ran away from home and became apprenticed to a Boston shipwright. Hodgkins was a rowdy youth, and he spent his spare time drinking, smoking, and carousing. One night, he had an epiphany, as he recalled: "I . . . resolved never to use tobacco or intoxicating liquors again." He kept that vow for the rest of his life. In 1848, Hodgkins was swindled out of his life's savings, and that winter news reached Boston of the discovery of gold in California. He could not afford the passage, but in the spring of 1849, he found a company of gold seekers who had bought a sailing vessel and were in need of a ship's carpenter. He worked his passage around Cape Horn to the West Coast. Because carpenters were always referred to as "Chips," he acquired his lifelong nickname.[3]

A circa 1880 reenactment depicting a Wells Fargo messenger like Chips Hodgkins during the California Gold Rush. [*Tom Martin collection*]

After a sea journey of five and a half months, his ship arrived in San Francisco on September 16, 1849. Chips spent his first two years in California digging for gold in what are now Tuolumne and Stanislaus counties, known as the Southern Mines. He lived in gold camps of log cabins and tents perched precariously on the steep slopes of ravines and rivers. Society was primitive and comforts few. Gold was the common currency; miners carried gold dust in small buckskin pouches called "pokes." Food and supplies were scarce and expensive. Women were even scarcer, and miners were forced, many for the first times in their lives, to perform all domestic chores for themselves—cooking, washing, sewing, and housekeeping. Even the names of the gold camps reflected the forty-niners' rough, masculine culture: Poker Flat, Drunkard's Bar, Whiskey Gulch, Hangtown, Murderer's Bar, Dead Shot Flat, Git Up and Git,

Hell's Delight, Dead Man's Bar, Garrote, Robber's Roost, Wild Yankee, Rough and Ready, Brandy Flat, and, inevitably, Whorehouse Gulch.

Like most gold hunters, Chips never struck pay dirt and sought other work. On March 1, 1851, he started as a mounted messenger for Reynolds & Co. Express, which ran stagecoaches and express shipments throughout the Southern Mines. There was little or no U.S. mail delivery in the mining region, so private express companies sprang up to fill the void. Hodgkins made his headquarters in the company's office in the important mining camp of Sonora. Several times a month, the East Coast mail arrived, brought by river steamboat from San Francisco to Stockton, and then overland by stage to Sonora. Chips would stuff his saddlebags with letters, packages, and newspapers and ride out of town. His route, by horse or mule, took six to eight days, and passed through the rough mining camps of Calaveras, Tuolumne, Merced, and Mariposa counties. He delivered letters and papers to homesick gold diggers, and picked up packets of gold sent by the forty-niners to their families back home. Everything he and his rival messengers delivered was referred to as "express." Chips became extremely popular among the gold hunters, for he was their sole connection to their friends and families back in the civilized world. He became easily identified, for as he trotted into each gold camp on his mule, Polly, the miners would yell, "Here comes Chips!" They would rush forward and surround him, eager for mail and news from home.[4]

During the first two years of the Gold Rush, crime was relatively rare. But as many miners failed to strike it rich, or found panning and shoveling too arduous, some of them turned to an easier way to make their fortune. Thus began a rapid rise of banditry and violence, which, during the 1850s, resulted in the highest recorded homicide rates in American history. But given the initial low crime rates of the Gold Rush, Chips, during his earliest months as a messenger, did not even bother to carry a gun. That changed one day in June 1851.

He was delivering express on horseback from Tuttletown to Soldier's Gulch in Tuolumne County when he spotted a Mexican step out of a miner's cabin and mount a fine horse. The man rode leisurely toward Hodgkins, but as soon as he passed by, he spurred his horse into a gallop and thundered out of sight. Highway robberies were becoming increasingly common, and Chips feared that the stranger might be a bandit. He dismounted, peered into the cabin, and found that it had been ransacked. He rode up the trail to a large open pit where a group of miners were digging and told them what he had seen. They exclaimed that it was their cabin, and they all rushed back and found that a pistol, pocket watch, and money had been stolen. Chips mounted up and raced toward Tuttletown. He soon spotted the Mexican on the road, far ahead of him. As Chips recalled years later, "I followed him and went to a store where I was acquainted and could see him sitting on his horse in front of a Mexican store. I tried to borrow a pistol or shotgun to go for him, but could not get anything. About that time the Mexican looked up and saw me and left suddenly. I followed but lost sight of him, and went on and finished my trip."

A few days later Chips, still unarmed, was riding with his express bags from Sonora to Calaveras County. He crossed the Stanislaus River at Robinson's Ferry and started up the steep grade to Carson Hill. Suddenly, he spotted the same Mexican approaching on a mule, with a small boy on the saddle behind him. As soon as the Mexican passed, Hodgkins rode toward a group of nearby miners and borrowed a revolver. He raced after the robber, who saw him coming and dropped the boy off the mule. The Mexican put spurs to his mule, but Chips's horse was faster. The bandit cut loose a bundle from his saddle, hoping that the messenger would stop to pick it up. Chips kept galloping after the man, who unloosed another bundle, this time to lighten his load. As Hodgkins passed close to a pine tree, the Mexican drew a pistol and fired, but he missed. The messenger was undeterred. "I kept gaining on him," he recalled, "and he saw that I was bound to overtake him, so he jumped off his mule and made his escape into the bushes. I took up his mule and a good lasso that was dragging. I think he tried to get it ready to lasso me, but it slipped out of his hand. . . . I finished my trip, took my prize to Sonora about eleven o'clock that night. Up to this time I had never carried a pistol. A few days later the real owner of the mule came and proved his property."[5]

Two weeks later, on July 7, 1851, Chips was in Sonora when the same Mexican was brought in on a charge of horse stealing. Sonora had a very active vigilance committee; previously they'd had a blacksmith prepare a brand marked "H.T." (horse thief) for marking miscreants. California then had no state prison, and such branding was used both for punishment and identification. The bandido was tried by a miner's court, found guilty, and sentenced to 150 lashes and to be branded "H.T." on his face. But after he confessed his guilt, the sentence was reduced to one hundred lashes and no branding. As Hodgkins watched, the desperado was stripped and tied to a tree. Chips recalled, "The whipping was done by a Frenchman named John B. Delahe, and every time he made a stroke with the rawhide whip, the fellow would try to hug that tree very close. When he had given him twenty-five strokes, the president of the vigilance committee thought it was a plenty, and put it to a vote of the witnesses whether he should have more. The vote was 'No more!' He was then taken down, washed with beef brine, dressed, and his friends ordered to take him out of the country."[6]

Chips Hodgkins had learned his lesson about traveling in the mining region unarmed. Because there was precious little law enforcement in the early years of the Gold Rush, all men were responsible for their own protection. Chips bought a multiple-barrel pistol, known as a "pepperbox" revolver, which he always carried with him on his route. Years later, a friend recalled, "There were instances when the company's stages running from Sonora to Stockton carrying Reynolds & Co.'s express were threatened by robbers. In those days the miners were in the habit of sending home to their friends packages of gold dust and specimens which, together with the gold shipped for commercial purposes, made the shipments occurring on what was called 'steamer day' very large. On several occasions, we well remember, it became necessary to arm and equip a special convoy extraordinary, and among them 'Chips' always was to be found, with a gun [shotgun] and his pockets filled with Colt's revolvers and Bowie knives."[7]

Reynolds & Co.'s biggest rival was Adams & Co. Express. One day in the summer of 1851, Hodgkins was at the steamboat landing in Stockton, on his way to San Francisco for a short holiday. Stockton was then one of California's most important towns, the principal port on the San Joaquin River and the gateway to the Southern Mines. While waiting to board the river steamer, Chips learned that Adams Express had just received a large shipment of the latest East Coast and foreign newspapers, and one of their messengers had left for Sonora on horseback with his saddlebags stuffed full. However, the newspapers for Reynolds & Co. had not yet arrived, for the rival steamer was delayed. The news-hungry miners placed great value on eastern periodicals. An issue that sold for two cents in New York went for between fifty cents and three dollars in the mines.

Chips forgot all about his holiday in San Francisco; he could not bear to see his employer bested by Adams. He stepped into the Reynolds express office and told the agent "that I could get the papers of Adams & Co., if he would furnish me a good horse, and [I] would beat that fellow into Sonora or lose a month's salary."

The agent replied, "All right. Go ahead and get the papers."

Hodgkins went into the Adams express office and told the agent he wanted to buy all the spare newspapers they had. The agent had no idea who Chips was, and he began stacking the papers on the counter. At that point, an Adams stagecoach driver walked into the office. Spotting Hodgkins, he said, "Hello, Chips. What are you doing here?"

Hearing their competitor's name, the agent snatched back all the newspapers, saying, "We have none to spare."

Hodgkins was unfazed. He got a friend to buy two hundred newspapers from the unsuspecting Adams agent. Loading them into his saddlebags, he mounted a fast horse, first tying a long coat around his waist, with the coattails covering the saddlebags. It was dusk when he thundered out of Stockton toward Sonora, sixty-five miles distant, in hot pursuit of the rival expressman. "I was well acquainted with the road," he recalled, "and between eleven and twelve at night overtook my man and saluted him with, 'Good evening, sir, you are traveling late.'"

Pilsbury "Chips" Hodgkins, Wells Fargo's pioneer messenger.
[*Courtesy of Robert J. Chandler*]

The Adams messenger didn't know Chips. The two rode along together, the Adams man telling Chips that he was hurrying to Sonora to deliver the latest papers before Reynolds & Co. could do so. Chips said nothing about being a messenger himself, and because he had concealed his saddlebags, the rival didn't know his errand. Hodgkins told the Adams expressman that he liked to travel at night because the days were so hot. It was daybreak as they neared Jamestown, four miles from Sonora. As they reached a fork in the road, Chips bid his competitor good-bye and took a different route. As soon as the Adams rider was out of sight, he put spurs to his horse. "I knew all the short cuts and trails from there to Sonora. At Jamestown I got a fresh horse and went into Sonora, making good time." He then delivered all his newspapers, even sending a few to the Adams express office.

"After having breakfast, and seeing that my horse was well cared for, I waited for the arrival of my opponent. Between eight and nine a.m. he came, his horse covered with sweat. He jumped off, dragging his two big canvas bags in, telling the agent that he had late papers for him. While he was going through that ceremony, there were seated all around him sporting men and others reading papers from the same supply I had brought in two hours before, which he discovered much to his chagrin and annoyance, and wondered how they obtained them. Their agent told him how they came. Then he knew I was the one who accompanied him during the night, and after that he would never speak to me."[8]

Reynolds & Co. was bought out by Todd & Co. Express, and in March 1853, Chips was assigned to Todd's express office in Stockton. That September, Todd's was purchased by the new and much larger firm of Wells Fargo, destined to become the principal express company in the United States. Hodgkins now became a Wells Fargo man; company officials later said that when they acquired Todd's Express, they "bought Chips with it." Because he had worked for Wells Fargo's two predecessors, Chips was thereafter considered one of Wells Fargo's first messengers. He now undertook what he called "four years of very hard work" as a porter in Stockton, loading and unloading express shipments on stagecoaches and river steamers. In 1857, Wells Fargo assigned him back to messenger duty, guarding shipments on the riverboats of the California Steam Navigation Company. In his first year alone, he transported almost $4.5 million in gold coin and dust on the San Joaquin River from Stockton to San Francisco. During the next twelve years, Chips guarded and delivered many more millions of dollars on this route. In 1858, he married Louisa Shattuck, and they had three sons, all of whom would work for Wells Fargo.[9]

Bitter rivalry between competing firms was not limited to express companies. On January 28, 1862, Chips was aboard the river steamer *Helen Hensley* when she departed San Francisco for Stockton. The captain and passengers were eating dinner when the opposition riverboat *Nevada*, also headed for Stockton, came up on the starboard side to overtake her. Under navigation rules, this was the wrong side for passing. Suddenly, the *Nevada* ran its prow into the *Helen Hensley*'s paddle wheel, tearing apart her bulwark and stanchions. The *Nevada* steamed off, leaving the *Helen Hensley* to fend for herself. The ship, with Chips and his express cargo, limped into Stockton hours late. He later called the collision a "vicious act," saying it was a deliberate attempt to run them into the rocks. Complaints by the officers and passengers on the *Helen Hensley* led to the prompt suspension of the *Nevada*'s two pilots.[10]

Steamship travel on the Sacramento and San Joaquin rivers was accompanied by other dangers. On September 29, 1866, Hodgkins was aboard the side-wheel steamer *Julia* as it left the wharf in San Francisco, headed for Stockton. The crew, numbering sixteen, were all below, most of them eating dinner. As the *Julia* rounded Alcatraz, the engineer reported to the captain that steam was escaping from the boiler. The captain gave orders for the *Julia* to turn about and return to the wharf. Chips, unaware of the problem, put his hand on the ladder rail to go belowdecks. Just then the captain rushed by and exclaimed, "Something is wrong." The words were barely out of his mouth when the ship was rocked by a terrific explosion. The boiler blew up, killing five crewman instantly, mortally wounding another six, and scalding several others. All were belowdecks, near the engine room. Chips gave all credit to the captain. "His speaking saved my life. Had I reached the foot of the stairs I should have gone with the rest who were below."[11]

Hodgkins's life as an express messenger was not an easy one. By 1869, he had spent eighteen years on horseback and shipboard, on stagecoaches and wharves, exposed to harsh weather, hard riding, and great privation. The hours were long, sometimes twenty a day. Back injuries from lifting heavy boxes and crates plagued him. His health suffered and he became so ill that Wells Fargo officials sent him to San Francisco for office duty. Chips moved his family to the city, where he lived for the rest of his life. By October 1870, he had regained his strength and returned to his messenger's duties. For the next seven years, he sailed on coastal steamers, guarding gold, silver, and cash between San Francisco, Los Angeles, and San Diego, at a salary of one hundred dollars a month. He carried the treasure in a heavy iron box, or pony safe, which he moved on and off shipboard with a dolly. It can be seen to this day on display in the Wells Fargo History Museum in San Francisco.[12]

In May 1876, Henry Wells, one of the founders of Wells Fargo, suggested to Hodgkins that he hold a reception honoring his twenty-five years in the express business. Chips and his wife sent out invitations, and a huge banquet was held in his honor in a public hall in San Francisco. As testament to his wide popularity, five hundred friends and their wives attended. Henry Wells gave the keynote speech, and poems lauding Chips, written for the occasion, were read. Aaron Stein, a prominent Wells Fargo agent, presented him with a magnificent case of silverware from the company. Hodgkins's friend Billy Pridham, then Wells Fargo agent in Los Angeles, sent a memento, which became one of Chips's most prized possessions. It was a miniature Wells Fargo treasure box, made of silver and engraved on the lid, "Chips, 1851–1876."[13]

In September 1877, he completed his last ocean voyage for Wells Fargo. Billy Pridham praised his faithful service, saying, "Never lost a penny. Never lost a package." Chips was again assigned to San Francisco office duty, this time in the forwarding department, organizing Wells Fargo shipments for all the Pacific Coast steamers. From 1886 to 1891, he worked in the collection department, where he collected debts owed to Wells Fargo customers. In December 1891, he came down with a deadly flu, exacerbated by heart disease, and his health began to fail. This forced his retirement from Wells Fargo. After many months of illness, he died in his San Francisco home on September 4, 1892, age sixty-seven.

Toward the end, Chips became delirious, but his final thoughts were about his life as a Wells Fargo man. Just before he died, he gasped, "That express has gone wrong!" Those were his last words.[14]

2

THE FIRST WELLS FARGO DETECTIVE

Henry Johnson

On a breezy spring day in 1868, the side-wheeler *Montana*, smoke billowing and steam hissing, churned through San Francisco Bay toward the huge Pacific Mail wharf at the foot of Brannan Street. Her deck was jammed with passengers, eager to see the booming city after the long Pacific voyage from the Isthmus of Panama. This was one year before the completion of the transcontinental railroad, and the trip to California was a long one by sea or by wagon train. A newspaperman watched a tumultuous scene as the *Montana* slowly pulled up alongside the dock for mooring. He found the wharf crowded with "the roughs, thieves, baggage-smashers, and jay-hawkers who infest San Francisco," all attempting to charge through the gates and prey on the disembarking passengers. He declared that "they manage to spot strangers who are unused to the ways of cities, and follow them up to places where they can commence their operations more safely. The class of hackmen known as 'Scalpers' and their stool-pigeons are especially active on such occasions, and woe be to the stranger who falls into their clutches with any money in his possession."

Amid the din, the journalist spotted Henry Johnson, special officer for Wells Fargo and the Pacific Mail Steamship Company. His beaver hat, high collar, and natty suit belied what he carried under his coat: a holstered six-gun, a pocket billy club, and a set of handcuffs and nickel-plated nippers. Johnson knew more crooks, thugs, and garroters than any lawman on the Pacific Coast. In a loud Scottish brogue, he barked orders to his officers and lawbreakers alike. The reporter could only admire the way Johnson and his men swept through the crowd of ruffians, manhandling those foolish enough to resist and sending the rest packing. "Detective Johnson and his assistants rendered valuable service to more than one passenger in saving him from being victimized, but they had more than their hands full."[1]

For fifteen years, Henry Johnson had his hands full as Wells Fargo's pioneer detective. The company built its reputation on safety and security. From the time of its founding, it guaranteed delivery and paid its customers for all losses suffered in transit, whether due to theft, fire, or accident. The vast riches carried by the company were a magnet for robbers, and it quickly became evident that the company needed detectives to investigate thefts and recover stolen property. A common misconception is that the famous western lawman James B. Hume was the first Wells Fargo detective. In fact, San Francisco police officers Isaiah Lees, Leonard Noyes, and James Gannon, as well as Sacramento lawmen Dan Gay and Charles P. O'Neil, all worked as Wells Fargo sleuths long before Hume's start in 1873.

It was during the Gold Rush of the 1850s that Wells Fargo officials hired Henry Johnson as their first detective. Born in Glasgow, Scotland, in 1818, he was a lifelong law officer. Johnson joined the Glasgow police as a young man, in about 1840, and rose to the rank of detective at a time when the profession of policing was in its infancy. He later emigrated to Australia, where he served as a police detective in Sydney and Melbourne. Johnson and his young bride, Elizabeth, sailed by clipper ship to San Francisco in 1855. Within a year, he became a special policeman, paid by private businesses to protect their property.[2]

American policing was then very new. Before 1845, there were no organized, professional police forces in the United States, for law enforcement had traditionally been handled by volunteer watchmen at night and by constables by day. As eastern communities became urban, the old system could no longer cope with booming population and the resulting increase in crime, social unrest, and rioting. Philadelphia and New York City were among the first cities to form full-time police forces manned by paid officers. Soon these departments were divided into patrol divisions for the prevention of crime and detective bureaus for the investigation of crime. The latter became known as "detective police." The result was a rapid rise in urban police professionalism.

But because of the transient and unstable nature of frontier communities, professional policing developed far more slowly in the American West. Only in San Francisco, where a small group of highly experienced career officers controlled its police department from the Gold Rush until the end of the century, did law enforcement reach a degree of professionalism by the late 1850s. There, Henry Johnson's experience and talent as an investigator quickly became apparent. He was appointed a San Francisco police detective and worked closely with Isaiah W. Lees, destined to become one of America's greatest sleuths. Johnson and Lees handled countless cases, from small-time thefts to major crimes and homicides. In that freewheeling era, on-duty San Francisco police frequently performed private detective work for banks, express companies, and merchants. Because American law enforcement was so new, clear rules separating public and private policing were often nonexistent.[3]

Although Johnson later said that he performed his initial detective work for Wells Fargo in 1855, newspapers did not report his first such case until two years later. On the night of February 1, 1857, a thief entered the Wells Fargo office in Fiddletown, in the Mother Lode country. The office was located in a corner of the United States Hotel, owned by Jerry Kendall, and the safe rested at one end of the bar. The burglar opened it and stole nine thousand dollars in gold dust and coin. Because the safe was undamaged, the Wells Fargo agent suspected that the thief either picked the lock or used a false key. The loss caused an uproar in Fiddletown. Because of the lack of effective law enforcement, vigilance committees were very active during and after the Gold Rush.

San Francisco Police Detective
Isaiah W. Lees, about 1860. He
worked with Henry Johnson as a
Wells Fargo detective.
[*Author's collection*]

A band of vigilantes seized two strangers and strung them up in an effort to choke out a confession. The pair insisted on their innocence and were set free.

Wells Fargo officials then sent Henry Johnson and Isaiah Lees to Fiddletown to investigate. They found a typical rough gold camp in which saloons outnumbered every other business. One third of its population of one thousand was Chinese. The camp had been founded in 1849 by Missourians. "They are always fiddling," declared one of the founders. "Call it Fiddletown." Stagecoaches stopped in front of the United States Hotel, the most imposing building in town and one of the few with glass windows. According to an early account, "The barroom was also sitting room, dining room, and bedroom, the beds being potato sacks stretched across poles, furnished with blankets, but no pillows, a man's boots being expected to serve that purpose. The floor was the original red soil, sprinkled, swept, and trampled every day."[4]

The company's superintendent, Samuel Knight, went to Fiddletown also and promptly repaid the owners of the stolen gold. Soon after

Knight and the detectives arrived, a lynch mob led by the Fiddletown justice of the peace, Stephen Kendall—a brother of the hotelkeeper—seized another suspect, named Stepperfield, and dragged him to the outskirts of town. He denied any involvement "and expressed the fear that if he was hung it would kill his mother and sister." He asked one of the mob to write down his last words and send them to his mother. When one of the lynchers tried to comply, others shoved him aside and exclaimed, "The man had better be praying, for his time is mighty short." Stepperfield was then strung up until he lost consciousness, then let down. This happened three times, until a local doctor and a deputy sheriff showed up and cut him down. He lived but was permanently paralyzed. It turned out that Stepperfield had had nothing to do with the theft.[5]

Johnson and Lees ignored the vigilantes' primitive attempts to solve the crime by strangulation, and they soon left Fiddletown to pursue a lead in Sacramento. While they were gone, a loafer known as "Drunken Joe" came forward with crucial information. He had been allowed to sleep in a room next to the hotel bar, and on the night of the theft, he awoke and saw the justice, Kendall, remove several sacks from the safe and hand them to a carpenter named Leroy Warden and another man, whom he did not know. Because Kendall was authorized to open the safe, Drunken Joe thought nothing of it until he saw the justice leading the lynch mob. Justice Kendall, Leroy Warden, and a ruffian called "Big John" were all jailed. One of them revealed the location of the gold, which was found hidden under a brick oven behind the hotel. Kendall and Warden were brought to trial in June and both were acquitted, illustrating that justice was extremely uneven during the Gold Rush: Innocent men were strangled half to death by a mob, while the guilty culprits went free. Though Henry Johnson did not crack the case, it marked the beginning of many investigations he would make for Wells Fargo.[6]

By the late 1850s, stage holdups had become an increasingly common problem for Wells Fargo. Stagecoach robbery first appeared in the far west in the mid-1850s. A widely believed myth holds that in

April 1852, a gang led by "Reelfoot" Williams pulled California's first stage holdup near Illinoistown (now Colfax), escaping with $7,500. This story had its genesis in a popular book, *The Diary of a Forty-niner*, which was first published in 1906 and then reprinted in several later editions. Although this so-called diary is obviously bogus and was debunked in *The American Historical Review* in 1921, many gullible writers relied on it. California never had an outlaw named Reelfoot Williams and the state never saw a stage holdup in 1852. And an 1853 newspaper report that the infamous Joaquin Murrieta gang robbed a coach near Stockton and killed two passengers was immediately disproved by the editor of the *Calaveras Chronicle*.[7]

The first robbery, actually a theft, involving a California stagecoach took place on September 5, 1853. A stage left Sonora, in the Southern Mines, bound for Stockton; in the rear boot was an Adams & Co. express box holding $25,000 in gold bullion. Along the way, someone cut the straps to the leather boot and removed the luggage and the strongbox. The culprit was never caught. Three years passed before robbers pulled the first recorded holdup of a California stagecoach. On August 4, 1856, near Coloma, in El Dorado County, two armed horsemen ordered a stage driver to halt. Peering inside the coach, they saw that it was full of passengers. During the Gold Rush, most travelers were armed, and the highwaymen, fearing resistance, lost their nerve and galloped away. A week later, on August 12, the notorious Tom Bell gang tried to stop the coach running from Camptonville to Marysville, in the Northern Mines. A messenger for Langton's Pioneer Express guarded $100,000 in gold bullion. In a bloody gunfight between the bandits and the messenger, a woman passenger was slain and three others wounded. Numerous writers have claimed that this was the West's first stage robbery, but that is wrong on two counts. First, as we have seen, one coach had been robbed and another held up before this. And, second, it was an attempted robbery, for the Tom Bell gang had fled without robbing the stage.[8]

These events inspired other desperadoes who wanted to get rich quick. On the night of June 9, 1860, five masked robbers held up a stage six miles south of Chico, in Butte County, in Northern California. As one of the highwaymen opened the Wells Fargo box, he declared, "The company is rich, and we have a particular use for this money." After making that statement, which succinctly explained the reason for the ensuing fifty-eight years of Wells Fargo robberies, the outlaw and his comrades galloped off with fifteen thousand dollars in gold. Company officials offered heavy rewards: seven thousand dollars for return of the stolen treasure and one thousand dollars for each bandit. It turned out that shortly before the holdup, five armed strangers had ridden up to the nearby ranch of Captain J. M. Maxey and bought liquor from him. A few weeks later, Captain Maxey happened to visit San Francisco and spotted one of the men who had stopped at his ranch. He notified the police, and immediately Henry Johnson and Isaiah Lees began searching for the suspect. On the night of July 14, they found him on the Oakland ferry, heavily armed. He tried to fight, but the two detectives quickly overpowered him. The man turned out to be Owen Masters, alias Owen Castle. Detective Lees and Dan Gay of the Sacramento police took him north by stage to Butte County, where he was convicted and sentenced to ten years in San Quentin Prison. The rest of the gang was never captured.[9]

In 1865, Johnson resigned from the San Francisco police and began working full-time as a detective for Wells Fargo and the Pacific Mail Steamship Company. This was eight years before Jim Hume took the same job. The two companies were closely connected: Wells Fargo was the freight agent for the Pacific Mail. Johnson made his headquarters in Wells Fargo's building on Montgomery Street and held a commission as a special police officer so that he would have the power to make lawful arrests. Private detectives in that era were often obstructed by competitors, jealous lawmen, and even by criminals who sought to bring false charges against them. Johnson was arrested several times in such cases. Once he was charged with carrying a concealed weapon, but he proved that as a special policeman he had that authority. Other times he was arrested on allegations of trying to collect a bad debt, making a witness disappear, false imprisonment, and taking money under false pretenses. In each case he was vindicated in court by proving that his actions were lawfully performed in the line of duty. Wells Fargo and the Pacific Mail paid no attention to such bogus complaints and kept him on their payrolls. And San Francisco's major banks were so pleased with Johnson's work, they presented him with a magnificent gold pocket watch valued at a then-whopping $650.[10]

In May 1866, Wells Fargo officials in San Francisco became alarmed by several irregular transactions by Peter D. Hedley, the agent at Gold Hill, situated just south of Virginia City, in Nevada's Comstock Lode. They sent their Virginia City agent to examine Hedley's accounts. Hedley showed him the books, then remarked that he had to leave the Wells Fargo office for a few minutes. He walked home, picked up a pistol, and shot himself in the head. The wound wasn't serious, and a lengthy audit eventually showed that Hedley's office accounts were short $62,000. This was an enormous sum, the equivalent of more than two million dollars today. Wells Fargo officials were determined to bring him to justice, but he had powerful friends, among them the governor of Nevada. The company had Hedley tailed until he foolishly visited San Francisco on September 11, 1866. Wells Fargo's superintendent, Charles E. McLane, immediately swore out a warrant for his arrest and handed it to Henry Johnson and Isaiah Lees.

The two detectives, surmising that Hedley would take the evening steamer to Sacramento, staked out the riverboat wharf. As soon as Hedley walked up the gangplank, Johnson and Lees stepped forward and arrested him. They took him to the city prison, where he broke down and made a full confession, admitting that he had lost the money speculating on risky Nevada mining stocks. Hedley was quickly brought to trial, convicted of embezzlement, and sentenced to three years in San Quentin. One newspaperman reported that when booked into the prison, "he sank into a chair, and cried like a child."

Hedley's lawyers appealed to the California Supreme Court, arguing that he could not be prosecuted in California for a Nevada crime. The court upheld his conviction and ruled that although the thefts had been initiated in Nevada, they had been completed in California. The

Nevada governor and many prominent citizens of Virginia City and Gold Hill then signed petitions requesting clemency. California's governor pardoned Hedley after he had served fewer than ten months of his term. This result was grossly unfair, for poor vaqueros and cowboys who stole a single steer routinely served prison terms of three years or more, while Hedley had stolen more than a workingman could earn in four lifetimes. The *San Francisco Bulletin*, in commenting on Wells Fargo's huge loss, remarked that "it is to be hoped that this may be the last of such cases." But that was wishful thinking. Theft by employees would comprise a major part of the caseload of every successive Wells Fargo detective for the next half century.[11]

On December 2, 1867, two masked road agents stopped a stage going from Ione to Jackson, in the mining region of Amador County. One was a huge man carrying a shotgun, and the other, much smaller, wielded a pistol. After chopping open the Wells Fargo box with an ax, they ordered the whip to drive on. Inside the box was $8,500 in gold coin, which had been sent by John Surface, Ione's tax collector, to the county treasury in Jackson. The highwaymen vanished and a posse soon arrived at the scene. The possemen followed the trail of two horses across ground muddied from recent rains. One set of tracks led three miles to the house of George Ringer, a respectable property owner who lived near Ione. The other trail led into Amador City. The posse determined that those tracks matched the hoofprints of a horse owned by James A. "Big Jim" Falkenberry, a miner from Amador City. Big Jim was a friend of John Surface and knew that the tax money was being shipped to Jackson.

When Henry Johnson received news of the robbery in San Francisco, he immediately dispatched William R. "Billy" Warnock, a Wells Fargo messenger who had formerly guarded the stage routes in Amador County and knew the country well. The company promptly offered a four-thousand-dollar reward for recovery of the treasure and arrest of the bandits. Two days after the holdup, Warnock sent Johnson a wire advising that the two suspects, George Ringer and Big Jim Falkenberry, had been identified. Johnson rushed to Jackson, arriving the next day, December 5. Johnson, Warnock, and Surface went to a justice of the peace and swore out warrants for the arrest of Ringer and Big Jim. Then Johnson, Surface, and the county sheriff rode to Amador City after Big Jim, while Warnock and a constable headed to Ringer's house.

On arriving in Amador City, Johnson learned that Big Jim was working at a mine a mile or two from town. The three officers got into a wagon and started up the trail to the mine, but they spotted Falkenberry coming toward them. As Henry Johnson later told the story, Big Jim acted "perfectly cool" and shook hands with Surface, who in turn introduced him to Johnson. The detective told Falkenberry "to consider himself under arrest for the robbery." Big Jim demanded to see the warrant, which the sheriff produced and read aloud. He then ordered Big Jim to climb aboard the wagon. According to a contemporary account, "He demurred at first, but on receiving a significant hint from Johnson not to indulge in any nonsense, he got into the wagon. . . . On the way he was sullen, denied all knowledge of the robbery, and refused to enter into conversation."

After reaching Ione, Big Jim asked to speak privately with Surface, and the two went into his office. There Falkenberry demanded to know the evidence against him. When told that he and George Ringer had been tracked from the holdup site, Big Jim asked "whether Johnson was authorized to make a binding agreement for Wells Fargo & Co." Surface told him that Johnson did have that authority, and Falkenberry replied that he "would make a clean breast of the matter." At that, Johnson, who had been eavesdropping behind the door, stepped in and promised that if Big Jim revealed everything and turned over the gold, Wells Fargo would not prosecute him. Falkenberry then admitted taking part in the holdup. He blamed the affair on George Ringer, saying that Ringer convinced him to find out when the gold was to be shipped. The night before the holdup, the two met at the Ione graveyard and planned the robbery. They had buried all but two twenty-dollar gold pieces, which Big Jim had spent.

The three officers then took Falkenberry to a spot near Amador

City to uncover the buried treasure. After searching the hills for several hours, Big Jim declared he had found the spot. When they dug down, nothing was there, and the robber insisted that someone must have removed it. Henry Johnson was not falling for that. He told Big Jim that "he had fooled just long enough, and that he could turn up the money at once or take the alternative." Falkenberry then walked a short distance and pointed out the hiding place. Johnson dug up the gold and found that all the loot was there except for forty dollars, just as Big Jim had said. Meanwhile, Warnock picked up Ringer, and the two stage robbers were then lodged in the county jail in Jackson. Ringer's bail was set at six thousand dollars, while Falkenberry was held as a material witness.

Johnson and Warnock, worn-out and disheveled, returned to San Francisco by stagecoach and riverboat. A reporter who met them at the wharf wrote, "They had not been undressed since leaving San Francisco, and looked like men who had been hard at work." Meanwhile, the district attorney of Amador County, unhappy with Wells Fargo's agreement, filed robbery charges against Big Jim. Although Wells Fargo officials often paid private lawyers to act as special prosecutors, they could not control whether or not a district attorney chose to file charges. In February 1868, Big Jim Falkenberry pled guilty and was sentenced to four years in prison. Due to his cooperation, the governor pardoned him after he served only two months. George Ringer, however, went scot-free. Under the law, Falkenberry's testimony alone was not enough to convict him; there had to be additional corroborating evidence. Since there was none, other than the horse tracks that led to his house, he was set free.[12]

But not all Wells Fargo stage robberies were pulled by road agents. On several occasions in the spring of 1868, money was found missing from the treasure boxes on coaches running between Santa Rosa and Healdsburg, on California's North Coast. Wells Fargo's assistant superintendent, Solomon D. Brastow, learned that in each case the driver had been Edwin Bogart, twenty-four, whom the stage company had hired a year earlier. Brastow sent Henry Johnson to investigate. Johnson found that on three occasions money had gone missing from the strongbox, but there were no signs of forced entry. On July 5, 1868, he interviewed Bogart and managed to obtain a full confession. Bogart revealed that he had found a key that had been lost by Wells Fargo's agent and had used it to pilfer the boxes of $650. He had become infatuated with a young woman and needed the money to win her favor. Despite his confession, he refused to plead guilty and instead was tried, convicted, and sentenced to a year in San Quentin Prison. His lawyers appealed to the California Supreme Court, which reversed his conviction on the flimsiest of grounds: The indictment failed to specify whether Wells Fargo & Co. was a partnership or a corporation. In fact, Wells Fargo had become a corporation in 1866. Much to Johnson's disgust, Bogart was released from prison after serving six months of his term.[13]

Wells Fargo was not the only express company plagued by dishonest employees. In March 1868, John Borden, a young clerk in the American Express Company office in Syracuse, New York, absconded with a money packet containing $812. Although the loss was comparatively light, American Express had suffered so many employee thefts that its officials were determined to bring Borden to justice, regardless of expense. The company put detectives on his trail and they learned that Borden and a young friend, Ira Seymour, a former American Express employee, had skipped out for California on shipboard. The superintendent of American Express sent a telegraphic message to Wells Fargo headquarters in San Francisco, providing descriptions of the pair and asking for aid in capturing them. Because Henry Wells and William G. Fargo controlled both American Express and Wells Fargo, there was close cooperation between the two companies. Henry Johnson was immediately assigned to the case.[14]

Johnson began searching the passenger lists for all incoming ships and found that two young travelers, using the names Moore and Bailey, had arrived in the city several weeks previous. Their descriptions matched those of the wanted men. Johnson learned from American Express officials that the fugitives' friends in Syracuse might send letters to them in San Francisco. Johnson put a detective in the main post office to watch in case they tried to pick up their mail. Weeks went by and Johnson, ready to give up, pulled the detective from his post. Then, on June 27, 1868, he got word from the postmaster that a young man was there, asking for letters addressed to John Borden and Ira Seymour. Johnson rushed to the post office and saw that the suspect matched Borden's description. He tailed the youth to the American Exchange Hotel. While his quarry read a newspaper in the lobby, Johnson quietly asked the hotel clerk if the suspect was staying there. The clerk replied, "No, but he was here six or seven weeks ago with another young man."

Johnson did not want to make an arrest until he had located both men. However, a bellboy overheard his conversation with the clerk and told him, "The other man is upstairs in bedroom 135. The chambermaid cannot get him up."

Johnson immediately stepped up to the youth in the lobby and, addressing him as Borden, reached out to shake hands. "My name is Bailey, sir," the youth said, lying. "You have the advantage of me."

Over Borden's protestations, Johnson placed him under arrest. He then went up to room 135 to arrest Seymour, but he found that the bellboy was mistaken: The occupant was not Ira Seymour. Johnson took Borden to the city prison, where he continued to deny his identity. Borden claimed to have arrived that morning from Santa Clara, forty-five miles south, but would admit nothing else. Johnson summoned Isaiah Lees and the two left for the South Bay. After finding no clue in Santa Clara, they continued on to San Jose, where they learned that a man matching Seymour's description had been seen at Woodworth's stage station, eight miles from the coast town of Santa Cruz. It was then eleven o'clock that night, and the two officers rented a buggy and team and drove over the Santa Cruz Mountains to Woodworth's station.

They arrived at 3:30 A.M. and knocked on the station door, asking Woodworth for feed for their horses. As they took a drink at the bar, the stationmaster mentioned that he had hired two new employees six weeks earlier and that one had gone to San Francisco.

"Where is the other now?" asked the sleuths.

"In the barn, asleep," Woodworth replied.

The detectives walked into the stable and wakened a man rolled up in a blanket. They asked his name and he replied, "Ira B. Seymour. I know what you want, but I had nothing to do with it."

Johnson and Lees placed him under arrest and took him back to San Francisco on the night of June 29. After booking him into the city prison, they let him see Borden. "Hello, Johnny," Seymour exclaimed. "They've got you too, have they? How these fellows found me I can't tell. I thought we were out of the world, but it all comes of your going after that letter. I told you not to meddle with it."

The next day, Borden and Seymour boarded a New York–bound steamer in the charge of a special officer for the long journey back to face prosecution in Syracuse.[15]

Meanwhile, other officers coveted Henry Johnson's lucrative job with Wells Fargo and the Pacific Mail. On August 3, 1868, San Francisco's mayor, police commissioners, and police judge held a private meeting, in which they revoked Johnson's special police appointment. The *San Francisco Daily Alta California* complained that this action was motivated by jealous detectives and declared that neither Wells Fargo nor the Pacific Mail "will allow any new appointee to be foisted upon them against their wishes and interest." The two corporations undoubtedly used their influence to retain Johnson, for the very next day he was reinstated.[16]

Four months later, on December 2, 1868, a distinguished gentleman stepped into the Union gun shop on Pacific Street in San Francisco and asked to see a fancy revolver. He announced that he was a Wells Fargo detective from Nevada and wanted to buy a gift for his brother, who owned an interest in the Bank of California. He displayed a note from Wells Fargo, written on a blank telegram form, which identified him as Thomas W. Lovelady, a company detective, with a right to free passage on its stagecoaches. Lovelady offered to buy the ornate pistol, but then, saying that he had forgotten his wallet, he started to put the gun back on the counter. The gunsmith turned to

Thomas W. Lovelady, the fake Wells Fargo detective. This photo was taken after Henry Johnson arrested him in 1868. [*Author's collection*]

wait on another customer, and when he looked back, both the gentleman and the revolver were gone.

He raced after Lovelady and caught up with him in the Wells Fargo building, where the purported detective was telling employees that he needed to see Henry Johnson. No sooner had the gunsmith demanded the pistol than he spotted Johnson and told him what had happened. Johnson questioned Lovelady, who insisted that he was a real Wells Fargo detective and that other employees in the building could vouch for him. When none of them did, Johnson placed him under arrest. On searching his pockets, Johnson found a purported pass for the

Central Pacific Railroad, which identified Lovelady as master mechanic, plus several other forged documents. Johnson believed that Lovelady wanted to meet him so he could thereafter recognize and avoid the real Wells Fargo detective. Lovelady was promptly convicted of petty larceny and sentenced to ninety days in jail.[17]

Henry Johnson continued serving Wells Fargo until 1871, when he and Thomas Ansbro, a former San Francisco police detective, formed a private investigation firm. Apparently, it was not a success, for in 1874, Johnson obtained an appointment as a regular police officer, but city doctors then rejected him on physical grounds. He did not need the work. Over the years he had collected numerous fees and rewards for the capture of thieves and murderers, and he wisely had invested in real estate and other ventures. He amassed money and property worth $64,000, then a small fortune and more than enough to support his wife and four children. That was fortunate, because his health was failing. On July 30, 1875, he died in his San Francisco home at the age of fifty-seven.[18]

Though totally forgotten today, Henry Johnson richly deserves a place in history as the first Wells Fargo detective.

3

FROM FIRST STAGE DRIVER TO SHOTGUN MESSENGER

Henry C. Ward

Every day thousands of people—office workers, tourists, and passersby—flock past the huge front windows of the Wells Fargo History Museum in the bank's main office on San Francisco's Montgomery Street. Dominating the view inside is a magnificent Concord stagecoach, once the Cadillac of American transportation. Many stop to admire it, but not one of them knows that in the 1870s this very stage raced at breakneck speed over rugged mountains and rough roads, its six-horse team handled by Henry Ward, one of the most courageous men who ever rode for Wells Fargo. Ward was widely regarded by his peers as the first stage driver on the West Coast. His long career as a jehu and Wells Fargo shotgun messenger began in 1849 and lasted through the entire frontier period, until he retired in 1895. Thus his story, like that of Chips Hodgkins, mirrored and exemplified the history of Wells Fargo.

Henry Chester Ward hailed from Connecticut, where he was born in July 1828. An adventure-seeking youth, he jumped at the chance when news of the California gold discovery arrived in late 1848. The following year, he landed by ship in San Francisco and quickly got work—not as a gold miner, but as a stagecoach driver. California's earliest stage route ran between San Francisco and San Jose. In 1849, no stagecoach road had yet been built, and the journey was fifty miles across rough trails. In September 1849, the twenty-one-year-old Ward took the reins of the first coach to leave Portsmouth Square in San Francisco, bound for San Jose. A huge crowd turned out to cheer his departure. The trip was a slow one, taking nine hours. His coach, which he later described as "an old French omnibus," was drawn by a mixed team of docile mules and wild California mustangs. Later that rainy winter, the stage service was canceled because the ground became so soft that coach wheels sank to their hubs. Early in the spring of 1850, the line started up again, and Ward was one of its three drivers, each of whom was earning three hundred dollars a month. The passenger fare was thirty-two dollars or two ounces of gold dust.

A natty dresser much admired by women, Henry Ward was handsome and made friends easily. He recalled, "Passengers riding on the seat with the drivers was supposed to treat the driver to drinks and cigars on the road." At first, there was no mail or express delivery, so drivers like Ward were paid extra for carrying letters and packages. However, in 1850, numerous small express companies began to spring up in Gold Rush towns. Ward was both a pioneer stage driver and an express messenger.[1]

With the founding of the California Stage Company in 1854, Henry Ward became one of its leading whips. Though only twenty-six, he was widely known by his facetious nickname, "Old Wardy." He drove the routes in the Northern Mines from Marysville south to Sacramento, and northeast to Camptonville. Ward was a great lover of dogs, and his stage dog, Pony, developed a reputation equal to that of his master. Pony was an Irish setter mix that Ward found running behind a coach on the Camptonville road in 1854. Ward recalled that "he was notorious as the wild dog that followed stages, and drivers considered it good luck to have him with them. He would come into town ahead of the leaders, his head and tail in the air." At first, Pony was so untamed he would not let Ward touch him, but over time he became the driver's pet. "When he started with a coach, he always went through," explained Ward. "Sixty miles was an easy day's run for him; he has followed me fifty miles every day for months without missing a trip."[2]

By the late 1850s, the stage line through the Sacramento Valley was gradually extended from Northern California into Oregon. Ward moved north, driving coaches from Yreka, California, to Salem, Oregon. Pony always went with him, and Ward could not get him to ride in the coach. On one occasion, Pony trotted from Yreka to Salem, a distance of three hundred miles, in four days and nights. The only rest he got was when the stage stopped for meals and to change teams. Ward said that after they arrived in Salem, "He was entirely played out. His feet were bleeding and raw, and he was not able to move. We gave him up for dead but in two weeks he was on the road again and was making fifty miles a day with me."[3]

In the fall of 1860, the California Stage Company completed the first stage route between Sacramento and Portland. Wells Fargo began to employ jehus like Ward to act as messengers in delivering express matter. This was his first service for the company. On September 15, 1860, Old Wardy was at the ribbons of the first stagecoach out of Portland on the new route to California. In 1862, he went east to The Dalles and drove coaches on the Columbia River road, always accompanied by Pony. That year, gold was discovered in Idaho, and the road between Portland and Walla Walla, Washington, became a major entry point to the new El Dorado. Ward drove between The Dalles and Umatilla and then to Walla Walla. He raced his teams so fast that he made better time than the Columbia River steamers. In 1863, Pony made his last run with Ward from Walla Walla to the river port of Wallula and back, a round trip of sixty-two miles. The next morning, he died in Ward's arms. He had served his master faithfully for nine years. "Poor old Pony," recalled a mournful Ward. "He was the pioneer stage dog on the Pacific Coast."[4]

A few years later, Ward started working for Wells Fargo as a driver and shotgun messenger on the stage line from Boise to the mining camp of Silver City, Idaho. Shoshone Indians made the route especially

Henry C. Ward, the pioneer stage driver and shotgun messenger for Wells Fargo. [*Courtesy of the Department of Special Collections, Stanford University Libraries*]

dangerous. Ward recalled that the road was "infested by roving bands of Indians. They generally went in small bands (about twenty) attacking anything they thought they could capture. They often attacked stages and invariably from ambush. . . . The attack was generally made by two Indians hid in the rocks a few feet from the road and where the stage would be moving slow. The Indians [were] each armed with a rifle, one to kill the driver and the other one of the lead horses; the balance of the band of Indians in hiding nearby to attack the stage." Ward recalled that this was the method used to slay his friend and fellow jehu William Younger. On March 23, 1867, Shoshones attacked the Boise and Owyhee stage, killing Younger and two passengers. A year later, in May 1868, Ward was riding with driver Robert Dixon one day before the latter was shot and killed by Shoshones on the Boise to Silver City route.[5]

Despite the dangers of his work, Old Wardy never lost his sense of humor. He was given to occasional sleepwalking, and one night in 1867, he arose from his hotel room in Walla Walla, stepped onto the balcony, and fell two floors to the street below. Through seriously injured, he joked that he "had driven stage many years but never had done better time than while going that twenty feet." Like most frontiersmen, Ward liked to imbibe. On June 3, 1867, he was in Walla Walla for the general election. Frontier elections were exciting, intensely partisan events accompanied by copious drinking and fighting. The widespread brawling spilled over to the next day, when Ward got roaring drunk and with two cronies drove a buggy along the sidewalks, blowing a celebratory horn. A policeman led the horses off the sidewalk, but Ward whipped his team back. The officer then tried to arrest one of his friends in the buggy. The man pulled a pistol, fired, and missed. The policeman shot back, but his aim was also poor. He then tried to arrest Ward, who yanked his six-gun, pointed it in the air, and shouted that "there weren't enough men in town to arrest him." The popular expressman escaped serious punishment.[6]

On the night of September 22, 1868, Ward was riding shotgun on a stage near Wagontown, ten miles west of Silver City, Idaho. A second Wells Fargo shotgun messenger, George W. French, was on board, which was customary when either an Indian attack was expected or the coach carried a heavy treasure shipment. Ward rode on the seat next to the driver, while French sat behind them on top of the stage. Five passengers were inside. The coach was moving through a narrow cut when the off, or right front, wheel struck a small rock. The impact stopped the wheel and forced the stage toward the right bank. The coach careened so far up the bank that it flipped onto its side, rolling over one and a half times until it slammed into a tree. French's head was caught between the coach and the tree, killing him instantly. The impact threw the jehu forward onto the team, but he was not seriously injured. Ward was trapped beneath the front of the overturned coach, his legs pinned, so he could not move. Reported a local journalist, "Had he not been a man of powerful frame, he would doubtless have been crushed to death, as at one time the entire weight of the stage was upon him." The passengers, unhurt, lifted the stage to extricate Ward. This freed one of the terrified wheel horses, which began kicking him in the face. With great strength, Ward seized the animal's hoof, lessening the blows. Nonetheless, he was painfully injured as he struggled to hold the horse's lower leg.[7]

The hardy messenger quickly recovered and Wells Fargo officials assigned him to safer steamboat duty on San Francisco Bay. Then in the spring of 1869, the company's superintendent, John J. Valentine, sent Ward to the White Pine mining district in eastern Nevada. His new route was the short stage road between Hamilton and Treasure City. According to James Otey Bradford, an old Wells Fargo man, Valentine "was annoyed by the slow time made by our outfit between those two points" and he ordered Ward "to run opposition to the Pacific Union Express Company and to beat it."

Treasure City was located atop Treasure Hill, three miles south of Hamilton, which was situated at the base of the hill. Drivers used a light wagon to carry express from Hamilton up the hill, which they considered an easy trip. But the downhill trip was steep, treacherous, and very slow. Ward first met with the stage agent in Hamilton. He recalled, "I told him that I wanted a pair of strong horses, but they must be active as I had to drive fast down the mountain." His wagon ready, he made the trip easily up the hill to the express office. Explained Bradford, "The time for the return trip having arrived, Wardy hitched up his team and drove them with considerable pride to the front of the office. He was arrayed in a new suit of clothes, boiled shirt, new hat and diamond pin in his blue cravat—blue was his favorite color—for Wardy was a great dresser and favorite among the ladies."

But now, Ward's only thought was to beat the competition. As he pulled his horses in front of the Wells Fargo office, he called out to the expressmen inside, "Boys, you need not be in a hurry. I will give the Pacific Union a long start and then beat it into Hamilton."

Ward later said, "I thought ten minutes would be enough and I waited for the last letter. The Pacific Union had been gone some time when I left." Then he whipped his team at breakneck speed down the mountain. Declared Bradford, "They passed the Pacific Union outfit as if it was standing still and nearly crowded it off into a canyon." Hamilton townsfolk saw a cloud of dust racing down the trail; some thought it was a stampeding band of wild horses. "I went through town like soap through a sink," recalled Ward, "and brought up in a corral at the lower end of town a little ahead of time."

Bradford declared that Ward was a sight to behold. He had been thrown to the floorboards and his trousers were torn to shreds. "He was covered with dust," Bradford reported. "The mares had kicked him from his seat and in their fright on the last half of the excursion had made water all over him, making it necessary to have the new suit and the boiled shirt renovated."[8]

With the Pacific Union bested, Old Wardy returned to steamboat duty on San Francisco Bay. On the evening of December 3, 1869, he was on the wharf in Vallejo, climbing the gangplank to the San Francisco–bound steamer *New World*. As he lugged two heavy Wells Fargo treasure boxes, he suddenly slipped and fell. Ward managed to cling to the gangplank, but the strongboxes plunged into the bay. Reported a journalist, "One of the boxes was partially fished up from its watery grave but fell again to the bottom, and when the steamer left Vallejo neither had been recovered." Ward was more than relieved when the two strongboxes arrived in San Francisco the next day. Ten minutes after his steamer had shoved off, the express boxes were found and hauled out of the water.[9]

In 1872, Henry Ward went into business on his own. He and a partner, George Colegrove, started a stage line between Watsonville, California, and the coastal lumber town of Santa Cruz, driving their first coaches in January 1873. The two partners bought and sold several stage lines running between San Jose and Santa Cruz, but in 1874, Ward left to join a Wild West show. That venture lasted but two months. Though Colegrove was furious at Ward for quitting, the pair immediately renewed their staging partnership. On a journey over the Santa Cruz Mountains, a newspaperman described Old Wardy's talent with the ribbons: "Ward, a veteran among California stage coach veterans, handles the reins over six splendid and sure-footed animals. Under his skillful guidance these horses seem to fly as they whirl the coach down steep hills, and around the shortest of curves."[10]

He and Colegrove operated their stage company until 1877, when Old Wardy returned to Wells Fargo as a shotgun messenger. Company officers assigned him to the Nevada stage routes out of Winnemucca, Carson City, and Hamilton, as well as the boomtown of Bodie, California. Bodie was a very rich and wild camp, and Wells Fargo sent two other famous messengers, Mike Tovey and Aaron Y. Ross, to help Ward guard its express shipments. On New Year's Day 1878, Ward was in Hamilton when his shotgun accidentally discharged, sending a full load of buckshot into one hand. A doctor amputated one of his fingers. The shotguns carried by messengers all had exposed hammers, which meant that if something struck a hammer while it rested on a live cartridge, the weapon could fire. This resulted in occasional accidents and was probably the cause of Ward's wound.[11]

A posed photograph of a stage robbery in California circa 1880.
[Author's collection]

In 1881, Ward was sent to Boise, Idaho, and the next year he returned to Nevada. In August 1882, lawmen arrested a pair of stage robbers, Robert Catterson and Charles Nicholes, and lodged them in jail in Hamilton, Nevada. They soon escaped by kicking through the flimsy wall but were quickly recaptured. This time, they were locked up in the supposedly more secure jail in Eureka. On November 5, they cut a hole through the jail wall, slipped outside, stole a handcar, and started north on the narrow-gauge railroad tracks toward Palisade. The pair pumped the handcar for twenty-five miles, until they became exhausted on a long upgrade. Just before reaching the summit, twenty-seven miles north of Eureka, they pulled the handcar off the tracks and fell asleep in the brush. Unknown to them, another mile would have brought them to a fourteen-mile downgrade and to safety. Meanwhile, Henry Ward had been notified of their escape, and he boarded a northbound train in pursuit of the desperadoes. He soon spotted the abandoned handcar next to the tracks. Ward ordered the engineer to stop, and he began searching the brush. The sleeping fugitives wakened, looking down the yawning barrels of Ward's sawed-off shotgun.

He took them back to jail in Eureka and made arrangements for a local photographer to take their mug shots. The photographer recognized that they might not willingly sit for the camera, so he told them, "Boys, there is a young lady in town who is very anxious to have your portraits. Now if you want to have them taken I will pay for it and will bring the gal in and you can give her one." The outlaws agreed and were taken to the photo gallery, where their images were taken, according to the town's newspaper editor, "before they had time to drop on the little racket." The duped desperadoes were returned to jail, convicted, and sentenced to nine-year terms in the Nevada State Prison.[12]

In 1885, a rash of stage holdups took place in Sonoma County, on California's North Coast. On February 9, two road agents stopped a stage near Cloverdale and escaped with the Wells Fargo box. On March 26, a lone highwayman repeated the feat. On April 7, a bandit tried to stop a coach twenty miles north of Cloverdale. When he fired his pistol into the air, the team spooked and raced off. Eleven days later, a stagecoach was robbed by a lone road agent near Cloverdale. No shotgun messengers had been aboard any of the stages. Wells Fargo sent Henry Ward to Cloverdale to deal with the robbers.

At that time, Cloverdale was served by railroad, but travel from the train depot west to the coast was by stage. At eight o'clock in the evening of May 8, driver James Romaine, with Ward riding next to him, picked up three passengers and started for the coastal town of Mendocino, seventy miles distant. The express box held $27,000. Nine miles from Cloverdale, after passing the Mountain House, Ward spotted two armed men ahead. One was standing in the road, the other on an embankment at the same level as the driver's seat. The man on the embankment shouted, "Halt! Halt, I say!"

At that, Ward told Romaine, "Pull up. I want to interview the gentleman."

In shotgun messenger's parlance, an "interview" meant shooting it out with bandits. As Romaine pulled back on the reins, the robber on the embankment fired his Winchester rifle at a range of just nine feet. Ward replied instantly, swinging up his shotgun and letting loose with one barrel. He thought he had missed, but a woman passenger saw the bandit drop. Ward, blinded by the concussion and the gun smoke, turned his shotgun on the highwayman in the road. Before he could shoot, the second bandit fired a shotgun blast. Several buckshot slammed into Ward's right hand, shattering his trigger finger. The rapid firing spooked the horses and they broke into a run. The shooting happened at such close range that Romaine's face was blackened with gunpowder and his hat was blown off.[13]

The coach raced to the next station, where Old Wardy boarded a return stage for Cloverdale. A witness who saw him arrive in town reported, "He came in blood-bespattered clothes, powder-burned face, with his right hand hung in a sling and with the torn buckskin glove still on the hand. He smoked a cigar with astonishing coolness, joked and laughed, and considered himself extremely fortunate in his narrow escape from death."[14]

The holdup men managed to disappear. Whether Ward had killed or wounded one of the bandits remained a mystery. However, a mail robbery on the same road in February 1886 led to the arrests and convictions of two highwaymen, who were sent to San Quentin. One of them, John Hamilton, confessed to Wells Fargo detectives that he and three accomplices, Charles Prescott, Samuel Eades, and George Clark, had held up Ward's stage. Hamilton admitted that he had been wounded by Ward, and he showed Wells Fargo detectives a bullet scar on one of his legs. The detectives looked into his story and became convinced that he was indeed the man shot by Ward. They concluded, however, that Hamilton was trying to get revenge against his three former comrades and was lying about their involvement. Nonetheless, all three were arrested and charged with attempting to rob the U.S. mail. During their preliminary hearing in federal court in San Francisco, they proved an alibi and were released.[15]

Although Wells Fargo's chief detective Jim Hume later declared that Ward had been "permanently crippled" by his wound, he was soon back on duty. A few months later, on August 4, 1886, the Ukiah stage was stopped three miles north of Cloverdale by two masked road agents, who made off with the Wells Fargo box. By this time, Ward was riding the stage route from Milton to Sonora in the mining region. He and Wells Fargo detective John N. Thacker rushed to Cloverdale by train. They set out on horseback to the holdup site and quickly cut the bandits' trail. Joined by two possemen, they tracked the highwaymen fifty miles east through rugged country to Lower Lake, and then another thirty miles across the Coast Range to Sulphur Creek, in Colusa County. There, on the night of August 7, Ward and the posse captured George Wilson and Thomas Cole. The pair confessed, pled guilty, and were sentenced to ten years each in San Quentin.[16]

Old Wardy seemed to be indestructible. In January 1888, he was thrown from a lurching stagecoach near Ukiah and hit the ground so hard, he broke his shoulder. Just three months later, on April 28, two bandits held up a stage between Cloverdale and Lakeport, then shot to death a constable who had been leading a posse in pursuit. In the exchange of gunfire, one bandit was killed and the other shot and

The notorious stage robber Ham White,
who shot it out with Henry Ward in 1891.
[*Author's collection*]

captured. Ward, despite his shoulder injury, was soon on the scene with
John Thacker to help investigate. He provided testimony against the
surviving robber, Joe Frey, who pled guilty and received a twenty-five-
year term in San Quentin.[17]

By 1891, Old Wardy was sixty-two, but still a highly capable guard,
assigned to stage routes throughout the upper reaches of California.
On March 7, his coach left Weaverville, bound for Redding, with Ed
Graham at the reins and Ward next to him, a Wells Fargo box under
the seat and four passengers inside. It was 7:30 P.M. when the coach
reached the "Double S" turn, two miles from Redding. Suddenly, a
masked robber appeared on the four-foot road embankment to the
right, aiming a revolver and yelling, "Halt!"

Ward had no way of knowing that the bandit was Ham White of
Texas, one of the Old West's most prolific stage robbers. Since 1877,
he had held up twenty-two coaches in Texas, Colorado, and Arizona,
and had never met resistance in any of those incidents. That was because
he had never met Henry C. Ward.

Graham brought his coach to a halt, and Ham White called out,
"Drive up a little further."

Graham obeyed, and White ordered, "A little further, or God damn you, I'll shoot."

As Old Wardy raised his shotgun to his shoulder, Ham White fired at a range of only a few feet. The pistol slug struck Graham in the right side and lodged in his breast. Unfazed, Ward pulled the triggers of his shotgun, but it misfired. Throwing the weapon onto the road, he jerked his six-gun. By this time, the terrified team had broken into a dead run. From his seat, Ward fired back over the top of the lurching coach. Ham White unloosed one parting shot as the stage raced to safety in the darkness. A manhunt for the highwayman failed. Twelve days later, White successfully robbed the same coach when Ward was not on the box. The bandit was soon captured in Los Angeles. Instead of being charged with the California holdups, Ham White was sent to Arizona, where he received a ten-year term for mail robbery.[18]

Wells Fargo officials soon obtained lighter duty for the aging messenger, replacing Ward with another noted Wells Fargo man, "Buck" Montgomery. In January 1893, they appointed Old Wardy superintendent of stables for Wells Fargo's Pacific Department. His office was first located in Portland, Oregon, and later in San Francisco. The company described his duties as "traveling inspector of wagons and stock." During the Chicago World's Columbian Exposition of 1893, Wells Fargo created a huge exhibit of items related to the company's colorful history on the frontier. A photograph of Henry Ward as well as his messenger's shotgun were prominently displayed. In June 1895, he became ill and was looked after by the company's president, John J. Valentine, and by detective John Thacker. The latter wrote to him, saying, "Just had a talk with Mr. Valentine and he says that you need have no fears. He will see that you have everything you want." Later that year, Ward retired on a pension from Wells Fargo and moved to Ukiah, in Mendocino County.[19]

Ward's condition improved and he lived another eight years. He liked San Francisco, where he had many friends, and made it his final home. In late 1903, when his health started to decline, his old Wells Fargo comrades looked after him. On January 4, 1904, superintendent

Solomon D. Brastow sent him a note: "Owing to your feeble condition, please stay in the house, as you are liable to get hurt on the street. I will be out to see you in a day or two." Ward continued to fail, and in February he was taken to the state hospital in Agnews, where he suffered a stroke and passed away on March 4, 1904. The *San Francisco Bulletin* eulogized Henry Ward as "one of the picturesque figures of pioneer days" who was "one of the most skillful and daring stage drivers of the west." He was, declared the *Bulletin*, "the hero of holdups on the road, and encounters with the Indians, who commanded the respect of the Argonauts. . . . Ward was a valued and trusted employee of Wells Fargo & Co., making a fine record for bravery as their shotgun messenger on different stage lines. He never surrendered in his battles with highwaymen."[20]

4

✦━┼━✦

TWELVE-GAUGE JUSTICE

Daniel C. Gay

Dan Gay leaped down from the doorway of the Concord coach, the hammers of his twelve-gauge shotgun at full cock. Loud shouts, the explosion of gunfire, and muzzle flashes shattered the cold night air. Sprawled before him in the muddy roadway moments later were the lead-riddled bodies of two armed stage robbers. They had made the fatal mistake of tangling with one of the deadliest law officers of the California Gold Rush.

Dan Gay was the first Wells Fargo detective to kill a man in the line of duty. Like Henry Johnson and Isaiah Lees, he worked for the company on a case-by-case basis during the late 1850s. Gay set the standard for relentless and fearless manhunting that would be the hallmark of all company detectives who followed him. He was born Daniel Conway Gay in Licking County, Ohio, in 1827, the son of Charles S. Gay, who moved his family to northwestern Missouri in the late 1830s. In 1838, the elder Gay was one of the founders of the village of Gentryville and built Gentry County's first sawmill. Eight years later, when Dan Gay was eighteen, he married his sweetheart, Barbara Jane Smith. The Mexican War was under way, and in April 1847, he enlisted in the Third Regiment, Missouri Mounted Volunteers. When his regiment moved out for New Mexico, Gay left behind a pregnant bride. He was promoted to sergeant and rode with his company through much of the Southwest. At the end of the war, in 1848, he was discharged and returned to his wife and infant son in Gentryville.[1]

Soon, news from California of the gold discovery swept through the Middle Border states. Gay, overcome with gold fever, and despite his wife's objections, was determined to "see the elephant," the popular expression for joining the Gold Rush. The expression originated with the apocryphal story of a farmer who, on hearing that a circus was coming, loaded his wagon with produce and started for town. Circuses featuring elephants were rare, and few Americans had ever seen one. The farmer encountered the circus parade on the way, and his horses, terrified by the elephant's scent, bolted and overturned his wagon, spilling his produce across the road. Bruised and shaken, the farmer declared, "I don't give a hang. I have seen the elephant."

In the spring of 1849, Dan Gay and many others joined the wagon trains that passed through Gentry County on the way west. A witness described it as "a scene to beggar all description. There was one continuous line of wagons from east to west as far as the eye could reach, moving steadily westward, and like a cyclone, drawing into its course on the right and left many of those along its pathway. The gold hunters from Gentry County crowded eagerly into the gaps in the wagon trains, bidding farewell to their nearest and dearest friends, and many of them never to be seen again." Gay reached California but found no riches in the placer mines. He discovered his calling in 1852, when he obtained appointment as a Sacramento police officer. A young man of imposing presence, he stood six feet tall and weighed two hundred pounds. He loved California and returned to Missouri several times to try to persuade his wife to join him. She refused and divorced him in 1857.[2]

Policing in the Gold Rush was extremely dangerous, for almost all men carried pistols and bowie knives, and consequently, most arrestees were armed. Dan Gay had many encounters with desperadoes. In 1854, a notorious outlaw, "Tipperary Bill" Morris, escaped from San

Charles P. O'Neil, Dan Gay's partner and fellow Wells Fargo detective, circa 1859. [*Author's collection*]

Quentin Prison. He eluded pursuit and made his way to Sacramento. There, on December 4, 1854, he got roaring drunk in a saloon, mounted his horse, and opened fire on an unarmed policeman. The officer ran to the station house, where Dan Gay was on duty. Gay, on foot, pursued Morris to the corner of Tenth and L streets and called for him to halt. Tipperary Bill jerked his pistol and fired; the bullet whined by Gay's head and slammed into a fence behind him. Gay fired back and hit Morris's horse in the thigh. The outlaw galloped off, but another policeman shot him in the back, a serious but not fatal wound. The officers returned Tipperary Bill to San Quentin, where he soon recovered. In 1858, he was pardoned for his assistance in preventing escapes, but the next year he was arrested and convicted in San Francisco for shooting a man in a saloon. On June 10, 1859, Tipperary Bill died on the city's gallows.[3]

As a result of Gay's exploit, Sacramento officials promoted him to lieutenant of police, and later to detective. He made countless arrests and came to know intimately many of the brigands and ruffians who infested the Mother Lode region. In 1856, he played an important role in breaking up the infamous Tom Bell gang of highway robbers. In the spring of 1857, he and his partner, Detective Charles P. O'Neil, made plans to capture a band of white and black freebooters operating around Folsom, twenty-three miles northeast of Sacramento. Two of its most dangerous members were Edward Jackson, an African-American, and the notorious Bill "Mountain" Scott, a New Yorker of Jamaican descent. The officers gradually identified most of the bandits, and in July, with the help of constable Ben Bugbey, raided their hideouts in Robbers' Ravine, a mile north of Folsom. The raids took several days and netted eleven felons. O'Neil and Bugbey captured Mountain Scott, and soon after, Gay and Bugbey arrested Edward Jackson, who ran a brothel on a Folsom hilltop. Before taking Jackson to Sacramento, Gay let him eat a meal. As they left the house, Jackson's wife threw her arms around him and slipped a pistol into his hand. Jackson bolted, and in a running gunfight, Gay broke his leg with a pistol shot at a range of more than a hundred yards. Jackson was handed a term in San Quentin, but a year later he attempted to escape with several other convicts, and prison guards shot him dead.[4]

Gay and O'Neil were rewarded by the city of Sacramento by having their pay docked for each day they had been absent from town. Police officer appointments in that era were often made based on political connections rather than on merit. In Sacramento, policemen served for only three months and then had to be reappointed. In November 1859, when Gay refused to make a ten-dollar donation to a city politician, he was dismissed from the force. The *Sacramento Union* bemoaned the fact that "an old policeman . . . whom one more efficient cannot be found in the State, has been thrust aside to make room for some political favorite. . . . Such disregard of the public interest is enough to disgust every good citizen." Such criticism resulted in Gay quickly being reappointed.[5]

Meanwhile, Gay, oblivious to the political controversy, was investigating a band of stage robbers at the behest of Wells Fargo. There had been numerous highway robberies on the roads outside of Sacramento, plus a number of stage holdups in nearby Placer County. James H. Latham, the Wells Fargo agent in Sacramento, had received a tip that a gang of brigands, headquartered in Stockton, was planning to rob the stagecoach from Foresthill to Auburn, in Placer County. He hired Gay and O'Neil to work up the case. From the same tipster, the detectives learned the date of the planned holdup. On November 8, 1859, Gay and O'Neil rode to Foresthill and warned the town's Wells Fargo agent of the plot.

That night, the two officers boarded a stagecoach bound from Foresthill to Auburn. A driver known as "Little Dave" was at the reins. When the coach stopped at Todd's Valley, three miles from Foresthill, Gay had the treasure box removed and ordered the passengers off the stage. The coach left at 3:00 A.M., with only two passengers aboard: Gay and O'Neil, armed with revolvers and double-barreled shotguns. The stage had gone less than a mile and was slowly climbing a steep grade when four bandits rushed out from the roadside trees. Two of them were Isaac Bryant, alias Frank Smith, a dangerous burglar and highwayman, and Francisco Nunez, a noted bandido. One robber seized the lead horses while two stood on either side of the coach with drawn six-shooters to intimidate the passengers. A fourth highwayman ordered the driver to throw down the Wells Fargo express box.

ISAAC BRYANT, alias FRANK SMITH, alias FRANK MURDOCH.
noted Burglar and Highwayman, shot on Tuesday, while attempting to stop the Sta...

Isaac Bryant, stage robber. He was killed in the 1859 gunfight with Dan Gay and Charles O'Neil. [*Author's collection*]

Gay and O'Neil reacted instantly. Throwing open the coach doors, the shotgun-wielding lawmen jumped into the roadway. They could barely see the outlaws in the dim light from the coach lamps. O'Neil opened fire on the robber closest to him. Isaac Bryant dropped, instantly killed by a load of buckshot. Dan Gay and Francisco Nunez both fired at each other simultaneously. Gay's aim was true, and Nunez fell, riddled with buckshot. At that, Little Dave leaped down from the box and tried to seize the fallen bandit's six-gun. Nunez was determined to die game, and he fired again, striking the driver in one hand. Suddenly, the other two highway robbers opened up on Gay and O'Neil. The officers dropped their empty shotguns and responded with a barrage of pistol fire. They exchanged twenty shots before the two road agents fled into the blackness. The detectives chased them a short distance, then prudently returned to the stage. There, Francisco Nunez called Gay and O'Neil to his side, shook their hands, and died. The two highwaymen were buried in Todd's Valley.[6]

After Wells Fargo paid Gay and O'Neil a fifteen-hundred-dollar reward, the two detectives continued investigating the gang of highwaymen. No doubt through the same stool pigeon, they discovered that the stagecoach from Angel's Camp, a celebrated mining town in Calaveras County, was to be robbed on its way to Stockton. O'Neil went to Stockton, where he secretly followed the ringleader, a robber known as "Cherokee Bob," and his partner, a hard case from Los Angeles called "Boss," around town for two or three weeks. Gay and O'Neil intercepted a letter to one of them that gave details of the plot. On January 13, 1860, Cherokee Bob, Boss, and two other desperadoes boarded a stage driven by Walter Moore and took it to Angel's Camp.

Meanwhile, O'Neil left Stockton and joined Dan Gay in Angel's Camp. In the early-morning hours of January 15, the down stage, again with Walter Moore at the ribbons, was loaded for its trip to Stockton. In the Wells Fargo office, Gay and O'Neil, knowing that the gang was watching the stages, put two bags holding fifty pounds of lead shot into the Wells Fargo box. When Moore and the express agent loaded the heavy box onto the stage, any observer would have thought it was a large shipment of gold from a local mine.

It was close to 4:00 A.M. when the coach left Angel's Camp. Gay and O'Neil, carrying shotguns, took seats with the passengers. The stage had gone two miles when they told the passengers that it was going to be robbed. Upon reaching the Cherokee House, the detectives instructed Moore to stop and ordered all the passengers to get off. Gay and O'Neil rolled up the leather side curtains so the brigands would think that the coach was empty. Then they crawled into the leather boot at the rear of the stage and told Moore to drive on. The passengers followed on foot at a safe distance. The coach had rumbled forward half a mile when a gunshot suddenly rang out from the roadside brush. Four road agents appeared and ordered the driver to halt.

As the coach rattled to a stop, Gay and O'Neill burst out of the boot. Cherokee Bob had his six-gun aimed at the jehu when the two detectives cut loose and dropped him with blasts of buckshot. Gay spotted a robber on the other side of the stage and fired, wounding him. The outlaws and lawmen exchanged between twenty and thirty shots with six-shooters at close range. Cherokee Bob, desperately wounded, managed to drag himself into the brush and disappeared with two of his fellow bandits. The fourth robber raced on foot back up the road toward Angel's Camp and ran into the passengers. He cried, "Oh gentlemen, protect me. They are trying to kill me!"

In the darkness, they thought he was one of the detectives and let him pass. But a few minutes later, Gay and O'Neil ran up in pursuit of the highwayman. They closed in on him and exchanged more shots, but the desperado escaped. At daybreak, no trace of the wounded road agents could be found. But Gay and O'Neil were certain they had slain Cherokee Bob, and they reported this fact to the newspapers.[7]

Reports of the shootout, following so closely on the heels of the first holdup attempt, created a public sensation. Gay and O'Neil were widely praised in the press. However, the editor of the *San Andreas Independent* claimed that the officers' account was "very exaggerated"

ANCISCO NUNEZ, (a Mexican) one of the Robbers killed in attempting to sto
a Valley Stage, on the 5th inst.

Stage robber Francisco Nunez, shot to death by Wells Fargo
Detective Dan Gay on November 8, 1859. [*Author's collection*]

and that "nobody was scratched." A correspondent to the *California
Police Gazette,* who claimed to have been a passenger on the stage,
charged that the holdup was a sham to secure a Wells Fargo reward
and that "none of the killed have been found or seen." These claims
were belied by the fact that the driver, Moore, and several of his passengers gave eyewitness accounts of the holdup and gunfight. The dispute was put to rest a few days later when the buckshot-riddled corpse
of Cherokee Bob was found in the chaparral near the holdup site.[8]

The San Francisco editor of the *California Police Gazette* raised a
more serious charge against Dan Gay and his partner. He suggested—
without any evidence—that Gay and O'Neil had "employed a class of
debased characters" to rob the two stagecoaches so that they could
"attain notoriety [and] receive rewards." This was essentially the "thief
taker" scam, in which crooked law officers in eighteenth-century
England enticed naïve young men to commit robberies on the king's
highways and then arrested them for the standing rewards. However,
the three men Gay and O'Neil had slain—Francisco Nunez, Isaac
Bryant, and Cherokee Bob—were all hardened desperadoes and cer-

tainly needed no inducement to commit a robbery. There had been numerous stage holdups between 1857 and 1859 in which large shipments of gold were taken from unguarded coaches. The stolen loot had greatly exceeded any rewards that Wells Fargo had offered. Therefore it is improbable that such career criminals would trust two detectives to split a small reward when far greater sums could be obtained by a simple highway robbery with no risk of betrayal.[9]

Dan Gay returned to his duties as a Sacramento police detective. In 1861, he remarried, this time to Fanny Clark. Gay, like many forty-niners, liked to gamble and imbibe with his cronies. His heavy drinking did not sit well with his wife, and was probably a factor in the failure of their marriage. Within a few years, they divorced. In 1862, he investigated a gang of arsonists, capturing the ringleader in Victoria, British Columbia. The next year, Gay performed his final duty for Wells Fargo, arresting a suspect in a stage robbery near Dutch Flat. Soon afterward, he became a police officer on Sacramento River steamboats, but he grew increasingly unhappy with the insecurity of police work. This led him to obtain a license as a river pilot, and later as a steamboat captain. On October 12, 1865, he was second pilot aboard the famous side-wheeler *Yosemite* when she left the wharf at Rio Vista. Her boiler suddenly exploded, killing fifty-four people and wounding many others aboard. Gay, who had just left the pilothouse, escaped without a scratch in one of the biggest steamboat disasters of the era. The next year, he married for a third time, to Sarah Truman. They quickly had a son, but he died in infancy. More bad luck came when Gay became temporarily blind from straining his eyes on the river night watch. He regained his eyesight after ten months, but it was too weak for him to continue on the river.[10]

Gay gave up his steamboat captain's job in 1873, and he later obtained an appointment as a detective for the Central Pacific Railroad. Although he was one of the most experienced sleuths on the Pacific Coast, he still lacked any financial security. Early in 1879, the railroad reduced its detective bureau and Gay was laid off. He and his friend Bob Harrison, a former Sacramento police detective, promptly opened a private detective agency in San Francisco.[11]

Dan Gay's last case was the mysterious attempted murder of two eighteen-year-old girls, Ida Dunn and Cora Heslep, at a farmhouse in Wheatland, thirty-five miles north of Sacramento. On the night of June 9, 1879, someone entered their bedroom while they were asleep and savagely bludgeoned their heads with an iron bar. A two-thousand-dollar reward was offered for the assailant. Local officers promptly employed the then popular technique known as the police dragnet and rounded up the usual suspects: an African-American vagrant, a demented Frenchman, and three Chinese laborers. There was no evidence against any of them.

Dan Gay was then in dire financial straits. He and his wife lived on the edge of poverty in a single room in a boardinghouse on Broadway in San Francisco. He was so desperate for work that ten days after the assault, he entrained to Wheatland in hopes of earning the reward. Gay and his partner, Harrison, began a long investigation, assisted by their friend James B. Hume, Wells Fargo's chief detective. Gay and Harrison quickly became convinced that the assault had been committed by a jealous woman. Ida Dunn was very beautiful, and her attacker had beaten her face to a pulp, almost killing her. Cora Heslep had also received numerous blows to her face. The detectives believed that the disfiguring injuries, inflicted at close quarters with a metal bar, rather than with bare fists, made it likely that the culprit was a female who knew the victims.

The girls lived with the family of Hugh Roddan, a well-to-do farmer. Cora's sister, Flora, was married to Roddan's son, Will, and the couple had recently had a baby. Gay learned that Will Roddan had been attracted to Ida Dunn, and that Flora suspected them of infidelity. Gay believed that Flora had attacked the sleeping Ida in a jealous rage and had also beaten Cora to eliminate her as a witness. The two girls survived, but with total loss of memory of the attack. Dan Gay created a sensation when he swore out warrants for the arrest of Will and Flora Roddan. During the Roddans' preliminary hearing, on September 26, 1879, Gay was the prime witness. Under cross-examination, he quarreled with the defense attorney, who accused him of trying to blackmail Hugh Roddan into testifying against Will and Flora. Gay and the lawyer exchanged loud threats and almost came to blows before they were separated by a bailiff.

Dan Gay was so upset at the attorney's charge that he began drinking heavily. A year earlier, he had made a solemn vow to his wife that he would not touch liquor for three years. Now, the more he drank, the more depressed he became. He realized that the case was a weak one and he would probably not earn the desperately needed reward money. Two days later, he returned to San Francisco, still drinking. On the night of September 30, footpads jumped the drunken detective on the street, striking him over the head and robbing him of two pistols and his silver pocket watch. Gay waited until he was sober before returning home. Then, on the morning of October 2, 1879, while his wife was out visiting friends, he wrote her a letter professing his love and confessing that he had broken his vow. After carefully placing his Mexican War veteran's medal on top of the letter, he swallowed a fatal dose of morphine.[12]

It was a tragic end for a pioneer western peace officer and one of Wells Fargo's first detectives.

PART TWO

———————

THE STAGE ROBBERY ERA

5

FROM PONY EXPRESS TO WELLS FARGO

"Shotgun Jimmy" Brown

The acrid smell of cigar smoke wafted through the spring air as a large crowd gathered in front of the Pony Express office in St. Joseph, Missouri. Businessmen in top hats, boatmen in stained cotton overshirts, and leather-jacketed frontiersmen mingled with women and children, rich and poor, all eager to see off the young pony rider. Jimmy Brown, his heart pounding with excitement, carefully draped the leather mochila over his pony's saddle, then strapped his holstered Colt Navy revolver around his waist. The mochila's pockets were crammed with letters, telegrams, and news reports, all bound for distant California. His mount could sense the excitement and nervously pinned back its ears and cocked a hind hoof as Brown lithely swung into the saddle. With a wave of his hat, he dug spurs into the horse's flanks and the throng erupted into cheers. Jimmy Brown thundered westward, the beginning of a lifelong adventure that would mark him as one of the great expressmen of the American West.

He was born James W. Brown in Nelson County, Kentucky, in 1839. During the 1840s, his gunsmith father, Evan B. Brown, moved the family west by wagon to Savannah, Missouri, thirteen miles north of St. Joseph. Jimmy Brown, one of seven children, grew up on the

Middle Border. St. Joe, situated on the Missouri River, was the jumping-off place for westbound wagon trains on the Oregon Trail. It was an exciting place for a young boy. The border town teemed with freighters, rivermen, emigrants, and adventurers. Everyone was headed west. In the Gold Rush year of 1849, more than two thousand covered wagons crossed the Missouri River at St. Joe. The excitement was not lost on young Jimmy Brown, for he would spend the rest of his life on the frontier, on the rough edge of civilization.[1]

Like many youths of the border states, he became an expert horseman and a fine marksman; he knew how to hunt, fish, cook, and survive on the plains. He was twenty-one when the Pony Express was established in 1860, soon after the arrival of the railroad in St. Joe. Crowds of young men flocked to the Patee House to apply for jobs. Thirty riders were hired, Jimmy Brown among them. Most of them, like Brown, hailed from nearby farms and ranches in Missouri and Kansas. Brown—small, wiry, and extremely handsome—was an ideal candidate for an express rider.

When the first Pony Express rider raced out of St. Joseph, Missouri, on the evening of April 3, 1860, a great saga of the Old West began. At that time, communication between the East and West coasts was extremely slow, taking three weeks. Mail was brought to and from California by steamer or across the Southwest by the stagecoaches of the Butterfield Overland Mail Company. The Pony Express, however, promised to deliver letters and newspapers from Missouri to California in ten days. Way stations, 190 in all, were set up along a trail almost two thousand miles long. Horses and riders had to be strong, tough, and fast. The pony riders braved extreme weather, poor roads and trails, and the constant menace of Indian attack. Eighty express riders were employed at any given time. Though the Pony Express lasted but eighteen months, it immediately captured the public's imagination in a magnitude far beyond its impact on western transportation and settlement.

The Pony Express was so famous and romantic that for generations men falsely claimed that they had been pony riders. Jimmy Brown was not one of them. A quiet, confident youth, he started his expressman's career on April 13, 1860, riding the second pony out of St. Joe. Years later, he would become one of Wells Fargo's finest shotgun messengers. "Shotgun Jimmy" Brown is mentioned in almost every book written about Wells Fargo, but to date virtually nothing has been known about his life. For Brown was a modest man who, unlike other Pony Express riders such as Buffalo Bill Cody, never tried to cash in on his adventurous career.

While most of the pony riders were sent out to distant stations in the West, Brown and a few others remained in St. Joseph. His assignment was to ride the first relay section to Seneca, Kansas, a seventy-mile journey. After crossing the Missouri River by ferry, he raced toward the four stations along the way, at Troy, Kennekuk, Kickapoo, and Granada. At each, he would gallop in and peel the leather mochila from his saddle. The hostler would affix the mochila to the saddle of a fresh mount; then Brown would swing up and charge away at top speed. At Kickapoo, Granada, or Seneca, his relay rider would be waiting to continue west. Brown would stay at the station, and when the eastbound rider arrived with express from California, he returned the mail-stuffed mochila to St. Joseph.[2]

In October 1861, the transcontinental telegraph was completed and the Pony Express, instantly obsolete, went out of business. Jimmy Brown hired on as a stage conductor for Ben Holladay's Overland Mail & Express Company, headquartered in Atchison, Kansas. Like Wells Fargo's shotgun messengers, a conductor sat next to the driver and guarded express shipments. Because Holladay owned all the coaches, his messengers also guarded the lives of the passengers. Holladay's stages followed the Overland Trail from Atchison, Kansas, west to Fort Collins, Colorado, then through southern Wyoming to Fort Bridger, and finally southwest to Salt Lake City. The distance was more than one thousand miles. Brown and the other conductors each worked a route about 250 miles long, earning $61.50 a month. Before long, he would play an important role in one of the bloodiest encounters with Indians in the history of the Overland Mail.[3]

Wells Fargo revolvers issued to messengers and detectives. At top is a Colt Single Action Army Model from 1907; middle is a Smith & Wesson Schofield Model from the 1880s; and bottom is a cut-down Colt Army Model 1860, made in 1869 and known as a "belly gun." [*Author's collection*]

During the 1850s, the Overland Trail had largely avoided raids by the Plains Indians. That suddenly changed in March 1862, when Indians began attacking isolated Central Overland stations in southern Wyoming. They drove off horses and mules, destroyed stations, and killed several men. In response, Holladay's stages traveled in pairs with a heavy guard. On April 16, two westbound Concord coaches, heavily laden with mail pouches, rolled out of Sweetwater Bridge station. This spot, which included an army fort and a bridge across the Sweetwater River, was midway between present-day Rawlins and Lander, Wyoming, on what is now Highway 287. The stages held nine men: Jimmy Brown, Overland Mail division agents Lem Flowers and William Reid, Agent T. S. Boardman, two drivers, two other stage employees, and one passenger. All were armed with six-guns and one carried a rifle.

Due to heavy snow, they made only twelve miles to Plante's station, formerly a Pony Express stop, on the first day. Brown and his companions learned that most of the horses at the station had been stolen by Indians, so they were forced to rest their mule teams overnight. At daybreak on April 17, they left in a swirling snowstorm. After digging through several drifts that blocked the road, they made another twelve miles and reached Split Rock station at 10:00 A.M. Here they found the station abandoned. Two days earlier, it had been raided by Indians, the stock stolen, and two men slain. Brown and the others scrounged around the stable and found enough hay to feed the mule teams. Then the two coaches started off again. Four miles out, they reached a hilly spot where the sagebrush was thick on each side of the road. Suddenly, a shout rang out from one of the party: "The Indians are coming!"

Jimmy Brown spotted a band of warriors charging wildly toward the two coaches. At the same time, Indians in the brush opened a volley of fire on the stages. A bullet slammed into Arthur Stephenson, driver of the first coach, plowing across his chest and narrowly missing his heart. Escape was quickly blocked by Indians in front and behind. The drivers raced off the road to a slight elevation on their left. The two coaches stopped, side by side, about ten feet apart. As gunfire rattled the stagecoaches, one of the mules was shot in the mouth. The stage men unhooked the terrified teams and let them loose, hoping the Indians would be satisfied with the mules. Instead, the warriors kept up a hot fire and bullets and arrows rained down on the two stages.

Brown and the rest quickly dragged out mail sacks, buffalo robes, and trunks and piled them into two barricades at the open ends between the coaches. From their makeshift barricade, they fired back with six-shooters. As Jimmy Brown crouched behind one of the rear wheels, a rifle ball ripped into the left side of his face, just under the eye, tearing a path through his neck and lodging under his left ear. Blood gushed from the wound, and he dropped to the ground, gasping, "I'm killed!"

Moments later, two slugs hit Lem Flowers in the hip and the lower back. Another of the band, Phil Rogers, caught two arrows in his right shoulder. James Anderson, firing his rifle from inside one of the coaches, took a ball in the left leg, and William Reid dropped with a bullet in his back. By now, five of the nine men were wounded, four of them seriously. "Bullets pattered like hail upon the sacks that protected us," said Agent Boardman later. "We returned the fire with the rifle and our revolvers whenever we got sight of any of the foe, reserving most of our revolver shots for their charges. They charged upon us twice, but the volleys we poured upon them repelled them."

The battle raged for four hours. The Indian warriors numbered about fifty. Some of the defenders thought they were Arapaho, others believed they were Snake (a generic term for Bannock or Shoshone). Finally, at four o'clock, the Indians' firing began to die out and they started withdrawing in groups of two and three. The four stage men who were not wounded began digging breastworks, using a shovel from one of the coaches. They soon gave up and decided to try to make it to the next station. Boardman recalled, "Brown, whom we supposed dead, we found by assistance was able to walk, though very weak from the loss of blood." Flowers and Reid, however, were too badly wounded to walk. The men removed the front wheels and wagon tongue from the body of one coach, made a bed of blankets and buffalo robes, and put Flowers and Reid on it. Then they began pulling the makeshift conveyance down the stage road. "It was slow work," said Boardman, "and we had not gone more than a quarter of a mile when we saw the Indians returning. We lifted the two men from the truck, and by a man on each side of them, managed to walk on at quite a brisk pace."

The Indians rode directly to the abandoned coaches and soon, in the distance, the men saw smoke as they burned the stages. Brown and his comrades kept on, and after an exhausting eight-mile march, they reached Three Crossings station, a long structure made of boards and logs on the banks of the Sweetwater River. There the stationmaster and his wife tended to the wounded. "We were gratified to find that none of the wounds were likely to prove fatal," explained Boardman. After learning that the Indians had raided the station the night before and stolen all the mules, the stage men tore down an outbuilding and used the logs to fortify the station house. They spent five days holed up at Three Crossings, but the Indians did not return. On April 21, they hitched oxen to two wagons and started a two-week, two-hundred-mile journey through snow and freezing temperatures toward the protection of Fort Bridger. On the way, they learned that Indians had raided up and down the line. Several stationmasters and their families joined the little party as they headed southwest. At Green River, they learned that the Indians had killed that station's master. After much suffering, they finally arrived at Fort Bridger on May 3. Here Brown and the other wounded men were treated in the post hospital. They had undergone one of the most harrowing ordeals in the history of the Overland Mail.[4]

Most of the original group, including Jimmy Brown and Lem Flowers, continued on another hundred miles through almost impassable snow to Weber, Utah. There a witness described Brown "walking around with a terribly disfigured countenance," and added, "The ball struck him on the left cheek bone, and glanced round to under the left ear. In its course it has probably injured directly or pressed against one of the principal nerves of the face, causing considerable paralysis of the left cheek and temple. He thinks that he will have to go on to California to undergo the operation of extracting the ball." The bullet left the once-handsome express rider with a permanently scarred face, and the wound would plague him for the rest of his life.[5]

Jimmy Brown stayed on as a conductor for the Overland Mail for several years. About 1865, he joined the gold rush to Montana territory, settling in Bannack and Virginia City. He began riding for Wells Fargo as shotgun messenger in 1870. Brown's first shooting as a Wells Fargo guard had nothing to do with protecting the company's treasure. In June 1873, he was at a stage station near Bannack when a ruffian pulled a gun on him. Brown shot and wounded the man, and the case was quickly ruled self-defense. As a local journalist wrote, "Your reporter took some trouble to investigate this case, and from all the information attainable it is clear that Mr. Brown was fully justified in defending himself by resorting to the use of a shooting iron."[6]

A few weeks later, Wells Fargo officials ordered him to investigate a major bullion theft that had long been unsolved. Two years earlier, on July 8, 1871, an overland stage had left Helena, headed south on the 450-mile-long Montana Trail, which passed through eastern Idaho to the transcontinental railroad town of Corinne, Utah. Resting on the inside seat was an iron-strapped express box containing nineteen thousand dollars in gold bars and gold dust. Despite the large treasure shipment, no Wells Fargo messenger was on board. That was a mistake. When the coach arrived at Pleasant Valley stage station in Idaho, the strongbox was found empty, its lid pried open.

Suspicion immediately rested on George Rugg, a twenty-two-year-old hard case who worked as a stock tender at isolated Red Buttes station, north of Bannack, in western Montana. The stage, carrying no passengers, had stopped there for an hour on July 9 while the driver ate a meal and Rugg changed the team. Red Buttes station was owned by two Canadians, Henry Heinsman and Donald McLean. Wells Fargo messenger Al Graeter conducted an investigation that can only be described as primitive, though not atypical for the frontier. He led a posse to Red Buttes station, where they seized George Rugg and

George Rugg, stage robber in Montana and California.
[*Author's collection*]

threatened to turn him over to John X. Beidler, a Wells Fargo guard who had achieved fame—and notoriety—as a leader of the Montana vigilantes who cleaned out the Henry Plummer bandit gang in 1863–1864. Graeter told Rugg that Beidler would be there in one hour to hang him, but the young hostler refused to talk. Then Graeter produced a rope and strung him up three times, trying to choke out a confession, but that didn't work, either. Finally, they released Rugg. Wells Fargo sent detectives in, but despite the offer of a liberal reward, they could not solve the case. They were morally certain, however, that Rugg, Heinsman, and McLean were behind the theft.

The investigation stalled for two years. Then in the spring of 1873, some sharp-eyed expressmen in Utah noticed that George Rugg was sending letters via Wells Fargo from Ogden, Utah, to Donald McLean at Red Buttes station. They opened several of the letters and read that Rugg was demanding money from McLean. Then they intercepted McLean's return letters, and in one McLean offered to pay Rugg two thousand dollars. That was highly suspicious and could not be a dispute over back wages, for no stock tender like Rugg could have earned such a sum from honest labor. Meanwhile, Rugg confided in an Ogden friend, Charles Knoth, and asked him to go to Red Buttes station and demand from McLean six thousand dollars as his one-third share of the loot. Rugg admitted to Knoth that his partners had cheated him out of his cut.

Knoth, instead, saw a chance to collect the Wells Fargo reward. In July 1873, he informed the Wells Fargo agent in Corinne, Utah, who, in turn, assigned Jimmy Brown to work up the case. Brown decided to use Knoth as an undercover man to try to extract a confession from Heinsman and McLean. Brown and Knoth took a northbound stage to Red Buttes station. Here Knoth got off, while Brown continued on to the next stop without being seen by Heinsman and McLean. Knoth told Heinsman and McLean that Rugg was going to turn them in unless he received his share of the loot. The two stage men admitted involvement in the theft but claimed that very little of the booty was left. Heinsman gave Knoth one hundred dollars in cash, plus a check for two thousand dollars drawn on a Montana bank. Knoth turned the money and the check over to Jimmy Brown.

Then Brown sought out the sheriff of Beaverhead County and the two went to Red Buttes station. They placed Heinsman and McLean under arrest and jailed them in Bannack. George Rugg was picked up in Corinne and joined his partners in the Bannack jail. Brown persuaded the vengeful Rugg to turn state's evidence, and in exchange for a promise of leniency, he made a full confession. Rugg explained that when the stage pulled into Red Buttes station, Heinsman and McLean kept the jehu occupied as they fed him his meal. Rugg, while changing the team, sneaked inside the coach. He used an iron bar to pry off the front hasp of the express box and removed a sealed tin box containing gold bars and gold dust. Then he turned the strongbox over so that the driver would not see that it had been broken. After the stage left, Heinsman hid the tin box by sinking it in a nearby creek.

Rugg admitted that soon afterward he foolishly told Jim McCoy, another stage employee, what they had done. McCoy demanded a full share in return for his silence, and the others agreed. The four stage men were afraid to sell the gold locally, where it might be recognized, so they left it in the creek until the fall. Then McLean took the gold to Canada, where he exchanged it for cash. He returned to Red Buttes in the spring of 1872, telling Rugg he had only $2,500 left. McLean claimed that he had incurred heavy expenses and could not get a good price for the gold. After McLean gave Rugg $500, the frustrated stock tender left for Salt Lake City. Jim McCoy later joined him there and displayed $2,400 in greenbacks and gold coin that he had received from McLean. Now Rugg knew he had been cheated out of his share and began writing the letters that led to his arrest.

McCoy fled to Nevada, while Heinsman and McLean were brought to trial in Bannack. Rugg, Knoth, and Jimmy Brown were the star witnesses. The jury convicted Heinsman and McLean and sentenced them to ten years each. Both were pardoned in 1880 and thereafter lived respectable lives in Montana. Not so George Rugg. For his cooperation, he was pardoned and released in 1874, but Wells Fargo had not seen the last of him. He went to California, where he robbed a stage near Marysville in 1877. He was captured and sent to San Quentin, where he died of an illness in 1880.[7]

Years later, a popular story circulated about Jimmy Brown. One of his friends recalled that in the early 1870s he was riding a stagecoach from Helena to Virginia City, Montana. "On the coach coming up was a young lady in deep mourning, about the prettiest girl that we had ever seen here and as there was no treasure aboard Jimmy got pretty well acquainted with her. She could not have been more than 26 or 27 years old and she was that handsome that when she got to the tavern at Virginia City the boys went into the dining room and ate an extra supper all around just for the chance of seeing her. . . . That evening he was very attentive to her, and most of the boys hung about the place, half inclined to be jealous." The girl told Jimmy that she was a widow and had come to settle her father's estate.

The next morning, she boarded the outbound stage. As she was the only passenger, Jimmy rode inside with her on the long ride. The two faced each other on opposite seats as they talked. In midafternoon, their conversation was interrupted by a loud yell and gunfire. Jimmy poked his shotgun out the stage window, but before he could fire, the girl leaned forward and snatched one of his six-guns from its holster.

"No, you don't," she snapped, leveling the pistol at his head.

Brown was accustomed to thinking quickly. He had his shotgun pointed out the widow at an angle to the side of the girl, about eighteen inches from her pretty face. He suddenly pulled both triggers, knowing that the blast and its concussion would stun her. As she flinched, Brown yanked the six-shooter from her hand. Then, with a pistol in each fist, he leaped out of the coach and opened fire at the highwaymen. They fled into the brush and Jimmy chased them a short distance, then returned to the stage. The girl had disappeared, leaving behind only a small gold tassel that had fallen from her watch chain. He picked it up and wore it for several years as a memento. He often declared to his friends that "if he ever saw the woman again he would marry her anyway." If the story wasn't true, it should have been.[8]

Brown became a popular figure in Montana's mining camps, where he became famous as Shotgun Jimmy Brown or simply Shotgun Brown. When his friend, stage driver Charley Phelps, was murdered by bandits in a holdup in Portneuf Canyon, on the overland route in Idaho, he raised money for a proper grave marker. It is there to this day, in the cemetery at Malad City, Idaho. In the mining towns, Brown was a familiar sight, with two holstered six-shooters and a sawed-off shotgun. As one newspaper editor wrote in 1874, "Jimmy Brown, W.F. & Co.'s Express Messenger, came into Bannack the other evening, a complete walking arsenal. Road agents are requested to be careful." Late that year, he returned to his hometown of St. Joseph, and on Christmas Eve he married twenty-nine-year-old Lucy Welch. They took a seven-week honeymoon, and returned to Helena in February 1875. Two years later, they had a daughter, May, and Jimmy doted on her.[9]

Like his fellow shotgun guard John Brent, Jimmy Brown was a heavy drinker. Another Wells Fargo messenger, Aaron Y. Ross, recalled, "Brown and Brent got on a spree in Helena and started in and acted pretty bad down the road, and the stage company turned them in and they got laid off for about a month." Brown went to work for the Gilmer & Salisbury stage line in the Black Hills of Dakota Territory. He and Brent were replaced by two messengers from California, who performed poorly. Soon after this, Aaron Ross was in Ogden, Utah, when he ran into Wells Fargo's assistant superintendent, Solomon D. Brastow. The two shook hands and Brastow asked, "Where are Brent and Brown?"

"I don't know where Brent is," replied Ross, "but Brown went out to run on the Black Hills Road for Gilmer & Salisbury."

"Well, telegraph him to come back to Ogden," said Brastow. Ross did so, and when Brown returned, Brastow said he would rehire him "if he could behave himself." The next morning, Brastow met with messengers Ross, Brown, and Brent. Ross recalled that Brastow "put me in charge of the road. He told me the first man I saw taking a drink or knew of taking a drink, to let him out. So we started up, all three of us, to go to Helena." Ross said they did not take Brastow's admonition seriously: "We all had a bottle apiece with us." They met the down stage from Helena and were happy to find fellow shotgun messengers Eugene Blair and Mike Tovey on board. The two stages stopped while the five Wells Fargo men held a whiskey-fueled reunion. "We all took a couple of drinks," recalled Ross, as Blair and Tovey boisterously congratulated Brown and Brent for getting their jobs back. Then Ross and Blair engaged in what he called a "set to," rolling around in the sagebrush in a rough-and-tumble but good-natured brawl.

Finally, one of the impatient drivers called out, "You fellows have been at that long enough. Come on or we will go along and leave you." Brown and the rest said good-bye and boarded their respective coaches. Aboard the down stage were several drummers—traveling salesmen— and on their arrival at the Wells Fargo office in Ogden, they asked Brastow what kind of shotgun messengers he had working for him. "They are considered good men," Brastow replied.

"Yes, they are a nice lot of sons of bitches," said one drummer. "They all had a bottle apiece and two of them went out and broke down nearly an acre of sagebrush fighting. I thought they were Ross and Blair. They all got on the stage and rode off singing." As Ross later observed sarcastically, "That was carrying out orders."[10]

On July 1, 1876, four masked brigands held up a coach in Portneuf Canyon, scene of many stage robberies, and made off with the Wells Fargo box. It turned out to be empty save for a few letters. Brown investigated and two weeks later arrested a suspect in the holdup. The following year, Wells Fargo officials assigned him to the stage routes of eastern Nevada. Silver had been discovered in the 1860s, and holdups of stages became increasingly common. There his most famous exploit occurred during the holdup of the Eureka-Tybo stage by a gang led by the notorious Big Jack Davis, on September 3, 1877. As related in chapter 8, when Davis tried to kill Brown's friend and fellow messenger Eugene Blair, Shotgun Jimmy dropped the desperado with a fatal load of buckshot. In the ensuing shootout, Brown was wounded in the calf of his left leg, the bullet striking the bone. The wound was a serious one, and after a doctor performed surgery in Eureka, Brown failed to improve. Wells Fargo officials sent him to Sacramento, where surgeons removed several large pieces of bone, and he rapidly recovered. By late November he was able to walk without a crutch.[11]

In February 1878, Jimmy returned to his messenger's duties in Nevada. Months earlier, in the fall of 1877, a gold bar worth fifteen hundred dollars went missing from the stage between Hamilton and Eureka, Nevada. Wells Fargo offered a three-hundred-dollar reward, and a few days later a man appeared in Eureka with the missing bar. He was Frank Clifford, a notorious stage robber and jailbreaker. Clifford claimed to have innocently found the gold bar, and the Wells Fargo agent paid him the reward. Shotgun Jimmy, as soon as he arrived in Nevada, began a careful investigation of the affair. He collected enough evidence to show that Clifford had stolen the bar, and that his paramour, Mrs. Repp, known as "Shoo Fly," had helped him. In March 1878, he arrested Clifford in Ward, Nevada, and the bandit and his

Frank Clifford, the Nevada road agent arrested by Shotgun Jimmy Brown in 1878. [*Author's collection*]

woman were indicted for grand larceny. At trial, Clifford still insisted that he had merely found the gold, and the jury hung. However, the case was retried in June 1878 and he was convicted and sentenced to twelve years in the Nevada State Prison. For her part, Shoo Fly was handed a one-year prison term.[12]

The same year, Jimmy Brown left Wells Fargo and returned to the Gilmer & Salisbury stage line in the Black Hills. He and Lucy made their home in Deadwood, where he worked with such noted messengers as Scott "Quick Shot" Davis, Galen Hill, Boone May, and Jesse Brown. According to one account, Jimmy Brown was one of the shotgun guards waiting to escort the famous ironclad stage Monitor when it was attacked and robbed by bandits at Canyon Springs station on September 26, 1878. Galen Hill received serious wounds in the bloody encounter. Brown was reportedly one of the messengers who responded to Canyon Springs station after the robbers had fled.[13]

Despite his triumphs as an express guard and detective, Shotgun Jimmy did not see the same success in his marital life. His heavy drinking and frequent absences from home took a toll on his marriage. Lucy became homesick and made occasional trips to visit her family in St. Joseph. After returning from one visit to St. Joe, she confessed to some type of sexual incident involving James M. Hall, a wealthy real estate agent. The circumstances are unclear; either they had an affair or he attempted to seduce her. Brown was enraged and brooded for a long time. When Lucy's father died on February 17, 1880, the couple made the long trip by stage and train to attend the funeral in St. Joseph. They arrived on February 23, and Brown made his way directly to Hall's real estate office. He approached Hall and ordered him to "heel" himself. When Hall said he was unarmed, Brown exclaimed, "You damned son of a bitch, I'll kill you anyhow."

He jerked his pistol and fired four shots. Hall and one of his clients wrestled the gun away and knocked Shotgun Jimmy to the floor. Fortunately for Brown, none of his bullets hit the target. He was arrested and jailed, but old friends soon bailed him out. The incident created a sensation, both in St. Joseph and in Montana. No doubt because Hall wanted to avoid further publicity, he dropped the charges. Jimmy and Lucy returned to the Black Hills together. Brown continued his service with Gilmer & Salisbury for some months, until he was offered a position as guard at the Savage Tunnel, a mine located in Lead, about three miles from Deadwood.[14]

Meanwhile, his marriage continued to deteriorate. On the night of January 5, 1881, Brown and his family were preparing to retire in their house at the Savage Tunnel. He and his three-year-old daughter, May, went to bed, while Lucy began undressing. Suddenly, Jimmy heard his wife rush into an adjoining room. A single pistol shot rang out. He leaped out of bed and found her on the floor, bleeding heavily. A doctor raced to the house and determined that a bullet had entered her side and crossed through her body. Lucy lingered for two weeks and died on January 20. Though the Deadwood newspaper ascribed the shooting to "temporary insanity," it was obvious that an unhappy marriage caused Lucy's suicide.[15]

Jimmy Brown was more than distraught. To get his mind off the tragedy, he rejoined Wells Fargo and took an assignment in Tombstone, Arizona. On March 23, 1881, after leaving little May with friends in Deadwood, he left for San Francisco, and from there proceeded to southern Arizona. Wells Fargo was plagued by stage robbers who tended to flock to the newest El Dorado. Beginning in 1880, following the discovery of silver in southern Arizona, bandits and cutthroats descended on Tombstone. Wells Fargo salary records show that Jimmy Brown was paid for messenger work, off an on, from June 1881 through March 1882. Fortunately for Arizona's road agents, they never tangled with him.[16]

The next year, Brown left Wells Fargo for the last time. In December 1883, he returned to Helena, Montana. The local newspaper reported, "He is receiving a hearty welcome from his friends, who have not seen him for several years." Within a few weeks, he signed on as a bullion guard for the Gloster Mine, twenty-five miles northwest of Helena. His daughter, May, now six, lived with him, and the two were inseparable. In June 1885, he took his final guard post, at the Montana

Territorial Prison in Deer Lodge. By this time, his old wound from the Indian fight in 1862 was causing problems. His right side and right leg became partly paralyzed, but he shrugged it off and reported daily for prison duty.

In early November 1886, he lost the use of his right arm, whereupon he made arrangements to visit a resort in Hot Springs, Arkansas, for medical treatment. Leaving May with friends, he left Deer Lodge and stopped in Helena on his way. There he suffered a serious attack of paralysis and was admitted to Sisters Hospital. His friends sent a telegraph message to the prison, and the warden rushed with nine-year-old May to Helena. By then Shotgun Jimmy Brown was so far gone, he did not recognize her. Two days later, on November 10, 1886, he died at the age of forty-seven. The Masonic fraternity buried him in the Benton Avenue Cemetery in Helena.[17]

The editor of the Deer Lodge newspaper penned his most fitting epitaph. "Mr. B. has led a dangerous life, having been almost since boyhood an express messenger on the overland route, and had many savage encounters with Indians and robbers. He was a man of courage that never quailed and won golden opinion from his employers. . . . There are thousands in Montana who will hear with sorrow of the death of Jimmy Brown."[18]

6

THE RIFLEMAN

Steve Venard

The deafening crash of whitewater thundered through the canyon of the South Yuba River. Exploding spume splattered the lone rifleman as he carefully made his way along the rocky stream bank. It was mid-May and the river was cresting from spring runoff. Steve Venard knew that one false step would sweep him to certain death in the foaming current. He also knew that an even greater danger awaited him: a desperate gang of bandits who for months had been terrorizing the highways and byways of Nevada County in California's Sierra Nevada. Their muddy trail was easy to make out as he hefted his Henry rifle and followed the tracks around and across the granite boulders. Within moments, Venard, completely outnumbered, would test his mettle in one of the Old West's most extraordinary gun battles.

A long trail had led this quiet former schoolteacher to the granite gorge of the South Yuba that deadly day in 1866. Venard was born near Lebanon, Ohio, in 1824, and grew into a modest but rugged six-footer. When still a young man, Venard left Ohio and settled in Newport (now Fountain City), Indiana. There he taught school and displayed strong antislavery beliefs by playing an active role in the Underground Railroad. In 1850, he joined the Gold Rush, traveling overland by wagon train to California. During the ensuing years, Venard mined for gold, ran a grocery store, and served as a deputy sheriff and police officer in Nevada City, California. In 1864, he was elected to a one-year term as the town's marshal, or chief of police. Nevada County, the gold-rich heart of the Northern Mines, was filled with rowdy mining camps and even rowdier miners, and there Venard got plenty of experience as a lawman.[1]

In the spring of 1866, robbers ruled the roads of Nevada County, and George Shanks, alias Jack Williams, reigned as chief of the highwaymen. He hailed from New York and had come to California in the mid-1850s, working variously as a hotel waiter, cook, and ranch hand. He liked to boast that "his mother had said he would die with his boots on, and that he would make a liar out of her if he had half a show." In 1861, he enlisted in the Fourth California Infantry, but he soon deserted. Two years later, Shanks worked as a cook for the Barton brothers in Nevada City. When the brothers fired him, he returned the same night and shot and wounded William Barton through an open

Steve Venard, about 1870.
[*Author's collection*]

window. Shanks escaped from Nevada County and vanished for several years. Then, on the night of December 18, 1865, he terrorized the town of Colfax, fifteen miles south of Nevada City, and forced all the saloons to close. When a bystander, Lewis Kopp, tried to quiet him, Shanks jerked his pistol, shot Kopp in the chest, and fled.[2]

A few months later, Shanks got roaring drunk and raised a row in Elias Unger's saloon in Grass Valley. When Shanks beat up the saloonkeeper's son, Constable John Meek obtained a warrant for his arrest. The officer confronted Shanks in front of a crowd of fifty men, but the desperado held him off with his six-shooter. "I'm Jack Williams, the great American chief," Shanks declared, using the then-popular slang term *chief* for gunfighter.

Once again, he escaped. Shanks now embarked on a prolific spree of highway robbery on the mountain roads and trails outside Nevada City and Grass Valley. His partner was Robert Finn, a twenty-six-year-old Irishman who had worked as a bank messenger in San Francisco until he was caught, as a pioneer journalist termed it, "in flagrante delicto with the lawfully wedded but not contented wife of a Sunday school teacher." He later served two terms in San Quentin for grand larceny but escaped in January 1865. Finn fled to Nevada County, where he worked as a hard-rock miner and eventually joined up with Shanks. On February 22, 1866, Shanks and Finn halted a tax collector near Nevada City and robbed him of $250 in coin. The next evening, they stopped a boy several miles from Grass Valley and forced him to "pungle." Next the bandits commanded a teamster to stop, but the man replied, "Go to hell!" and laid the lash on his horses. Shanks and Finn fired several shots, wounding one of the animals, but the teamster easily outran them.[3]

Numerous other holdups took place, and Shanks, sometimes acting alone and always masked, was undoubtedly responsible. At one o'clock on the morning of April 19, he tried to rob a man named Smith, who fled on foot into Grass Valley. Shanks brazenly chased him into the center of town, firing two shots before Smith escaped with a bullet in his leg. George Hilton, a miner and fighting man in the nearby gold camp of You Bet, boasted that he was unafraid of the robbers and declared that he would walk the isolated road to Grass Valley alone at night. He started out on the evening of April 21, carrying a pistol and sixty dollars in his poke. George Shanks heard of the boast and decided to teach Hilton a lesson. Shanks took up a position a mile outside of You Bet and stopped each traveler who came along. After robbing them, he made each man sit down on the side of the road, until he had five in all. Next came George Hilton, who saw the six figures and thought they were all road agents. He meekly raised his hands and Shanks relieved him of poke and pistol.[4]

But George Shanks had greater ambitions. About the first of May, he and Bob Finn held up a stage driven by Sam Henry on Yuba Hill, west of Nevada City. They knew Henry and addressed him by name. The strongbox proved to be empty, so they relieved the jehu of a Colt revolver, pocket watch, and diamond ring. A week later, at three o'clock on the morning of May 8, Shanks and Finn stopped the coach from North San Juan in the mountains about three miles above Nevada City. They told the driver, John Majors, that they "did not want to injure him or take anything from him but were after Wells Fargo & Co.'s treasure." Nonetheless, they searched the two passengers, both Chinese, and savagely beat one who resisted. From his money belt they took four hundred dollars, probably his life's savings. The stage carried an iron pony safe, with an outer lock and an inner lock. The bandits pried off the outside padlock but could not open the inside lock. Shanks complained that "the expressmen were getting damned smart" and declared that "if he had known they carried such boxes he would have come better prepared."[5]

A week later, the brigands had better luck. They recruited a new man, George W. Moore, a forty-year-old escaped convict whom Finn had known in San Quentin. He had broken out only a month previous. At 4:30 A.M. on May 15, they held up the stage from North San Juan near Purdon Crossing on the South Yuba River, seven miles north of Nevada City. Shanks told the driver and passengers, "Gentlemen, we don't want anything from you, but we are after Wells Fargo & Co.'s treasure, and we mean to have it."

This time, Shanks and his masked partners were well prepared. One of them stepped into the roadside brush and emerged with two sledgehammers and a crowbar. While one robber held the seven passengers at gunpoint, another pounded away at the iron Wells Fargo safe, which was bolted to the floor, under the middle seat. But this strongbox proved to be even more secure than the last. Finally, one bandit went back into the brush and returned with a can of gunpowder. After ordering the driver to unhitch his team and take it up the road, he poured the black powder into the keyhole, tamped it down with mud, and lit a fuse. The explosion blew off the large padlock, and the highwaymen removed a leather bag holding $7,900 in gold. One of the road agents produced a bottle of brandy and passed it around to the passengers. Before slipping off into the darkness with his biggest haul, Shanks announced, "This job will be charged to Jack Williams, but he is not here."[6]

The coach raced into Nevada City, where Sheriff Richard B. Gentry quickly raised a posse. His most experienced deputy was forty-two-year-old Steve Venard. He was also the sheriff's deadliest rifleman. In his free time, Venard enjoyed hunting deer and black bear and became an expert tracker and marksman. Not long before, a friend had sold him a used Henry rifle, then America's most advanced long arm. Most firearms at that time were percussion guns that had to be loaded slowly with cap, powder, and ball. The Henry, on the other hand, was a sixteen-shot, .44-caliber, lever-action rifle that fired metallic cartridges. It was the precursor of the Winchester. Venard practiced so often with the gun that his friends joked that he "had Henry rifle on the brain." Recalled one of them, "He replied to all the jokers good-naturedly and continued his practice, raising and lowering the sights of his weapon and regulating it in various ways until he was master of it and could make it send a ball to any mark aimed at." His skill with the Henry rifle would be put to its most severe test.[7]

On that fateful morning, Steve Venard was asleep in his room in

George W. Moore, one of the three
stage robbers slain by Steve Venard
in the Yuba River shootout.
[*Author's collection*]

the National Hotel when Sheriff Gentry banged on the door and told him of the Purdon Crossing stage robbery. Within minutes, Venard was in the saddle with Gentry and four possemen, racing up East Broad Street, then through the mountains and down into the South Yuba canyon to Purdon Crossing. At the holdup site, they carefully looked over the ground but could not cut the bandits' sign. The officers concluded that the highwaymen had stayed off the road and had fled either up or down the river. Leaving the horses, Sheriff Gentry took three of his men and headed upriver on foot, while Venard and one posseman started down the granite gorge of the South Yuba. After clambering across the streamside rocks and boulders, they discovered the outlaws' tracks at Rock Creek, a mile downriver from Purdon Crossing. Venard sent his companion back upriver to get the rest of the posse, while he continued tracking the bandits downstream along the raging cataracts.

He went only five hundred feet before reaching the point where Meyers Ravine enters the South Yuba on his left. The roar of the river's whitewater drowned out almost every other noise. Then, above the din, he caught a faint sound up Meyers Ravine. At the entrance to the ravine rested a huge boulder, and just as Venard started into the gulch, he discovered a man sitting at its base, only twenty-five feet distant. It was George Shanks, and he spotted Venard at the same time. Both men went for their guns. Shanks yanked out his Colt Navy revolver and Venard instantly shouldered his rifle. As the deputy drew a bead on Shanks, he saw a second man—Bob Finn—leveling his pistol. Steve Venard squeezed his trigger and the .44 slug slammed into Shanks's heart, killing him instantly.

Finn dived for cover into a cleft of rocks. Venard levered another round into his Henry and waited. A moment later, Finn cocked his Colt Navy and raised it to fire. Venard first saw the pistol come up from behind the rocks, and he aimed carefully. As Finn's head appeared behind the gun barrel, Steve Venard fired a second time. The bullet slammed into the ruffian's head an inch below his right eye, pancaked, and tore out the back of his skull. Bob Finn died on the spot.

Venard knew that there had been three stage robbers, and he quickly scanned the brush and the rocks for the third man. Seeing nothing, he snatched up the outlaws' guns and two sacks of gold booty and tossed them under a pile of leaves. Then he jumped across the ravine and climbed fifty yards up its steep bank, all the while searching for the last highwayman. Within minutes, he spotted George Moore. The heavily bearded outlaw was a hundred yards up the ravine, Colt six-gun in hand, scrambling along the rocks to escape the gunfire. Venard took dead aim and fired. Moore fell onto his hands and knees. He kept crawling up the ravine, looking over his shoulder at Venard. The rifleman shot again and Moore crumpled. Venard kept his gun on him for a full minute, then cautiously stepped forward to make sure that the desperado was dead. He then climbed up the canyon walls to Purdon Road, on the ridge above the gorge, where he found Sheriff Gentry and the rest of the posse.[8]

When they brought the stolen gold into Nevada City, it created a sensation. Crowds gathered at the Wells Fargo office, shouting cheers for Steve Venard. The coroner, with a group of forty men, went out to

The ornate Henry rifle presented by Wells Fargo to Steve Venard for his valor in 1866.
[*Courtesy of Robert J. Chandler*]

the scene and brought the bodies into town. All three were immediately identified. While Venard had been hunting the bandits, Wells Fargo had posted a three-thousand-dollar reward. The company's agent offered him the entire sum, but he refused and insisted that all the possemen share it. They finally agreed that Venard would take half. The story of his killing three desperadoes with four shots was featured in newspapers throughout the country. Declared *Harper's Weekly* of New York City, "No romance could depict greater bravery." Wells Fargo officials presented him with an ornate Henry rifle with a silver plaque on the stock illustrating his exploit. The governor of California appointed Venard a lieutenant colonel in the National Guard, "for meritorious services in the field."[9]

The quiet lawman let none of the adulation go to his head. He continued serving as a deputy for Sheriff Gentry, and in June 1866, he became township constable at Meadow Lake City, a gold camp located near the crest of the Sierra Nevada. In 1869, he hired on as a payroll guard for the Central Pacific Railroad in Nevada, then returned to Nevada County, where he undertook an unsuccessful campaign for sheriff. Venard stayed in Nevada City, serving as a police officer. Then in September 1871, Wells Fargo officials contacted him with an undercover assignment. They wanted him to try to infiltrate a murderous band of stage robbers in Sonoma and Mendocino counties, on California's North Coast.[10]

The gang of highwaymen had been running rampant for almost a year. On the night of November 4, 1870, two of them stopped the stage from Mendocino, a picturesque fishing and logging village on the coast, to the inland ranching town of Cloverdale. One seized the lead horses, while the other covered the jehu with a six-gun. The Wells Fargo box held only a few hundred dollars. The three passengers were unarmed, but one, Joe Rawls, didn't need a gun to outwit the bandits. He leaped out of the coach and yelled, "I know these damned rascals! I know them!" The ruse worked, and the outlaws fled. Local officers picked up a Cloverdale hard case, John Lacy Houx, and charged him with the holdup. Houx, thirty-three, had come to California by wagon train from Missouri in 1856; his father ran a livery stable in Cloverdale. But there was not enough evidence, and he was released from jail.[11]

The gang learned from their mistake. Three months later, at four in the morning on February 16, 1871, three masked road agents held up a stagecoach a mile south of Cloverdale. Two seized the leaders by their bits while the third covered the driver and six passengers with a shotgun. After taking the Wells Fargo box, they ordered the coach on. Five months later, on the night of July 12, 1871, four of the gang halted the stage from Healdsburg to Cloverdale in the Russian River Valley. They used the same method as in the prior holdups: While one covered the driver with a shotgun, the others seized the team. They left the passengers alone but fled with four hundred dollars from the Wells Fargo strongbox.

Bill Reynolds, a Sonoma County deputy sheriff, suspected that John Houx and Lodi Brown, a twenty-one-year-old hard case from Hopland, north of Cloverdale, were two of the bandits. Four days after the holdup, he arrested Houx in Cloverdale and took him to the county jail in Santa Rosa. Two nights later, on July 18, Reynolds learned that Lodi Brown had been seen riding through Santa Rosa. The deputy and his brother John, a town policeman, mounted their horses and started in pursuit. After a long horseback chase on the road north to Cloverdale, they finally outran Brown and relieved him of a shotgun, pistol, and bowie knife. Brown joined Houx in jail, but two days later a judge released them both for lack of evidence.[12]

This escape from the clutches of the law greatly encouraged Houx and Brown. On the night of August 10, the pair, accompanied by a confederate, stopped the stage from Healdsburg to Cloverdale at the same spot as the last holdup. The coach held four passengers, and the driver declared, "You can't get anything out of this crowd. They are hunters." The robbers, thinking the passengers were well armed, allowed the stage to proceed and rode off empty-handed. A disappointed Houx was determined that their next job would be a success.[13]

Six days later, on the evening of August 16, 1871, John Houx, Lodi Brown, Elisha William "Bigfoot" Andrus, and a desperado known as "Rattle Jack" took up a position on an upgrade near what is now the Italian Swiss Colony winery in Asti, four miles south of Cloverdale. The repeated holdups had caused a public uproar, and many people feared traveling the highways out of Cloverdale. When the northbound stage left Healdsburg for Cloverdale at 9:00 P.M., the Wells Fargo agent, Charles D. Upton, climbed aboard with a repeating rifle, determined to guard the strongbox. Riding on top of the coach with driver Sandy Woodworth were Henry P. Benton and B. S. Coffman. Inside were eight more passengers, several carrying revolvers. Among them was Miers F. Truett, who had been one of the leaders of the famous San Francisco Committee of Vigilance in 1856. Truett owned a ranch near Cloverdale and carried a double-barrel shotgun.

As the coach approached the holdup site, Houx and his three companions, brandishing rifles, shotguns, and six-shooters, stepped into the roadway. They yelled, "Halt!" and one robber fired a warning shot into the air. Simultaneously, Charley Upton shot at the highwaymen and Sandy Woodworth cracked his whip over the team. As the stage lunged forward, the Houx gang opened up with a terrific barrage. Coffman, seated next to the jehu, tried to yank his pistol, but he caught a bullet in his arm and dropped the revolver. One buckshot tore into Woodworth's cheek and two more peppered his hat. A rifle slug slammed into Henry Benton's midsection, piercing his intestines.

Truett shoved his shotgun out the window and unloaded both barrels. Lodi Brown staggered with a minor wound to his breast, while

Rattle Jack screamed and dropped, riddled with buckshot. Wood-worth urged his team on as the wounded Coffman slumped against him. The bandits ran after the stage, keeping up a hot fire. A full charge of eighteen buckshot slammed into Coffman's side and face. Within moments, the coach was out of range. Houx, Brown, and An-drus loaded Rattle Jack onto his horse, then swung into their saddles and started off. They hadn't gone far before Jack gasped that he was dying and pleaded for them to kill him. The desperadoes did so, and after tying a rope to his neck to make it look like he had been lynched, they tossed his body into the Russian River.

The stage stopped at Truett's nearby ranch house, where Benton died the next morning. He breathed his last in the arms of his mother, who had also been a passenger on the stage. Though doctors expected Coffman to die, both he and the wounded driver recovered. This was the bloodiest California stage holdup in years and caused widespread indignation. Wells Fargo offered a reward of $3,500 and the State of California added another $1,000. But the express company did not es-cape criticism. "There was not more than $1,000 in the treasure box, which was saved at a fearful cost," declared the editor of Healdsburg's *Russian River Flag*. "The public will hold Wells Fargo & Co. respon-sible for this blood."[14]

Within days after the holdup, Steve Venard appeared in Sonoma County. He met secretly with Deputy Sheriff Bill Reynolds in Healds-burg. Reynolds explained his suspicion that John Houx's gang was responsible. They agreed that Venard, who was a stranger on the North Coast, would go undercover. For the next two months, he rode back and forth through the hills of northern Sonoma and southern Mendocino counties. He dressed in rough clothes and told folks that his name was Jones and that he was looking to buy a hog ranch. But he spent most of his time in the saloons and gambling halls of Healdsburg, Cloverdale, and Ukiah. Whenever a crowd of hard cases could be found in a saloon, "Jones" was in the middle, drinking and playing cards. He made it a point of befriending John Houx and his companions. When the des-peradoes were drunk, they talked too much, and Venard learned that a young teamster, Billy Curtis, had been one of the gang but had deserted prior to the murder of Henry Benton.

Steve Venard and Bill Reynolds held a clandestine meeting with Curtis and offered him immunity and a share of the rewards if he would rejoin the band and act as an informant. Curtis agreed and provided the names of the whole band: Houx, Andrus, Lodi Brown, his brother Johnny Brown, Tom Jones, and two spies who notified them of express shipments: Willis Samsel and Alfred Higgins. On October 10, Billy Curtis, with Venard's approval, helped John Houx stop a stage on an upgrade near McDonald's Hotel, eight miles north of Cloverdale. They broke open the Wells Fargo box and took $185, but in their haste they left $740 behind.[15]

Several weeks later, Curtis tipped Venard to Houx's most ambitious and reckless plan yet. At that time, California sheriffs were also county tax collectors. Houx intended to rob Mendocino County Sheriff David Crockett as he rode the stage from the coastal town of Big River to the county seat in Ukiah, carrying tax money he had collected on the coast. Venard knew he had to act quickly to avoid more violence. He and Reynolds met secretly with the district attorney of Sonoma County, who told them that in order to convict the Houx gang of murdering Benton, they needed one of the killers to testify against the others. Venard decided to arrest the whole gang as soon as Houx made a move to rob the sheriff. That would not be easy, for Houx had been watching Deputy Reynolds's movements.

On November 9, 1871, John Houx rode from Cloverdale to Healdsburg to make sure that Reynolds was at home. He found that the deputy was at his house with his family, apparently oblivious to Houx's movements. No sooner did Houx start back than Reynolds sent a telegraph message to Venard in Cloverdale, warning him that Houx was on his way, apparently to round up his gang and rob the sheriff. Then the deputy and another of his brothers, Hedge Reynolds, mounted their horses and raced toward Cloverdale. The unsuspecting Houx, on his arrival in Cloverdale, ran into Steve Venard and Billy Curtis. They invited him into the Cloverdale Saloon for a drink. As Houx raised a glass of whiskey to his mouth, he looked down the barrel of Venard's six-gun. "You are arrested," Venard exclaimed. "Throw up your hands or you're a dead man."

Houx, taken completely by surprise, wisely obeyed. Venard took three revolvers from the outlaw's gun belt. Moments later, the Reynolds brothers rode up to the saloon. Houx had many friends in town, so the officers put guards on all the roads to prevent anyone from warning the rest of the gang. Then Venard explained to Houx that Billy Curtis was his informant and that he had enough evidence to convict him of the stage robbery near McDonald's Hotel. Venard offered the bandit immunity if he would reveal the names of Henry Benton's killers. The treacherous Houx did not take long to save his own neck, and he named Lodi Brown and Bigfoot Andrus, but he refused to identify Rattle Jack, whose body had been found in the Russian River. He also admitted that Johnny Brown and Tom Jones had taken part in some of the other stage robberies.

While Venard guarded Houx, the Reynolds boys and Billy Curtis immediately picked up Tom Jones. Cloverdale was too small to have a jail, so a posse of citizens kept Houx and Jones under guard. At daybreak Venard, along with Curtis and the Reynolds brothers, rode to the house of Houx's ex-wife, where they believed Bigfoot Andrus was

Steve Venard's Model 1862 Colt revolver, converted to fire metallic cartridges. [*Author's collection*]

hiding out. The woman told them that Bigfoot and Lodi Brown were at a cabin in a remote canyon at the headwaters of Dry Creek, in the rugged hills about ten miles northwest of Cloverdale. She also said that Johnny Brown could be found at the house of John W. "Old Man" Houx, the father of the bandit chieftain. Venard and his posse located Brown at the Houx place, arrested him at gunpoint, and left him with Hedge Reynolds and the citizen guards.

Then Venard, along with Bill Reynolds and Billy Curtis, rode out to the remote hideout of Bigfoot Andrus, which to this day is called Big Foot Canyon. Bigfoot got his nickname from the oversized shoes he wore to confuse trackers. A local rancher guided them to the canyon, where the three possemen dismounted and proceeded on foot until they reached a small cave and spring surrounded by fresh horse tracks. They hid in the cave, hoping that the outlaws would come down to water their mounts. They waited only five minutes, at which point Lodi Brown walked down the canyon trail, leading his horse and carrying a rifle.

"Hold!" ordered Venard. The robber, seeing three shotguns aimed at him, surrendered quietly.

"Where is Bigfoot?" Venard asked.

"He's up the canyon about three hundred yards at the camp, getting dinner. You'll never take him unless you kill him," responded Brown.

Venard and Reynolds quickly came up with a clever plan. While Venard and Reynolds took cover, Curtis fired Brown's rifle in the air, then forced him at gunpoint to shout, "Bill, I've killed a big buck. Come and help me pack him in!"

Andrus soon came rushing down the canyon. As he passed Venard and Reynolds, they sprang from their cover and called, "Halt!"

Bigfoot froze, and Venard demanded, "Unbuckle your pistol. Drop it and step back!"

The outlaw had no choice but to obey. Then the possemen walked the two prisoners up the gulch to the cabin. There they found the ax used to open the express boxes, Bigfoot's extra large shoes, and an oilcloth mask. By midnight, all five stage robbers were safely locked in the Ukiah jail. Then the exhausted officers fell asleep, having rounded up the gang in twenty-four hours. When John Houx agreed to testify against Bigfoot Andrus and Lodi Brown, they both pled guilty to second-degree murder and each received a thirty-year jolt in San Quentin. Johnny Brown pled guilty to robbery and got three years in prison. Tom Jones, Willis Samsel, and Alfred Higgins were released due to lack of evidence. In December, a thirteen-year-old Indian boy who lived with the Brown family was arrested for robbing a stage with a dummy rifle he had carved out of wood. He revealed that Rattle Jack was the gang member who had been shot by Miers Truett.

When John Houx was released from jail in Santa Rosa, it caused a public uproar. He was rearrested and taken to Ukiah to stand trial for the holdup near McDonald's Hotel, which was in Mendocino County. However, the district attorney dismissed the case either because Houx had been promised immunity or because the only evidence against him was from Billy Curtis, a coconspirator. Under the law, then and now, that was not enough for a conviction in court. Complained the editor of the *San Francisco Daily Alta California*, "The deepest dyed villain of them all, John Houx, is now at large again." But justice did catch up with Houx. He returned to Missouri, where he died of smallpox a few years later.[16]

Steve Venard received statewide newspaper praise for his success in breaking up the Houx gang. He drifted north to Eureka, California, where in 1873, he was an unsuccessful candidate for sheriff of Humboldt County. Then he returned to Nevada City and worked off and on as a miner, lawman, and Wells Fargo detective. In January 1876, Jim Hume sought his help in tracking down three road agents who had pulled a pair of stage holdups in the Sierra Nevada foothills of Amador and El Dorado counties. The bandits were all noted outlaws: Charlie Pratt, "Texas" George Wilson, and "Old Jim" Smith. The latter had been a member of the Tom Bell gang during the Gold Rush. After a ten-day manhunt, Venard, Hume, and two other officers captured Texas George and Old Jim in a house near Folsom. Four months later,

Sheriff Harry Morse caught Charlie Pratt in Oakland. A judge sentenced them to twelve years each in San Quentin.[17]

In 1883, while serving as a constable in Nevada City, Steve Venard had one of his most dangerous encounters. He arrested a notorious ruffian, Joe Lawrence, who carried a bowie knife concealed inside his shirtsleeve. Venard searched Lawrence for weapons but missed the knife. The desperado whipped out the blade and stabbed Venard twice in the face and once in the neck. The lawman jerked his pistol, and instead of shooting Lawrence dead, he beat him with the gun until he dropped his knife. Venard quickly recovered. Two years later, he performed his final duty for Wells Fargo. After a stage was held up in Napa County in October 1885, Venard captured the suspect, Michael Donovan, in a Nevada City bordello.[18]

By 1888, Vernard's health began to decline and he became unable to work. He had never married and lived alone in a small cabin. Three years later, he was penniless and suffering from kidney disease. He entered the Nevada County hospital, where he died quietly on May 20, 1891, at the age of sixty-seven. His friends paid for his burial in Nevada City's Pioneer Cemetery. His death received wide coverage in the newspapers, with journalists recalling his extraordinary victory over the Shanks gang. One newspaperman provided Steve Venard's most fitting epitaph: "He was a man of modest demeanor, thoroughly temperate, of the strictest probity, and not afraid of anything."[19]

7

A SHOTGUN MESSENGER
IN OLD MONTANA

John X. Beidler

John X. Beidler was one of the most colorful and fascinating characters of the Old West. A leader of the Montana vigilantes in the 1860s, he played a major role in breaking up the outlaw gang led by Henry Plummer, the archetypical crooked frontier sheriff. He later became a peace officer and for three decades exhibited extraordinary courage in enforcing the law. The diminutive Beidler, as tough as any man who ever rode north of the Yellowstone River, cut a wide swath across one of the West's most rugged frontiers. Although his life story is prominent in Montana history, almost nothing has been written about his career guarding Wells Fargo's treasure. That is a significant omission, for Beidler, as he liked to boast, was "the shotgun messenger who never threw up his hands nor lost an ounce of gold dust for Wells Fargo."[1]

The long trail that brought him to Montana Territory began in Mount Joy, Pennsylvania. There John Xavier Beidler was born on August 14, 1831, to parents of German heritage. He had one sister and four brothers. A restless youth, he drifted from one job to another: shoemaker, brick maker, broom maker, and barkeeper. Following a failed love affair in 1854, Beidler departed for Elkhart, Illinois, where he ran a broom-making shop. Growing bored, he moved west to

Atchison, Kansas, running a saloon there and joining the antislavery forces in strife-ridden "Bleeding Kansas." He later claimed to have fought in the Battle of Osawatomie, which took place on August 30, 1856, and pitted pro-slavery Border Ruffians against abolitionists led by John Brown. Beidler said that he was "shot and left for dead on the field near Osawatomie" and that his wounds were so severe that he was "partially crippled for life." However, in another account, Beidler claimed that he fought in the Battle of Hickory Point, which occurred just two weeks later, on September 13 and 14, 1856. Either he had made a miraculous recovery or his stories were untrue.[2]

In 1858, he left Kansas to join the gold rush to Colorado, but he quickly gave up and returned to Atchison. The following year, Beidler went to Denver, where he first worked as a store clerk, then took up prospecting for gold. In 1863, he joined the new gold rush to Montana Territory, where he quickly made his mark. Henry Plummer was then sheriff at Bannack. A former marshal of Nevada City, California, he had been sent to San Quentin prison for murder, but the governor had granted him a pardon. In Montana, he led a double life and acted as chief of a large, organized band of road agents responsible for numerous robberies and murders. Montana was a wild country with very little law enforcement, and the outlaws had easy pickings until Beidler and many others formed a vigilance committee. From December 1863 to February 1864, they cracked down hard on the bandit gang, capturing and hanging twenty-two desperadoes in one of the most prolific lynching sprees in American history. Plummer and two of his henchmen were hanged on the sheriff's own gallows. Montanans lynched numerous other outlaws in the years that followed, and Beidler became widely known as the vigilantes' hangman. He would spend the rest of his life enforcing the law on the Montana frontier.

Because of his dangerous service as a vigilante, Beidler became a famous and much-beloved figure to many of Montana's pioneers. They addressed him by his favorite nickname, "X." One of his friends, in an 1867 letter to the *Helena Weekly Herald*, declared, "He is the great detective of the mountain regions, and works up every important theft;

John X. Beidler, about 1867, with buckskins, cross-draw six-gun, and bowie knife. [*Robert G. McCubbin collection*]

runs down every murderer; pursues every criminal who flees to escape justice; spots the wrongdoers often before they mature their villainy and disperses them to distant climes; takes a turn at Indians occasionally, usually at the cost of savage scalps; runs the militia when in the field, and can tell of every den of iniquity in the Territory, name its occupants, and sum up the record of their previous crimes. When important [pack] trains are to be guarded, he is called to the task, and his presence, with a picked command, has always prevented attack."[3]

Although a small man, standing but five feet, five inches tall, Beidler was strong, energetic, and fearless. He habitually wore a pair of Colt's revolvers and a large bowie knife on his gun belt. X was also gregarious and outspoken, with a sharp sense of humor and a penchant for practical jokes. Like many frontiersmen, he had a knack for telling exaggerated stories of his adventures. As one journalist explained, "It was a peculiarity of X that he was a blowhard—with the experience behind it." But Beidler also had his detractors. In 1870, while serving as a deputy U.S. marshal, he captured a Chinese suspect who was accused of murder. Instead of jailing his prisoner, Beidler turned him over to the vigilantes in Helena. Although there were strong doubts of his guilt, the Chinese man was strung up to Helena's infamous Hanging Tree. Beidler then claimed the six-hundred-dollar reward for the killer. Some Montanans were shocked, and Beidler received a death threat signed "200 Anti-Vigilantes." It read: "We shall live to see you buried beside the poor Chinaman you murdered."[4]

Beidler's earliest messenger service took place in the fall of 1866, when three Germans dug a colossal 2,180 pounds of gold in Confederate Gulch, southeast of Helena. Gold had been discovered there by former Confederate soldiers in 1864. The German miners hauled their yellow cargo from Diamond City to Helena, where they placed the gold under guard in a bank. Because of Beidler's fearsome reputation as a vigilante and deputy U.S. marshal, one of the German miners asked him to take charge of shipping the treasure 130 miles north to Fort Benton, the navigation headwaters on the Missouri River. The gold was locked in iron strongboxes, then loaded onto three wagons drawn by mules. Beidler and a special posse of ten guards rode horseback in front of and behind the wagons.

On the first night, they made camp in Prickly Pear Canyon, thirty-five miles north of Helena. Recalled Beidler, "While in camp a man came to me—an outsider who was posted about the treasure—and asked me if he would whistle would I whistle back. Then he would come and have the treasure taken off and I should get my whack. He started in to tell me his plans, telling me I was to fix the guns so that they could be stolen also, and that then there would be no killing done on either side. I told him I didn't want to hear any more plans. I knew the man and was and am very well acquainted with him. I told him I would kill him if I could."

Beidler said that he warned the German owners and they set guards to watch throughout the night. The wagons reached Fort Benton without further trouble. "No whistling and no money taken," as Beidler put it. The gold was loaded onto a steamer for a long trip by river and rail to the U.S. Mint in Philadelphia.[5]

Although Beidler later claimed that he started as a Wells Fargo messenger in 1866, in fact, he was a Madison County deputy sheriff from 1864 to 1865 and a deputy U.S. marshal from 1865 to 1870. He did not become a shotgun messenger until 1870, a position he held, off and on, until 1877. He guarded the company's shipments on the long route from Helena to the Union Pacific Railroad in Corinne, Utah. At that time, there were no railroads into Montana, and the main route to the territory was the Montana Trail, which ran from Corinne north through Idaho to the mining camps of western Montana. This wagon road from Corinne to Helena passed through 450 miles of isolated, rugged terrain. The stages would go night and day and cover the distance in three and a half days. Beidler made one trip a week.[6]

Beidler recalled that he often rode with a second messenger: "Mike Tovey was generally my companion and a good one he was." He said that there were so many holdups on the route between Helena and Corinne that Wells Fargo began running three messengers with each gold shipment. "From Pleasant Valley to Sand Hole station, in the night, two of us messengers had to ride horseback behind or at the sides of the coach, as the case might be, for the better security to the coach, and during the day we rode on the coach."[7]

X loved to recount stories of his adventures. Exaggerated storytelling was a frontier skill dating to the era of the fur trappers and mountain men. In Beidler's case, his stories were generally true, with touches of embellishment. But sometimes he spun the same yarn too often. Just before Christmas in 1867, he stepped into the El Sol Saloon in Virginia City, Montana. After a few drinks, he began regaling a group of comrades, who, one by one, quietly slipped away. When he looked up to emphasize the climax of his story, he was chagrined to find that he was alone. Beidler said nothing to his friends, but about ten days later, he remarked that he had just jailed a notorious outlaw. His companions were eager to see the desperado and followed Beidler inside the lockup, its outer walls constructed of rough-hewn timbers. He led them into the barred corridor, and once they were all inside, he quickly stepped outside the iron wicket and locked it shut. "Boys," he declared,

"I believe while I have time and everything is favorable, I will finish that little story of mine." Now with a captive audience, he leaned against the bars and leisurely finished the same old tale.[8]

Stage holdups were endemic on the Montana Trail. On the night of July 28, 1870, six road agents stopped a coach near the Pleasant Valley stage station, near present-day Humphrey, Idaho. They riddled the stage with bullets, wounding two men, but fled when a passenger returned fire. A week later, in the early-morning hours of August 5, three highwayman stopped the southbound stage at Little Dry Creek, fifteen miles south of Pleasant Valley. They looted the Wells Fargo box, took $4,200 from three Chinese passengers, and escaped. A few days later, X. Beidler rode as the lone shotgun messenger on the two-hundred-mile trip from Helena to Pleasant Valley station. Arriving there on the night of August 10, he was joined by two special messengers, "Big Nick" Freyer and Frank Orr, whom the Wells Fargo agent had hired because of the recent holdups. Both were hard cases, and the agent thought they had "sand" and would resist bandits. But Beidler disliked and distrusted them. He called Orr "a brockly-faced thief," and of Freyer, he said, "I had once arrested Big Nick for making bogus gold dust at Helena, but he broke jail and got out." Freyer's jailbreak had taken place two years earlier, in February 1868, but the charges against him were apparently dropped.[9]

Explained Beidler, "I was always in the habit of riding outside the coach with the driver. There were no passengers on the coach; they were generally afraid to travel with the treasure coach." As the stage was about to leave Pleasant Valley, with Tom Caldwell at the ribbons, Beidler decided to take a seat inside the stage, telling Orr to get up with the driver and Big Nick to sit inside. "They kicked and growled and said that I always rode outside and asked what was the matter with me. I told them I had been riding outside two days and nights and my eyes hurt me, and I thought I would ride inside because the wind was blowing so hard."

At that, Orr announced, "There's plenty of room and I will ride inside, too." Beidler ordered him to ride outside or stay behind. Orr obeyed and climbed up next to the jehu. Initially, the trip went smoothly, as Beidler later recalled. "The first run of twelve miles to Jenney's station at the mouth of Beaver Canyon we went all right, and while we were changing horses, Orr and Nick were whispering near the stable alone, which was an unusual thing for messengers to do and I watched them more closely."

It was three miles to Little Dry Creek, scene of prior holdups, and Beidler quietly told Caldwell that he was suspicious of the two special messengers. He told the driver that if there was a holdup, he was to whip up the horses and flee. They had proceeded about a mile when Big Nick turned to Beidler and asked, "What will we do if we are halted?"

"I am getting $250 per month to fight to save treasure and I will shoot at the first thing that crawls," Beidler snapped.

"X, I'll tell you a better plan," retorted Big Nick. "If we are halted, let us give up the money and ride off a half mile and come back afoot and catch the robbers."

Beidler said that he was now certain a holdup was afoot. He leaned out the window and called to Caldwell, "Hold your lines well in hand and let them run."

It was now 11:00 P.M. and the big sky was lit by a full moon. The coach charged forward and splashed across the creek, which was lined on both sides by large rocks. Suddenly, a figure arose from behind a rock and yelled, "Halt!"

Beidler said that he instantly shoved the barrel of his shotgun out the stage window. "He hadn't the word out of his mouth before he had eighteen buckshot in him. I only had to shoot about ten feet. He fell backwards and both barrels of his shotgun went off as he was falling; they looked like the smokestacks of a steam boat. The smoke from my gun had blown away and there stood my next good man—another road agent. I shot him with my other load, hitting him just about the groin. He fell over, and during this time road agents on the left hand side of the coach had fired several exciting, but harmless shots, and Frank Orr had fired one shot—I don't know what at—and Big Nick had fired one shot from a needle gun from the inside. This firing had set the team on a dead run; my gun was empty and I got my revolver out, but we were then out of range of the road agents."

Big Nick was lying on the floor of the coach, and Beidler thought he had been shot. He just laughed and told Beidler he was resting. "I called him some pet names and told him we would never be in another fight together," the Wells Fargo man recalled. The stagecoach raced eight miles into Hole-in-the-Rock station, where Beidler telegraphed a message to Salt Lake City: "Coach attacked; road agents repulsed." Wells Fargo's agent wired back that Orr and Big Nick were to bring the treasure shipment on and Beidler was to pursue the highwaymen. "I got saddle horses and three good men and started on the trail; found where one man had been buried, and found bandages and blood in their camp, where they had fixed up the wounded man. The road agents got too much start on us and we only followed them two days. It was, in fact, impossible to follow anyone in the Lava Bed country. We learned that the party consisted of seven men, four at the attack and three holding the ten horses."

According to Beidler, Big Nick Freyer and Frank Orr were immediately fired by Wells Fargo. Two months later, X learned that the second robber he had shot had died of his wounds on the Humboldt River near Elko, Nevada.[10]

It was the practice of Wells Fargo agents to maintain secrecy when large treasure shipments were made. On one occasion, Beidler learned that it was common knowledge in Helena that a big shipment of gold dust was to be sent to the railroad in Corinne. Just before the stage was to depart, Beidler told the agent to hold the shipment until the next day. The agent sent out the stage with a near-empty express box, and sure enough, the coach was held up and robbed near the Snake River. The next day, Beidler boarded a southbound stagecoach and delivered the gold shipment to Corinne safely. When he got there, he found a dispatch waiting for him from Theodore Tracy, the Wells Fargo agent in Salt Lake City, which read, "Beidler, why in hell ain't you there when our coaches are robbed?"

Beidler fired off a telegram in response: "Why in hell don't they rob them when I'm there?"

John X. Beidler, posing as a Wells Fargo messenger in 1889.
[*Author's collection*]

The messenger was furious and took a train into Salt Lake City to see Tracy and hand in his resignation. As soon as Beidler stepped into the Wells Fargo office, Tracy demanded, "Well, X, you got my dispatch?"

"And you got my answer," Beidler replied.

"Yes, and it was just as good as I sent. What are you doing down here?"

"I've quit," Beidler said.

"Oh, go on back to work," said Tracy resignedly. "I'll raise your wages."[11]

Another Wells Fargo story Beidler liked to tell was of a visit to San Francisco. There he was arrested by a detective who accused him of robbing a stagecoach in Nevada. His rough appearance was the only basis the detective had for making the arrest. Beidler asked to be released on bail, telling the jailers that Wells Fargo would provide his bond. They were stunned when a company official arrived at the city prison and bailed out their shotgun messenger. Beidler said that "when the facts became known in the newspapers the detective was made the laughing stock of the community." However, no such story appeared in the San Francisco newspapers of the period.[12]

In 1874, a railroad line was completed from Ogden, Utah, to Franklin, Idaho. Beidler was required to get off the stagecoach in Franklin and take his express box on the train to Ogden. He did this on every trip. A year later, he told a newspaper reporter in Helena, "The last time I went down they had a new conductor aboard. He came along to where I was, reposing as usual astride the treasure box, and yelled in my ear, 'Ticket!'"

Beidler was surprised and responded, "I have no ticket."

"Pass, then?" asked the conductor, for Wells Fargo messengers were issued railroad passes.

"No pass, either," said the messenger.

"Well, then, you'll have to get off this train."

"All right," replied Beidler. "I bet you two to one that I beat you into Ogden."

He laughingly finished the story: "And will you believe it, that [conductor] wouldn't take me up nor put me off just to let me show him how easy I could have won that wager!"[13]

The noted Western artist Edgar S. Paxson recalled what may have been Beidler's last ride for Wells Fargo in 1877. Paxson, twenty-five, was then a recent arrival in Dillon, Montana, where he worked for the Gilmer & Salisbury stage line. It would be twenty years before he would achieve fame as an artist. Beidler and Shotgun Jimmy Brown were guarding a large gold shipment and got wind of a planned attack on the stage. They armed the diminutive Paxson with a sawed-off shotgun, wrapped him in a buffalo robe, and had him hide inside the rear boot. The coach took off with the three guards ready for action.

Paxson recalled that it was a tense all-night ride, and he was greatly relieved when the road agents failed to appear.[14]

The same year, Beidler resigned his position as a Wells Fargo shotgun messenger to become a deputy U.S. marshal and Indian scout. His frontier life was grueling. Three years later, a friend wrote, "Beidler is getting prematurely old from hard riding, exposure, etc., and his services have almost always been but very poorly paid." As late as 1889, he took part in a manhunt for two robbers who had committed a double murder. Nonetheless, by the late 1880s he had largely retired from law enforcement. Beidler had not saved any of his wages, had never married, and lived in poverty, hobbling around Helena on a cane. By comparison, his brothers had been successful. Jacob Beidler was a prominent citizen of Battle Creek, Michigan; Henry M. Beidler prospered as a developer and first mayor of Texarkana, Arkansas; and George Beidler acted as first postmaster of Oklahoma City.

Though poor in pocket, X was rich in friends. They helped him financially and sponsored a bill in the legislature to award him a pension for his many years of service to the people of Montana. But the politicians voted it down several times. Beidler began writing his memoirs, hoping to raise money, but never finished them. In 1889, he posed for several photographs, including one that depicted him as a Wells Fargo messenger, and sold them as souvenirs. His friends tried unsuccessfully to get him appointed a guard at the territorial prison or night watchman at the capitol building.[15]

Beidler's health began to fail, and that winter he came down with pneumonia. He died in his lodgings in Helena on January 22, 1890. In those final months, his good nature had become somewhat bitter. He believed that the dangerous service he had provided—as vigilante, manhunter, shotgun messenger, scout, and lawman—was all but forgotten. "Fifty years from now no one will know anything about it," he wrote in his diary. Yet that was not true, for John X. Beidler remains one of Montana's most famous pioneers.[16]

8

"HONEST, FAITHFUL & BRAVE"

Eugene Blair

Eugene Blair had many adventures as a Wells Fargo shotgun messenger. One that he loved to relate was an encounter with stage robbers in Montana: "They had formed a sort of barricade on the edge of the road, which at that point ran along the side of a mountain. Back of them there was a slope of half a mile, rough, with rocks and fallen timber. We were jogging along at a comfortable gait when I spied a movement back of the shrubbery on the side of the road and seized my gun. 'Halt! Throw up your hands, there!' yelled two or three of them in chorus. I answered instantly with a volley from both barrels. We heard nothing more. The crash of the gun was terrific. When the smoke cleared away a little we saw those fellows going end over end down the mountain side. I never knew what became of them or how badly they were hurt. We found their guns and took them away with us. That was about the quickest work I ever did." As Blair concluded, "If they had had nerve they might have made us trouble."[1]

Eugene Blair came from Richmond, Maine, where he was born on November 5, 1845. His father was a farmer, an occupation that held no interest for his sons. In the early 1860s, his older brother John joined a ship's company as a cabin boy and worked his way around Cape Horn to San Francisco. He spent several years in the city, then departed for the Comstock Lode in Nevada. Eugene was desperate to follow in his brother's footsteps, and in 1866 he traveled to Virginia City, Nevada, to join him. The silver mines of the Comstock Lode drew many such adventurers, and the Blair boys labored in the hard-rock tunnels and shafts. John Blair was a businessman, more interested in owning mines than working them. He recalled many years later that he lost a fortune in one Comstock mining venture.[2]

In 1870, after several years as a hard-rock miner, Eugene became a police officer in Virginia City. A friend later described him as "very tall, long limbed and muscular, quick of motion, ready and perfectly brave." The following year, he and John moved to the new boomtown of Pioche, in southeastern Nevada. Isolated in the high desert, Pioche was one of Nevada's most important silver-mining towns and by 1870 had ten thousand residents living in tents and shacks. That year, a Pioche merchant complained, "About one-half of the community are thieves, scoundrels and murderers. . . . There is a fight every day and a man killed about every week. About half the town is whiskey shops and houses of ill fame." Recalled another pioneer, "It was like all the rest of the Nevada camps, only exceeding the worst of them in deviltry and wickedness, for it gathered to itself the scum of hell—desperadoes, highway robbers, thieves, gamblers, and prostitutes, and they made it just one of the liveliest towns that ever existed."[3]

Eugene spent two years in Pioche working as a deputy sheriff. In November 1872, Wells Fargo hired him as a shotgun messenger earning $125 a month. By 1874, the company assigned him to the Montana Trail, riding stages from the Union Pacific rail town of Corinne, Utah, north to the mining camps of western Montana. The greatest dangers were attacks by Indians and road agents. Blair's comrades and fellow messengers on this line were John X. Beidler, Shotgun Jimmy Brown, Aaron Y. Ross, John Brent, and Mike Tovey. Like the other guards, Blair generally wore a brace of six-shooters in addition to carrying his sawed-off shotgun.[4]

Many of the coaches did not have shotgun messengers on board;

Eugene Blair, in the early 1870s,
about the time he became a Wells
Fargo shotgun messenger.
[*Author's collection*]

they carried Wells Fargo's guards only if the company was shipping a
large amount of bullion or coin in the express box. Thus highway robbers would often lay off a stage if they saw a shotgun messenger on the
box. In later years, Blair liked to relate a humorous story of his encounter with such a highwayman on this route. He said he was "shotgun-
ning" a stage in Montana's wild country when he spotted an "old
fellow" on the road just head. "I knew he had no honest business in that
part of the country alone, for he plainly was not a traveler, and there
were no habitations within a day's journey. When we saw him I ordered the driver to halt, and I raised my gun, not as to fire, though.
The old chap threw up both hands at once and began to yell. I saw that
he was not especially dangerous and ordered the driver to proceed.
When we came up to where the fellow was we stopped again and I
asked him what he was doing."

The stranger replied, "Nothing."

"Where are you going?" Blair asked.

"Oh, just down the road."

"What is your business?"

"Haven't any."

"Are you in the habit of stopping stages?" Blair demanded.

"Never stopped a stage in my life," he insisted.

"Well, your actions are mighty suspicious for an honest man. You better get along now, and don't let me catch you here when I get back."

Blair ordered the jehu to start on, and the stranger watched the coach proceed a short distance, then ran after it with both hands up, calling for them to stop.

"Say, are you the shotgun messenger?" he asked.

"That's what they call me sometimes," Blair replied.

The man looked at Blair curiously for a moment and said, "I thought you was when I first see you coming down thar. I never happened to run foul of one of you fellers before, but I've heard of you. I'm glad to see you. Goodbye."

As Blair laughingly recalled, "He was one of the cheap kind of highwaymen you read about. Of course he had heard of the shotgun messengers and I presume to his dying day he never ceased to congratulate himself on having sense enough to discern me at a distance."[5]

Early in 1875, Wells Fargo sent Blair back to Pioche, where he soon encountered one of the most reckless outlaws of the Nevada-Utah border. "Idaho Bill" Sloan was a colorful, loudmouthed former Idaho stage driver. In December 1875, he robbed a coach at Desert Springs station (now called Modena) in Utah, about forty miles east of Pioche. Eugene Blair rode to the scene and made a careful search for the bandit. On December 31, he captured Idaho Bill in the high desert and took him to jail in Beaver, Utah. In the outlaw's preliminary hearing, the stationmaster testified against him, but Sloan's gang quickly bailed him out of jail.[6]

Soon after, on January 18, 1876, Idaho Bill returned to Desert Springs with a fellow desperado and took over the stage depot. They threatened the stationmaster and forced him to sign an agreement that he would not appear at the trial. A pony mail rider who passed through reported that the outlaws "were running it to suit themselves [and] were stopping everyone that came along the road, taking their arms and firing them off . . . turning the liquors loose, making everyone indulge, practicing with six-shooters on the window glasses and riddling the house generally." Idaho Bill brazenly road into Pioche, where he was seen "strutting around the streets like a walking arsenal." Blair was not fazed, recalled a friend, who said that Idaho Bill "submitted to arrest as peacefully as a lamb when Eugene Blair came for him." However, the *Pioche Daily Record* credited the desperado's February 9 arrest to a local police officer. Idaho Bill was lodged in jail where he threatened to "raise particular hell" with eighteen local citizens whom he considered his enemies.[7]

The governor of Utah issued a requisition for Idaho Bill, and on February 26, Eugene Blair put him in handcuffs and loaded him onto the Utah-bound stage. A friend of Blair recalled, "It was generally thought that Bill's friends would try to rescue him somewhere on the road." Eugene sat beside his prisoner and warned, "Bill, I've heard your friends are going to get you away from me. . . . Likely enough they will, but it's fair to tell you that it'll never do you any good, for I shall shoot you dead at the first break they make. It's well to have the matter understood between us."[8]

Idaho Bill's comrades had enough sense not to tangle with Blair. He took the outlaw to Beaver, Utah, where he was charged with stage robbery. Several weeks later, after Idaho Bill was convicted, Blair and the Beaver County sheriff took him to Salt Lake City. He was lodged in the state penitentiary but twice managed to escape. Idaho Bill then became notorious as a horse thief in Wyoming, where he was finally slain in a quarrel with his father-in-law in 1881.[9]

A few weeks after returning to Pioche, Eugene Blair encountered yet another dangerous outlaw. Andrew Jackson "Big Jack" Davis was one of Nevada's most notorious bandits. He had come to the Comstock Lode in 1859 as a respectable citizen and acted as the local mining recorder. He also ran a stamp mill, crushing silver ore from mines, in Six Mile Canyon, near Virginia City. But the temptation of easy money was too much for him, and on November 7, 1865, he led a gang that held up a stage in Six Mile Canyon and escaped with more than one thousand dollars. A year later, on October 31, 1866, Davis and three others robbed two stages on the Geiger Grade near Virginia City, using gunpowder to blow open a Wells Fargo safe. They fled with five thousand dollars in booty. Big Jack and his men were never suspected. On June 10, 1868, he and two men stopped another coach in Six Mile Canyon, taking bullion bars from the Wells Fargo box. This time, Davis and two comrades were arrested, but there was not enough evidence to hold them and they were released. Undeterred by this close call, in the fall of 1870, Davis and his gang robbed three more stages on the road between Reno and Carson City.

Finally, Big Jack undertook his most infamous job, when he and five of his gang pulled the first train robbery in the American West. On November 5, 1870, they slipped aboard a Central Pacific train as it pulled out of Verdi, Nevada, near the California line. Inventing a technique that would be used by train robbers for another fifty years, Davis and his men captured the crew and uncoupled the engine, coal tender, and express car from the passenger coaches. This prevented the many passengers, some of whom were armed, from interfering with the holdup. They proceeded down the tracks, where an accomplice was waiting with saddle horses and pack mules. At gunpoint, they forced the express messenger in the Wells Fargo car to turn over $41,000 in gold coins, then escaped into the night. Wells Fargo, the Central Pacific, and the state of Nevada issued enormous rewards, totaling forty thousand dollars, for the six bandits. Astute detectives managed to unravel the plot, and Big Jack and the rest of the gang were soon jailed. Sentenced to ten years in the state prison in Carson City, Davis was pardoned after serving only four.[10]

But Big Jack Davis could not leave stagecoaches alone. On the night of April 14, 1876, Eugene Blair was on the box of the stage from Eureka to Pioche, a 190-mile ride across the mountainous desert. The coach had reached a spot three miles from Pioche when a masked figure suddenly appeared in the roadway and ordered, "Throw down the box."

As the whip, Pat Ryan, halted the stage, Blair dropped down into the front boot, with his shotgun ready. Ryan threw down an empty express box, and the road agent, who obviously knew the driver, called out, "Ryan, is that the right one?"

Just as Ryan started to reply, Blair cut loose with his shotgun and the highwayman staggered to his side. The outlaw fired back, but Ryan whipped up his team and the stage jolted forward. Blair had him stop a short distance down the road; then he walked back to the scene. He found the express box in the road, but the bandit had fled. A hunt for the robber was unsuccessful. Although Blair was sure he had hit him, no blood was found at the site. More than a year later, Big Jack Davis would admit that he was the holdup man. And this would not be the last encounter between Eugene Blair and the notorious highway robber.[11]

A month later, on the night of May 12, 1876, a lone bandit tried to rob the stage from Hamilton to Pioche. Wells Fargo messenger Phil Barnhart opened fire on the robber, who fled without booty. Eugene Blair investigated the holdup, and on May 21, he found a suspect, who gave his name as George Mayfield, at a local ranch. Blair was suspicious of Mayfield because he had been "beating about in that vicinity for several days." Blair took him to the White Pine County jail in Ely, but the district attorney thought there was insufficient evidence to hold him and ordered him released. Blair, however, rearrested him on suspicion of stealing a horse from the stage company. He took Mayfield to the jail in Pioche. The desperado had in his possession a rifle, a flour-sack mask with two eyeholes, and two pieces of blanket that could be wrapped around his boots to muffle his tracks. Mayfield turned out to be John Williams. He was convicted of robbery and sentenced to five years in the Nevada State Prison.[12]

That November, Eugene took the railroad east to visit his parents in Augusta, Maine. When he got back, grateful Wells Fargo officials presented him with a gold pocket watch, inscribed "For faithful and resolute attention to the company's interests." Wells Fargo's gratitude was not misplaced. Soon after his return, on the night of February 27, 1877, he was aboard the stage from Hamilton to Pioche as it climbed a steep grade near the boomtown of Ward. Two masked, shotgun-wielding road agents, James Crawford and John Carlo, were waiting. Both were young miners in Ward. Carlo stepped out from behind a tree and shouted, "Hold up!"[13]

At the same time, Carlo fired a blast from his shotgun. Blair instantly responded. He emptied both barrels, sending a load of buckshot into Carlo, which pierced his chest and shattered his right arm. Eugene leaped down from the box, cracked open the barrels of his messenger's gun, and quickly reloaded. Crawford fired twice at him with his shotgun, missing the Wells Fargo man but wounding two passengers with buckshot. Blair fired back and the highwayman broke and ran. He chased the fleeing bandit for seventy-five yards before he lost him in the darkness. When he ran back to the stage, he heard the wounded robber calling that he was dying and wanted to surrender. As Blair approached Carlo, the bandit gasped, "Shoot me."

Blair refused, saying that he "was not such a coward as to shoot a man that he had the best of."

Carlo responded, "You won the fight but if you had come an hour earlier we would have got you."

Blair picked up the robber's shotgun, which had the barrels and stock cut down, so it was little more than a foot long. Then he helped the desperado into the stagecoach and quickly arrived in Ward with his bloody cargo. The two passengers were not badly injured, but Carlo's right arm had to be amputated. The highwayman told a friend, "I was on my knee when I leveled and fired my gun, which was to my disadvantage, or else I'd fetched him." Carlo's friend asked him why he wanted to kill Blair, and the road agent replied, "I have been in the business before. If I had not been coppered and my arm broken, I would have killed the whole outfit." Carlo asked his friend to write to his brother in Ohio. He lasted a little over a day, until the morning of March 1. Eugene was with him when he died and tried to get him to reveal the name of his partner, to no avail.

Blair gave townsfolk in Ward a description of the second man, and he was immediately identified as James Crawford, who had been about town with Carlo not long before the holdup. Then Blair and Fred Gilmer, the stage-line agent, set off after Crawford. They tracked him across the mountains and found him in the mining camp of Bristol, fourteen miles northwest of Pioche. Crawford was armed with a shot-gun, a six-shooter, and a bowie knife, but he surrendered quietly. He begged his captors not to take him to Ward, where he feared he would be lynched. Instead, Blair took him to the jail in Pioche. Crawford pled guilty and received seven years, which turned out to be a death penalty, because he died in prison in 1881.[14]

Because Eugene Blair had already been presented with a gold pocket watch, Wells Fargo officials now gave him a fine Remington shotgun. He would soon prove, once again, that the company's grati-tude was properly placed. That fall, Big Jack Davis was planning an elaborate stagecoach robbery. He met up with two ex-convicts he had known in the Nevada prison, Thomas Lauria and Bob Hamilton, who, in turn, recruited the latter's brother, Bill Hamilton. The four went to Eureka, Nevada, where they learned the schedule for the Gilmer & Salisbury stage line. The coach left late in the afternoon, headed south for Tybo, a gold camp named after the Shoshone Indian word for white man. The stage first stopped at Willows station, forty miles south, about 9:00 P.M. Davis and the Hamilton brothers headed for Willows station while Lauria remained in Eureka to wait for a stage guarded by a shotgun messenger, which would indicate a large treasure shipment on board. Lauria was to ride to the top of Bald Mountain, between Eureka and Willows station, and light one or more signal fires, show-ing how many messengers were on board.

On September 3, 1877, the stage left Eureka with Jack Perry at the ribbons. Blair and his old friend Shotgun Jimmy Brown sat on top of the coach, with two passengers inside. The Wells Fargo box contained a large payroll for the miners in Tybo. Lauria watched them leave, then leaped onto his horse and raced to the mountaintop, ten miles distant. Meanwhile, Davis and the Hamilton brothers took over Wil-lows station. They tied up the stationmaster and a local rancher and began watching the mountaintop, thirty miles off. Just before dark, Lauria lit two fires, but he placed them so close together that from Willows station they looked like one. An hour later, the coach rattled into Willows station. Blair sat next to the jehu, and Brown was on the front dickey seat, behind the driver. As Perry checked his horses, a shout rang out from the stable door.

"Eugene Blair, surrender!"

Blair didn't move, thinking the stationmaster was drunk and playing a practical joke. Then the command came again.

"Get down off of there and surrender!"

Shotgun in hand, he jumped down from the front boot. As soon as he hit the ground, two shotguns boomed. One blast came at Blair from the corner of the stable, directly in front of him, and another from behind the stage. The shots were so close to his head, he could feel the concussion. Blinded by the cloud of gun smoke, he fired toward the stable. At that, Big Jack Davis rushed forward and slammed the muzzle of his shotgun against Blair's breast and pulled the trigger. But in his excitement, Davis had cocked the hammer for the barrel he had already fired. The hammer snapped and Blair seized the gun and wrenched it aside.

The robbers were not prepared for two messengers. As Blair shoved Big Jack away, Jimmy Brown saw his chance. He could see Davis plainly in the stage's headlamp. From the dickey seat, he fired a full charge of nine buckshot into the outlaw's lower back. At the same time, Blair shoved his shotgun into Big Jack's chest, but before he could fire, the bandit cried, "I am shot! I surrender!" He crumpled to the ground.

Jimmy Brown jumped down from the stage. As soon as he hit the ground, a shot from one of the Hamilton brothers rang out from behind the stage, hitting him in the left calf and nicking the bone. He staggered as the Hamiltons fired four more blasts with shotguns and six-shooters. But Blair and Brown did not flinch. They emptied their shotguns, then jerked six-shooters and unleashed a barrage of gunfire at the two road agents. That was too much for the Hamilton boys and they fled into the night. Eugene then helped the wounded Brown and Davis inside the station and untied the two captives. Big Jack Davis writhed in great agony and begged Blair to kill him, but the nervy messenger refused. In the morning, the coach continued on to Tybo, while Blair and Brown returned to Eureka on the down stage

The notorious stage and train robber
Andrew Jackson "Big Jack" Davis. He
was slain by Eugene Blair in 1877.
[*University of Nevada Library, Reno*]

with the wounded robber. They tried unsuccessfully to get him to
name his confederates. He told Blair that this was the second time
they had exchanged gunfire, and the messenger thus learned for the
first time who had shot it out with him on the Pioche stage. A few
miles from Eureka, he was near death, and gasped that his name was
Jack Davis. Then he died.

They took his corpse to the Wells Fargo office and the news spread
like wildfire. The whole town was thrown into excitement. Declared
the editor of the *Eureka Republican*, "The two messengers, James
Brown and Eugene Blair, deserve the gratitude of the people of this
state for their matchless heroism. They have fought one of the greatest
battles that is ever recorded of the highway and their miraculous escape against such large odds, covered with double-barreled shotguns
and a dark night, can only be attributed to their unflinching bravery."
Blair and Wells Fargo detective John Thacker investigated and soon
picked up the Hamilton brothers and Lauria as suspects. All three
were brought to trial. Bill Hamilton's case resulted in a hung jury, but

Bob Hamilton and Thomas Lauria received fourteen years apiece in the Nevada State Prison. And Wells Fargo awarded Eugene Blair and Jimmy Brown three hundred dollars each for "gallantry in defense of treasure."[15]

By this time, Blair must have been concerned that road agents were targeting him deliberately. After all, Big Jack Davis had called out his name before firing on him. Within a few months after the Willow station holdup, he quit Wells Fargo, according to one newspaper account, "at the request of friends, who feared that he might be assassinated by desperate characters out of revenge for what he had done in the way of duty." Blair's new job was superintendent of the Hillside Mine, situated northwest of Pioche and owned by his brother John. Eugene ran the mine for almost two years, until it shut down in late 1879. He then opened a butcher shop in the nearby mining camp of Bristol, but that did not work out. By 1881, he had returned to his duties as shotgun messenger.[16]

"I have no regret for killing or maiming a highwayman," he once said. "But I should never forgive myself for firing on an innocent man. The nearest I ever came to it was in White Pine County, Nevada, in 1881. We were going through by night from Hamilton to Ward with about $40,000 in bullion and currency. The district was full of highwaymen and I had been warned that we would probably be stopped. It had been raining hard and the sky was still overcast. The driver and I were drenched to the skin. One of our lamps was out and our matches wouldn't work. We stopped once and tried to light the lamp from the other one with a piece of paper, but the wind blew out the paper and came mighty near extinguishing the lamp. We then concluded to experiment no more lest we lose all the light we had. Just as we got ready to start up I thought I heard voices."

Blair listened intently, and as the wind momentarily died down, he heard someone say, "Now, you look out for them."

He grabbed his shotgun and the stage proceeded slowly, but Blair could see nothing in the blackness. Suddenly, he heard a noise in the roadside brush. "I had my gun up instantly, and in a second it would have been discharged into what I believed was a nest of robbers, but something impelled me to pause. In that pause I heard a baby scream, and just then a woman rose up and asked us to help them. I lowered my gun, trembling from head to foot."

Blair managed to gasp, "Who are you?"

"We're going to Ward," she replied, "but we broke down back here a bit, and then got caught in the rain. My husband left us here to go and get assistance. He has just gone and you can call him back."

Blair did so, later recalling, "When he returned we loaded them all in and took them to their destination. There were three little children there, and one barrel of my gun would have killed a regiment of them. I didn't tell the father how near I had come to destroying the family he had just left. In my business you want to be sure you are right, and then you cannot shoot too quick."[17]

This was Blair's last recorded experience as a shotgun messenger. In 1882, he married twenty-three-year-old Nellie Leahigh. He soon left Wells Fargo again, taking up hauling wood, which was presumably a safer occupation. However, on February 3, 1883, as he drove a load of lumber from his brother John's ranch, he fell from his wagon and was crushed by a wheel. His ribs snapped and punctured his lung. The injury was exacerbated by tuberculosis. That winter, Eugene left for the warmer coastal climes of San Diego, but his health continued to fail. In January 1884, he and Nellie had a baby girl, but four months later newspapers reported that he was dying in San Diego. He recovered enough to move to Auburn, California, where he was looked after by his wife and Jim Hume. But he lasted only a few weeks and died in Auburn on June 27, 1884. Eugene Blair was but thirty-eight years old. He was buried in Old Auburn Cemetery. Wells Fargo paid for the funeral and had his headstone engraved "Honest, Faithful & Brave."[18]

Eugene Blair "lived in an atmosphere of danger for years," declared the editor of the New York *Sun*. "That he was spared to die quietly in bed is the marvel of all who knew him."[19]

9

CHIEF SPECIAL OFFICER

James B. Hume

Jim Hume was the most important and most famous express detective of the Old West. For thirty-one years, from 1873 to 1904, he served faithfully as Wells Fargo's chief special officer. He supervised a small bureau of detectives and established himself as a pioneer in the use of modern investigative techniques. A man of innate intelligence, he was an intuitive investigator and a relentless manhunter. In an era when many private detectives were disreputable porch peepers who spied on philandering spouses, Hume established a reputation for professionalism and unimpeachable integrity. He established close relations with local lawmen and coordinated their investigations in an era when many peace officers often undermined one another in jealous competition. And Hume would work just as hard to free an innocent man as to convict a guilty one. From his campaign against a renegade band of Confederate guerrillas in California in 1864 to his handling of the West's biggest train robbery investigations of the 1890s, he had a major impact on the development of American law enforcement.

James Bunyan Hume was born in New York State in 1827, the second youngest of ten children. When he was ten, his father moved five hundred miles west to LaGrange County, Indiana, and established a farm.

Jim's childhood was not a happy one. Although he attended school until he was fifteen, his father, a strict Scot and Presbyterian fundamentalist, treated him like a field hand. "I never had a holiday," he recalled. "It was work, work, work; plowing and grubbing from six o'clock a.m. until dark. When the ground was too wet to plow, we had to build fences or haul wood, or hull corn, or clean the barn—never an idle moment." Hume was twenty-one in December 1848, when news of the California gold discovery reached Indiana. Jim and his older brother, John, a newly minted lawyer, were overcome with gold fever. In the spring of 1850, they started west with a group of friends in covered wagons.[1]

After months of hardship, the Hume boys reached California and settled in Placerville, a cluster of rude log cabins along a gold-rich creek. It was one of the principal mining camps of the Sierra Nevada, the seat of El Dorado County, and better known by its vigilante-inspired nickname, "Hangtown." That appellation resulted from a January 1849 incident in which three desperadoes were captured on suspicion of robbery and murder. Social conditions were so new and raw that the town had no police, no jail, and no government. A crowd of miners tried the suspects, found them guilty, and strung them from a tree. This was the first lynching in the California mining country. Jim Hume would come to be deeply affected by the rampant crime and lawlessness of the Gold Rush.[2]

Like so many gold seekers, the Hume boys never struck pay dirt. Abandoning their shovels, picks, pans, and sluice boxes, John opened a law office and Jim a general store. But such mundane work held no interest for Jim Hume, and in 1860, he got an appointment as a tax collector in Placerville. Two years later, he finally found his mission in life when voters elected him the town's marshal, or chief of police. Hume quickly proved to be a born law officer and manhunter. He made numerous arrests, even tracking one murderer 130 miles to San Francisco, where he captured him in December 1863.[3]

A few months later, in March 1864, Jim became undersheriff of El Dorado County. It wasn't long before he tangled with Ike McCollum, one of the most dangerous desperadoes in the Mother Lode country.

Early in the morning of April 27, the burly McCollum, with "Scotch Tom" Christian and a ruffian named Clifton, broke out of the Marysville jail and fled south to El Dorado County. On May 13, Hume got word that the trio, heavily armed with six-shooters and double-barreled shotguns, had been spotted near Mud Springs (now El Dorado), four miles southwest of Placerville. Jim, with Deputy Sheriff Joe Staples and Constable John Van Eaton, started in pursuit. They found Scotch Tom, sick and abandoned on the trail by his partners, and took him to the jail in Placerville. Two days later, they got word that McCollum and Clifton were robbing Chinese miners near Frenchtown, ten miles south of Placerville. Hume, Staples, and Van Eaton started in pursuit on horseback. On the afternoon of May 17, they caught up with the outlaws near Fiddletown, in Amador County. The bandits fled into the brush, then opened fire on Hume's posse. In a blistering gunfight, almost forty shots were exchanged at a range of sixty feet. Deputy Staples's horse caught a slug in one leg and Constable Van Eaton dropped with a bullet in his right side. Jim thought that they had gotten McCollum, but when night fell, the two bandits escaped in the darkness. Hume was disgusted at having let the outlaws slip away, but McCollum did not live long. A month after, following a stage robbery near Georgetown, thirty-five miles north of Placerville, he was accidentally shot by one of his own gang. Ike McCollum died a few weeks later.[4]

The same month, Jim played a leading and much more successful role in tracking down the culprits in one of California's most important stage robberies. On June 30, 1864, a band of Confederate guerrillas held up two coaches eleven miles east of Placerville at a spot known ever after as Bullion Bend. The stages were loaded with passengers plus $26,000 in gold and silver bullion from the mines in Nevada. After looting the treasure boxes, they gave one of the drivers a receipt that stated the money was "for the purpose of outfitting recruits enlisted in California for the Confederate States Army." Then they fled on horseback. In the subsequent pursuit, the outlaws shot and killed Hume's friend, Deputy Sheriff Joe Staples. Though overcome with grief and rage, Jim helped organize a huge manhunt, which resulted in

James B. Hume, chief special
officer for Wells Fargo, in 1879.
[*Author's collection*]

the capture or killing of most of the band. The gunfights between lawmen and the guerrillas are rightly considered to be the westernmost
skirmishes of the Civil War.[5]

In late July 1867, three desperadoes—Hugh De Tell, Walter Sinclair, and a German named Faust—undertook a rampage of robberies
on the overland stage road, now U.S. Route 50, between Placerville
and the summit of the Sierra Nevada. Hume, correctly surmising that
the road agents would continue on to Lake Tahoe and Nevada, led a
four-man posse in pursuit eastward through the mountains. He set up
an ambush at Osgood's Toll House, at the foot of Meyers Grade, eight
miles south of present-day South Lake Tahoe. Late on the night of
August 2, Hume spotted three rifle-wielding horsemen approach. Jim
ordered them to halt and called out "that he was an officer and demanded their surrender." Hugh De Tell instantly swung up his rifle
and fired. The heavy slug tore into Hume's arm but inflicted only a
flesh wound. The undersheriff ordered his men to open up with their
shotguns and six-shooters, and they did so with a vengeance. When

the smoke cleared, Faust was dead, Sinclair was a prisoner, and De Tell had jumped into the Upper Truckee River and escaped.[6]

Hume quickly recovered from his wound and in the fall of 1869 won election as sheriff of El Dorado County, taking office in March 1870. Although he performed well as sheriff, Jim served only one two-year term and lost at the polls in September 1871. He left office the following March but was not unemployed for long. Two months later, in May 1872, he secured an appointment as warden of the Nevada State Prison near Carson City. Due to political squabbling, he resigned the following March. Soon afterward Wells Fargo officials hired him as their chief special officer, thus initiating his long career as an express detective.[7]

Hume's first big case began a few months later, on July 23, 1873, when a gang of bandits stopped a stage from Colfax to Grass Valley and escaped with seven thousand dollars in gold coin and bullion from the Wells Fargo box. The robbery resulted in one of the most bizarre happenstances in the annals of Old West outlawry. One of the passengers, a young mail-order bride named Eleanor Berry, was on her way to Grass Valley to marry a man she had never met before, Lewis Dreibelbis. At her wedding the next day, she fled in terror when she recognized Dreibelbis as the leader of the band that had robbed her coach. Dreibelbis vanished. On August 9, Hume got a tip that a wealthy stranger had recently appeared in Coloma, eight miles northwest of Placerville. He drank heavily, spent freely, and deposited one thousand dollars in gold coin and a small bar of bullion with a local hotelkeeper. Jim went to the Coloma hotel and examined the gold coins and bar, which matched those stolen in the robbery. He arrested Dreibelbis and took him to Placerville, where he quickly extracted a full confession. Dreibelbis had abandoned his wife and family in Iowa, then served a term in San Quentin for an 1865 stage holdup. He admitted his part in two recent stage robberies, the last being the Grass Valley job. This led to the arrests of the entire gang, four of whom were convicted and sent to prison. Dreibelbis, who had turned state's evidence and testified against his accomplices, was released without charge and immediately left for his old home in Iowa. He died there in 1888 and never saw Eleanor Berry again.[8]

Hume quickly established himself as a brilliant and dogged detective. His ingeniousness became fully evident in the attempted robbery of a stage from Yreka to Redding in the Klamath Mountains of Northern California on September 7, 1878. Three masked bandits stopped the coach, unaware that Wells Fargo messenger John Reynolds was riding inside. Reynolds shoved his shotgun out the stage window and blew one of the bandits to eternity. The other highwaymen fired back with a Winchester rifle and a shotgun, killing one of the wheel horses, then fled into the brush. Hume rushed to Callahan, near the scene of the holdup, arriving on the evening of September 10. He found that local officers had identified the dead bandit as Andy Marsh, a shoemaker and ex-convict, but they had already abandoned the manhunt. Jim examined the dead stage horse and found it riddled with buckshot. He ordered that all the shot be removed and turned over to him as evidence.

Hume learned that two men matching the description of the stage robbers had been seen at a miner's cabin on Picayune Creek, a few miles east of the holdup site. He promptly hired the two best trackers in Callahan and send them east toward Picayune Creek. At the same time, he sent a wire to Sisson (now Mount Shasta) and engaged a three-man posse to proceed west through the mountains toward Picayune Creek. Jim figured that the mountains to the north were far too rugged and remote for the fugitives, and that they would try to reach the settled areas east, west, or south of the robbery scene. Then Hume went south to the mountain town of Trinity Center to cut off any flight in that direction. Four days later, on the morning of September 14, Hume's manhunters captured and disarmed the two highwaymen at their camp near the headwaters of the Trinity River. They proved to be a pair of San Quentin ex-convicts, Tom Jackson and Martin Tracy.

At Jackson's trial in December, Hume produced the buckshot that had been removed from the dead stage horse and compared it to that in shotgun shells taken from the ex-convict. The shot was identical. That, coupled with clear evidence against Jackson, resulted in his conviction after a five-minute deliberation by the jury. Tracy, seeing the handwriting on the wall, pled guilty to attempted robbery and received half of Jackson's ten-year prison sentence. Jim Hume may not have realized it, but his use of primitive ballistics was one of the first in the American West.[9]

Hume's job was never easy. He was constantly on the move, traveling throughout the West by train and stage, investigating myriad thefts from Wells Fargo. He did get some free time, however, and one Sunday in January 1879, he accompanied a party of friends on a boat excursion from San Francisco across the bay to San Quentin Prison. Such trips were then the rage, with sightseers touring the prison, simultaneously repelled and thrilled to see the hard-faced convicts in their woolen stripes. One of the group was Lida Munson, daughter of a family he had known in El Dorado County. Lida was only twenty, pretty, and extremely vivacious, with an outrageous sense of humor. As the steamboat pulled up to the dock, a prison officer spotted Hume and called out, "Hello, Jim, is that you? You do not seem to have anybody with you for the state's boarding house this trip."

Hume laughingly replied, "Oh yes, I have," and seized the arm of young Lida. The girl blushed and laughed, but she was determined to pay him back. After a picnic and tour of the prison, they took the boat back to San Francisco. Jim, Lida, and their friends boarded a crowded streetcar to return to their homes. When the car stopped at Hume's lodging house, he arose from his seat. Lida took that moment to remark, in a voice loud enough to be heard by everyone on the car, "I do not think that man should ever have been pardoned. He should have stayed in prison every day of his term!"

The detective, beet red from embarrassment, rushed from the car to escape the disapproving stares of the passengers. He quickly forgave Lida. Hume had always been a bachelor, due mainly to the state's large gender imbalance. There just weren't enough women to go around. Despite huge immigration, in 1860 California was 72 percent male, and as late as 1880, it was still 60 percent male. Now, despite the fact that he was fifty-two—more than thirty years Lida's senior—the two began a five-year courtship. To Lida, Jim was handsome and daring, a wonderful combination of gentility and steel. They finally married in 1884 at the San Quentin home of Hume's good friend Charles Aull, a former Wells Fargo detective and at that time deputy warden of the state prison.[10]

On December 14, 1881, Jim got word of a daring train robbery near El Paso, Texas. The railroad had reached the rowdy, gunfighter-infested border town only six months earlier. The train's Wells Fargo messenger, Charles Barnard, reported that at one a.m. two masked bandits had entered his express car as the California-bound train was four miles west of town. They knocked the messenger down, gagged him, and took his keys to the safe. After looting the safe of fifteen hundred dollars, they leaped from the train and disappeared. Hume soon arrived in El Paso, where he made one of his typical painstaking investigations. Although Barnard claimed that the robbers were part of a gang of cattle rustlers, Hume found something in his story suspicious. He soon concluded that there was but one thief: the Wells Fargo messenger himself. Jim arrested him for embezzlement, and in October 1882, Barnard pled guilty and received a two-year term in the Texas state penitentiary.[11]

From El Paso, Hume proceeded by train to southern Arizona, where several stage holdups had taken place that fall and winter on the roads to silver-rich Tombstone. His description of the celebrated silver camp was more facetious than accurate: "Six thousand population. Five thousand are bad. One thousand of these are known outlaws." The prime robbery suspects were the Cowboys, a notorious loose-knit gang of bandits, smugglers, and cattle thieves then engaged in bloody war with Hume's friends Wyatt Earp and his brothers. Wyatt and Morgan Earp had both served as shotgun messengers for Wells Fargo on the Tombstone route. The apex of the conflict had taken place at Tombstone in October 1881 when the Earps and Doc Holliday killed three of the Cowboys in what later became known as the Gunfight at the O.K. Corral. On January 6, 1882, a trio of Cowboys, probably led by Charles Ray—better known by his alias, Pony Diehl—riddled the Tombstone to Bisbee stagecoach with gunfire and forced the Wells Fargo messenger to turn over $6,500. The next evening, Jim was at the

James B. Hume in the 1880s.
[*Author's collection*]

Southern Pacific train depot in Benson, where he boarded a stage for Tombstone to investigate the stage robbery. The coach held nine passengers, eight inside and one on the seat with the driver.

It was 1:00 A.M. on January 8 when the coach reached an arroyo six miles from Tombstone. Most of the passengers, including Hume, were sound asleep. Suddenly, two masked highwaymen appeared in the moonlit road and yelled, "Halt!"

Jim awoke with a start, only to find himself staring down the barrels of a shotgun in the hands of a masked road agent. The bandits demanded that the driver throw down the Wells Fargo box, but he told them "there was no treasure on board." The robbers then ordered the passengers out and lined them up. Hume saw but two bandits, but he thought there were two more in the darkness. He noted that one was tall, wearing a "tight fitting suit," and the other was shorter, wearing a large gunnysack with holes cut out for his head and arms, to conceal his clothing. From Jim they took a pair of silver-plated Smith & Wesson six-shooters, each adorned with a four-carat diamond. They searched the other passengers and relieved them of another pistol and seventy-five dollars in coin. Complained one of the outlaws, "What kind of a layout is this? It's the poorest crowd I ever struck."

Then the bandits waved the stage on. On reaching Tombstone, an embarrassed Hume went to the office of the *Tombstone Daily Epitaph* and gave an account to its editor. "Mr. Hume states that to attempt to use his revolvers under the circumstances—and being also under the impression that there were four robbers—would inevitably involve a sacrifice of the lives of several of the passengers, and as there was none of his employers' treasure on board, he considered he would be acting the part of wisdom to refrain from violent measures." When the detective's story reached San Francisco, a city newspaper caustically remarked that "a man of Hume's reputation and supposed 'sand,' armed to the teeth as he was, should have been able to take care of the two highwaymen." The editor of the *San Francisco Daily Report* promptly came to Jim's defense: "No person who knows him ever questioned Mr. Hume's valor, but he is cool as well as brave, and in this instance showed that discretion is the better part of valor."[12]

Wyatt Earp suspected that Pony Diehl and "Curly Bill" Brocius, the latter one of the leaders of the Cowboys, had robbed the first stage. He led a posse, which tracked the outlaws to Len Redfield's ranch on the San Pedro River. Redfield and his brother Hank were friends of the Cowboys and were known to harbor fugitives. Their nephew, Frank Carpenter, who later admitted that Curly Bill was a frequent visitor to the ranch, defiantly told the posse, "Gentlemen, you cannot scare or bribe me into telling where they are." Wyatt was unable to capture the highwaymen. However, two months later he shot and killed Curly Bill at Cottonwood Springs in the Whetstone Mountains.[13]

During the next ten years, Jim Hume took part in the successful manhunts for some of the West's most notable express robbers: Charles E. Boles, alias "Black Bart," train robbers Chris Evans and John Sontag, and the Dalton gang. Yet his brilliance as a detective and his pioneering methods in the use of forensics are best illustrated by the case of stage robber and killer Lee Sykes. It began on the evening of October 21, 1887, when a stagecoach left Redding, in Northern California, headed for Alturas, 140 miles northeast. The Wells Fargo box was empty of cash. Next to the driver sat a prominent businessman, George Henderson; two other passengers rode inside the coach. Just as the stage reached the top of the Churn Creek grade, three miles from Redding, a lone bandit carrying a large revolver stepped into the highway and yelled, "Hold on there!"

As the driver started to rein in his team, the robber fired. The bullet whined by the jehu's chest and tore through Henderson's right hand, then slammed into his abdomen and lodged in his intestines. The terrified horses bolted and the stage careened down the grade, leaving the bandit behind. The outlaw fired one parting shot, but the coach was soon out of range. The whip raced three miles to Loomis Corners, where Henderson was carried from the stage and a doctor summoned from Redding. The physician could do nothing and Henderson died the next morning. A huge manhunt swung into action, and two days later Jim Hume arrived on the scene. Even though Wells Fargo had not been robbed, he began one of his most exhaustive investigations.[14]

Jim examined the bullet that the doctor had removed from Henderson's body. He noted that it was a .45-caliber "swedged" ball of the type often used in the Colt Model 1873 Army revolver. Local officers believed that Henderson had been assassinated in a private feud, but Hume was certain it had been a robbery attempt. He thought that the holdup man was an amateur, for only the stages headed into—not out of—Redding carried treasure, and only an amateur would have fired at the coach for no reason. Hume posted reward notices for the killer throughout Redding.[15]

Meanwhile, the search for the culprit came up dry. Months passed and the investigation petered out. Then, on March 12, 1888, Jim received a letter from A. M. Goodenough, who owned a ranch one mile from the holdup site. Goodenough wrote that he had learned who the killer was and would reveal it in exchange for the thirteen-hundred-dollar reward that had been posted by Wells Fargo and the governor of

California. Detective and rancher exchanged several letters before Jim sent Goodenough a copy of the reward circular and arranged to meet him in person. Then Hume took a train north to Redding, where he found that Goodenough had an interesting story to tell.

Two months before the holdup, Goodenough had employed three young men—Lee Sykes, Ed Beck, and Leslie Jones—to cut lumber and haul it into Redding for sale. Sykes and Beck were hard cases, but Jones had an education and worked off and on as a schoolteacher. On October 18, three days before the murder, Sykes quit the ranch and said he was going to Idaho. Eight or ten days later, Beck told Goodenough that he had received a letter sent by Sykes from Idaho. On November 21, a month after the holdup, Beck and Jones also quit Goodenough. They went into Redding, where Beck got roaring drunk. As they walked down the street toward the train depot, Beck tore down three of the Wells Fargo reward notices and crumpled them into his pocket. When Jones asked why he'd done that, Beck replied, "I know who killed Henderson, and I harbored him in Goodenough's barn the first four nights after the murder."

Beck refused to reveal anything else, explaining that he "was afraid to tell in Redding." Beck was broke, and Jones, hoping to earn the reward, bought him a train ticket and accompanied him to his family home in Fresno County. Jones met secretly with Charlie Fraser, a Fresno deputy constable whom he knew, and related Beck's admission. But Fraser told him that the newspapers had published reports that a suspect had already been arrested in Oregon. Jones concluded that Beck had made the whole story up to wangle a free train ticket home. Disgusted and chagrined, he put the incident out of his mind. Then, early in March, he wrote a newsy letter to Goodenough and mentioned Beck's story. Goodenough went immediately to his barn, and in the haymow found dried grapes and empty cans of salmon. Convinced that someone had been hiding there, and suspecting that Lee Sykes had not gone to Idaho after all, he promptly wrote to Hume.

The Wells Fargo detective, after his meeting with Goodenough,

Lee Sykes, stage robber and murderer, as he looked in San Quentin prison. [*California State Archives*]

tracked down Leslie Jones and asked for a meeting with him at Jim's San Francisco office on March 28. From Jones, Hume learned that Sykes hailed from Live Oak, a small town one hundred miles south of Redding. Jones also revealed that Beck had given Lee Sykes a revolver. When the weapon malfunctioned, Beck had ordered a new mainspring from Ladd & Co., a San Francisco gun dealer. Sykes had taken the gun with him on his supposed trip to Idaho. Hume walked a few blocks to the gun shop on Kearny Street, where he found that the mainspring Beck had ordered was for a .45-caliber Colt Model 1873 revolver—the same type of weapon he believed had fired the fatal shot.

Jim immediately went to Live Oak in search of Lee Sykes. The latter's family had not seen him in months. Hume was also unable to find Ed Beck, whom he believed was the key witness in the case. He returned to Redding, where he again interviewed Goodenough and learned that Beck had stolen a silver watch from a neighboring rancher. Hume procured a warrant for Beck's arrest and sent it the Fresno deputy constable, Charlie Fraser. The latter suspected that both Beck and Sykes were hiding out at a mining claim owned by Beck's father, in the mountains thirty miles east of Fresno. Beck's family had been mixed up in a horse-stealing case, so Fraser decided on a ruse. He obtained a subpoena for Ed Beck as a witness in the theft case and rode to the mining claim to serve it. Fraser hoped that this would allow him to discover whether Sykes was there. He found Ed Beck at his father's cabin, but Lee Sykes had "skipped out" two weeks earlier. Fraser served subpoenas on Beck and several other witnesses and returned to Fresno.

On June 15, Ed Beck showed up in Fresno to testify. Constable Fraser immediately arrested him and slipped him onto a northbound passenger train. Jim Hume was waiting for them in the depot at the railroad hub of Lathrop, and the two officers took Beck to Sacramento and lodged him in jail. There the prisoner readily admitted to stealing the watch and also confessed his role in hiding Lee Sykes. He said that Sykes had come to him an hour after the murder and lay concealed in the haymow for four days. Beck added that he had recently received a letter from Sykes in Bakersfield, and that when Sykes had left his father's cabin, he was wearing a coat and pants made of the same pattern as Beck's vest. Jim ordered Beck to remove the vest, which he kept as evidence.

Then Hume telegraphed the Wells Fargo agent in Redding to swear out a complaint charging Sykes with the Henderson murder and send it to him on that night's express train. The agent quickly responded by wire, saying that the district attorney refused to issue the complaint because another suspect, John Curtis, was under arrest in Redding and charged with the crime. Hume was certain Curtis was innocent. He sent Constable Fraser to Bakersfield to hunt Sykes and took Beck to Redding in hopes of convincing the prosecutor that he had the wrong man. Jim reached Redding on the morning of June 18 and immediately met with the district attorney and the county sheriff. Hume had Beck repeat his story. Then they proceeded to Goodenough's ranch, where Beck showed them the hiding place and the discarded provisions in the barn. The Redding officers were convinced, and they released John Curtis.

When Constable Fraser had no luck finding Lee Sykes in Bakersfield, Jim headed there by train on June 23. He took with him Beck's vest, which he cut into pieces, and he handed these to the Wells Fargo agent and local lawmen with the request that they look out for Sykes. They promised to do so. Two weeks later, on July 2, Sykes stopped a stage near Hildreth, thirty-five miles north of Fresno. Wielding a shotgun, he disarmed the Wells Fargo messenger and escaped with ten thousand dollars in gold ingots. He hid an eight-thousand-dollar brick in a tree stump and left for Bakersfield with the rest. Sykes arrived in town on the Fourth of July, flush with money and "parading the streets in a drunken condition," but the local officers were so busy keeping the peace, they didn't spot him.

A few weeks later, on July 23, a young man walked into the Wells Fargo office in Bakersfield with a saddle and a valise. He told the agent that he wanted to ship them to Hildreth. He was coatless, and around his waist was a gun belt and a large Colt revolver. Though the alert agent immediately suspected that he was the Hildreth stage robber, he calmly received the items and wrote out a receipt. The stranger then opened his valise and took out a coat. The agent saw that the material was identical to the swatch that Hume had given him. As soon as his customer left the office, the agent ran to warn the sheriff. He and two lawmen found the stranger in a livery stable, getting ready to leave town. The man was Lee Sykes, and he gave up his pistol without a fight.

Word of the arrest was telegraphed to Hume, who was then working a case in Chicago. After recommending that Lee Sykes and Ed Beck not be jailed together in Redding, to prevent them from conspiring, Hume had Beck removed to the county jail in Tehama. The Wells Fargo detective attended Sykes's preliminary hearing in Redding on August 23, and the judge found that there was ample evidence to hold him for trial. Jim had developed an ironclad case against Sykes. The statements he had obtained from Beck and Goodenough were more than compelling. And the revolver taken from Sykes was a Colt Model 1873, the same as was used in the murder. To save himself a prison term, Beck turned state's evidence, and Sykes, to avoid death by hanging, entered into a plea bargain. In exchange for a life sentence in San Quentin, he pled guilty to murder.

Jim Hume showed outstanding detective work in the Sykes case. Once again he had had used primitive ballistics to help solve a crime. He had worked closely with local lawmen and made sure that the Wells Fargo rewards were publicized. He had used swatches of clothing to help trap the fugitive. And he had saved an innocent man from facing the gallows. As the *Sacramento Daily Union* commented, "Mr. Hume alone is entitled to all credit which may attach to the successful result of this case, for without his energy, skill and discretion, the murderer of Henderson would, in all probability, never have been brought to justice. As it is, it forms one of the most interesting cases of detective pursuit that has occurred on the coast."[16]

Next to Black Bart, Charley Dorsey was probably the slipperiest stage robber Hume ever hunted. Dorsey, a former Confederate soldier, claimed to have ridden with William Clarke Quantrill's guerrillas during the Civil War. Quantrill and his bushwhackers, who at times included Jesse and Frank James, had committed the 1863 raid on the Union town of Lawrence, Kansas, killing more than 160 men and boys in cold blood. Dorsey first entered San Quentin on a burglary rap in 1865. On his release in 1867, he made the mistake of pulling a robbery in El Dorado County, where Hume, then undersheriff, helped arrest him and send him back to San Quentin. Dorsey's term expired in 1871, and a few months later he and another desperado went on a robbery spree near Knight's Ferry, on the San Joaquin River. They held up several travelers, then broke into a farmhouse, chloroformed the women and children, and ransacked the place. He was later captured and sent back to San Quentin on a fifteen-year jolt. Incredibly, the governor commuted his sentence and he was freed in 1878.[17]

A reporter who interviewed Dorsey in later years described him thus: "His face is one of a thousand. High cheek bones, lantern jaws, stiff and stubby gray mustache and sunken cheeks, all give him a repulsive yet strangely attractive expression. The eyes, though, are the greatest feature. They are almost coal black, and very deep set. They appear to be constantly on the alert for some approaching danger, and are never at ease. Dorsey is fully six feet in height, broad-shouldered, and muscular looking. He is unusually intelligent and a most interesting conversationalist."[18]

Upon his release, Charley Dorsey joined up with a former prison mate, John Collins, alias John Patterson. On September 1, 1879, they held up a stage near Nevada City, in the Northern Mines. One of the passengers, a banker named William Cummings, had two gold bars worth $6,700 in his valise. As Collins and Cummings struggled over the valise, Dorsey killed the banker with a shotgun blast. This was one of California's most infamous stage robberies. The bandits evaded a giant dragnet and made their way to New Orleans, where they sold the gold. Dorsey ended up in Union City, Indiana, where he charmed his way into polite society. After cashing a one-thousand-dollar check at the local bank, he purchased a saloon and a lumber company and quickly became one of the town's prominent businessmen.

Meanwhile, Jim Hume was busy investigating the murder. From a local prostitute, he learned that she had carried food to a pair of strangers who were hiding out in a deserted mining tunnel. She noticed that they possessed a gold bar. From her description, Jim believed the two men were Charley Dorsey and John Collins. Despite heavy rewards and the huge manhunt, the pair vanished for more than two years. Finally, in 1882, Hume learned that Collins had been arrested for burglary in St. Louis, Missouri. He put Charles Aull, then a Wells Fargo detective, and Isaiah W. Lees of the San Francisco police on the trail. In St. Louis, they learned that a man named Charles Thorne of Union City, Indiana, had provided an alibi for Collins in his burglary case. The detectives proceeded to Union City and located Thorne. Aull, who knew Dorsey well from San Quentin, recognized him instantly. The arrest of the prominent businessman created a sensation.

Aull and Lees returned the fugitives to Nevada City to stand trial for murder. Both were convicted. Even though the witnesses identified Dorsey as the man who had killed Cummings, he received a life term, while Collins was sentenced to death. Under the law then and now, each was a principal in the robbery and was therefore equally guilty of any murder that resulted. Collins was hanged on the gallows in 1884. As Hume explained, "It transpired on the trial that Dorsey had been one of Quantrill's men. One man on the jury was an ardent admirer of Quantrill, his men and their deeds, and resolved that Dorsey should not hang." Dorsey himself later said, "One of the jurymen was a soldier with me in the rebel army and he held out against the other eleven jurors and thus saved my neck."[19]

The killer was lodged in San Quentin. Recalled Hume, "Dorsey had the reputation, deservedly, of being a bad man, the worst man of all the 1,200 in that prison." He became friends with fellow convict George Shinn, one of the leaders in the Cape Horn Mills train holdup on the overland railroad in 1881, California's first. Shinn was a trusty, assigned to haul trash out of the prison in a wagon. In a driving rain on December 1, 1887, Shinn drove out the gates, with Dorsey hidden in the wagon bed. They fled to Chicago, where they survived on odd jobs and burglaries. In 1889, Dorsey and Shinn went back to California, where they pulled several saloon holdups and three stage robberies. In one holdup, Dorsey

The notorious road agent and killer Charley Dorsey. [*Author's collection*]

shot and wounded a Chinese victim; in another, Shinn had to dissuade him from killing a stagecoach passenger. Jim Hume was certain that Dorsey and Shinn were the culprits, but he was unable to locate them.

In June 1890, the two outlaws returned to Chicago, but a few weeks later, Dorsey, in a remarkable coincidence, was spotted by an ex-con from San Quentin. Jim Hume later got word of the Dorsey sighting and boarded a train for Chicago, arriving on October 1, 1890. There he quietly engaged the help of Pinkerton's National Detective Agency. "I have been very cautious," explained Hume later, "for they both know me well, they have reason for remembrance. I sent both to prison. So I enlisted the services of Billy Pinkerton. I employed the best men he had." Hume supplied the Pinkertons with photos of Dorsey and Shinn. While Jim stayed out of sight, five Pinkerton detectives spent two weeks searching for the desperadoes. Finally, on the evening of October 15, they found Shinn in a house at 292 Jackson Street and arrested him without a fight. An hour later, they picked up Dorsey while he was eating supper at 56 Gurley Street. He was taken completely by surprise. "I guess it's a ground hog case," he said with a grim smile. "Come on, I'm ready."

While detectives kept them under guard at Pinkerton headquarters, word of the arrests leaked out. Reporters flocked in to interview Hume, expecting to see a wild and woolly westerner. Instead, they found the sixty-three-year-old lawman impeccably dressed in a double-breasted suit and starched collar. Wrote one surprised journalist, "He is a white-haired, kindly faced old gentleman, as far removed in appearance from the traditional detective as can well be imagined." In response to questions, Jim said modestly, "I hate detective stories like poison, and this is not much of a story anyhow. It is interesting so far as the community will care to know that two dangerous characters have been caught and will be taken away." Hume gave the journalists a long account of the careers of the two outlaws, but was closemouthed about how he had tracked them down. The story of the capture was featured in newspapers nationwide.

Two officers from San Quentin arrived in Chicago to assist Hume in taking the prisoners back to California. Jim was taking no chances with his slippery customers. Each man was handcuffed and a fourteen-pound Oregon Boot fastened to his lower leg. The Oregon Boot, or Gardner Shackle, had been invented by the warden of the Oregon state prison and featured a heavy iron ankle collar, which was impossible to remove without a key. Hume and his men guarded the desperadoes night and day on the long train journey home. Shinn was lodged in Folsom Prison, while Dorsey found himself back in San Quentin. Over the years, he gradually reformed. In 1911, the muckraking San Francisco newspaper publisher Fremont Older befriended the old bandit and got him paroled. Dorsey worked for years on Older's fruit ranch near San Jose and died in Los Angeles in 1932, at the age of ninety-three. He outlived all the lawmen who had hunted him.[20]

As Jim Hume aged, though plagued by health problems, he kept up a relentless pace. Yet the constant train travel, especially to Texas and the Southwest, took its toll. With the epidemic of train robberies in the 1890s, he was joined by a new man, Fred J. Dodge, who established an office in Houston, Texas. Even then, there were only three full-time Wells Fargo detectives—Hume, Thacker, and Dodge—to cover the entire West. Still, Jim made time for his family. He and Lida had a son, Sam, born in 1885, and he was Jim's pride and joy. Sam Hume became an important theater producer and his wife, Portia Bell Hume, achieved prominence as a pioneering psychiatrist.

After 1900, as his health continued to decline, Hume became less and less active, and John Thacker took over many of his duties. But he was still in harness as Wells Fargo's chief special officer when he died in his Berkeley home on May 18, 1904, aged seventy-seven. "This country has produced few men who have made such a remarkable record in the persistent and successful pursuit of that class of robbers who prey specially on the express and transportation companies as that made by James B. Hume," declared the *San Francisco Chronicle*. "For more than a generation his name has been a terror to stage and train robbers. They learned to know him as a keen, intelligent officer who was as untiring and relentless as the United States Government in following and punishing offenders."[21]

10

— ╬ —

RIVERMAN, EXPRESSMAN

Andy Hall

Though all but forgotten today, Andy Hall was one of the Old West's remarkable figures. He played important roles in two of the most dramatic frontier episodes: John Wesley Powell's 1869 expedition down the Colorado River, and service as a Wells Fargo shotgun messenger in Arizona Territory. He came from rugged Scottish stock, born Andrew Hall in Liddisdale, Roxburghshire, Scotland, in 1848. His father, William Hall, died when he was very young. In 1854, his mother, Mary, brought her three children, Ellen, William, and the youngest, Andy, to Kewanee, Illinois, where she had relatives who could help support her brood. Andy was a wild and adventurous boy, known to his friends as "Daredevil Dick." In 1862, as the Civil War raged, he tried to enlist in the 124th Illinois Volunteers with his sixteen-year-old brother, William. Andy was rejected because he was only fourteen.

Two years later, overcome with wanderlust, he joined a wagon train headed west. On the prairies and in the mountains he drifted from one job to another: hunter, trapper, Indian scout, and bullwhacker, or teamster. Hall took part in numerous fights against Plains Indians. In a letter home, he wrote that "many an Indian would be glad to get my scalp as my hair is about fourteen inches long." In the fall of 1867,

Andy was in Fort Leavenworth, Kansas, where he was arrested and fined five dollars for, as a local newspaperman put it, "indulging in a little too much '40 rod' [whiskey] and getting on a public drunk generally." At one point, he was apprenticed to a gunsmith in Denver, but that work proved too tame for the rowdy youth. By October 1868, young Hall was at Green River, Wyoming, hauling wood for the Union Pacific Railroad, which was laying tracks westward. He built a small rowboat, which he used to ferry wood across the Green River.[1]

Six months later, in May 1869, Maj. John Wesley Powell spotted the youth at Green River, resting on the oars of his self-made boat. Powell, a geologist and Civil War hero who had lost his right arm in the Battle of Shiloh, was leading the first expedition to explore the Colorado River and the Grand Canyon. He was impressed with the young boatman and thought that he would be a good addition to his crew. "Young as he is," wrote Powell, "Hall has had experience in hunting, trapping, and fighting Indians, and he makes the most of it, for he can tell a good story, and is never encumbered by unnecessary scruples in giving to his narratives those embellishments which help to make a story complete. He is always ready for work or play and is a good hand at either."[2]

Powell's expedition left Green River on May 24, 1869, in four specially made boats. Andy Hall was the youngest of the ten-man crew. The journey would take them down the Green River to its confluence with the Colorado, and then through the Grand Canyon. The Grand Canyon was then a complete unknown; no one had ever dared to challenge its remoteness and its deadly whitewater. Just before they pushed off, Andy penned a quick note to his mother in Illinois: "I can not write to you any news at present for I have not time to write to you now. I am going down the Colorado River to explore that river in boats with Major Powell, the professor of the Normal college in Illinois. You need not expect to hear from me for some time ten or twelve months at least."[3] At that, Andy and the rest started off on one of the greatest adventures of the American frontier.

Hall and another young man, Billy Hawkins, piloted one boat.

Another crewman called them "as jolly a brace of boys as ever swung a whip over a lazy ox" and described Andy as "a rollicking young Scotch boy." The three-month, thousand-mile trip through the biggest rapids in North America became the stuff of legend. Three of the expedition, terrorized by the massive whitewater, quit at Separation Rapid, hiked out of the canyon, and were slain by Indians. Andy Hall was not one of them. No matter how great the danger, he never thought of deserting. Instead, he used his hunting and fishing skills to feed the crew and lifted their spirits with cheerful humor and constant pranks. He even conjured a name for the Canyon of Lodore on the Green River after a poem he knew from his school days, "The Cataract of Lodore." At journey's end, near present-day Las Vegas, Nevada, only two of the four boats had survived. Major Powell and his brother walked out overland, while Andy Hall and another crewman took one boat another three hundred miles downriver to the Gulf of California. Then, rigging a sail from a wagon sheet, they floated back upriver to Fort Yuma, Arizona Territory. Hall and his companion were the first to run the Colorado from the Green River to its mouth.[4]

While John Wesley Powell went on to international celebrity, Andy Hall began an obscure, nomadic life on the Arizona frontier. In Fort Yuma, he found work as a bullwhacker, then in 1870 drifted north to Ehrenberg, also on the Colorado River, where he was a laborer and teamster. By 1873, Hall had moved farther north to the mining town of Prescott, where he ran the Grey Eagle Stable. During the army campaign against Apaches that year, Andy offered to raise a band of thirty volunteers to fight the Indians. He then returned to southern Arizona and from 1874 to 1875 drove a mail wagon in Mohave County. That winter, he went to Tucson and served as a special constable. In the spring of 1876, Andy rode back north to Florence, seat of Pinal County. Situated sixty miles southeast of Phoenix, Florence was the center of an important mining region. There Andy ran a pack train and met a Mexican woman, Francisca. They married and lived in Florence with her two children.[5]

On the evening of March 18, 1879, Hall was eating dinner in a Chi-

Andy Hall, Colorado River explorer and Wells Fargo shotgun messenger. [*Author's collection*]

nese restaurant in Globe, fifty-five miles northwest of Florence. When he stepped outside, a vicious dog lunged at him. Several times Andy kicked it away, but when the dog kept charging him, he jerked his pistol and shot the animal dead. Then he walked down the street to a general store. Meanwhile, Gee Fan, the Chinese cook and owner of the dog, found his dead pet. Overcome with rage, he grabbed a pistol and started off in search of Hall. He found him in the general store. As a crowd gathered, he berated Hall in broken English for killing his pet, then pulled his six-gun.

"Look out, Andy!" one of the bystanders yelled.

"Now don't do that," Hall warned, but the cook raised his pistol to fire. Andy was quicker and pulled the trigger, killing Gee Fan instantly. He surrendered to a deputy sheriff, and at his preliminary hearing the next day, a justice of the peace ruled that it was self-defense. The judge and the prosecuting attorney decided that the hearing was irregular because no witnesses had been brought in to testify on behalf of the dead man. Five weeks later, the county grand jury indicted Hall for murder. The case was so weak that the prosecutor never brought it to trial. But he did not dismiss the charge, which hung over Andy Hall like a dark cloud.[6]

The following year, he got work as a shotgun messenger for Wells Fargo, guarding treasure on the ninety-mile route between Globe and the railroad depot at Casa Grande. He also worked as a deputy for his close friend Pete Gabriel, sheriff of Pinal County, and became a local constable. In September 1881, Sheriff Gabriel, with Andy Hall, several Florence citizens, and fifteen Pima Indian policemen, made a horseback scout after Apaches on the Gila River. They found no hostiles and returned to Florence empty-handed. Hall was a popular figure in Florence, much admired for his good nature and sense of humor. The editor of the *Florence Enterprise* described one of Andy's happy visits to his office: "Andy Hall drew two bottles of Milwaukee [beer] on us and called for a surrender. There's nothing like being a printer in Florence."[7]

On the night of November 29, 1881, Hall was aboard a stage on the Globe to Florence route when a suspicious character stepped out in front of the coach. As the driver reined in his team, Andy covered the man with his Wells Fargo shotgun. The stranger blurted out several nonsensical questions, then fled into the blackness. Commented a Florence newspaper editor, "It is the supposition that he intended to rob the stage, but lost his courage when he discovered a messenger on board training a double barreled mountain howitzer on him." It may have been this incident that led Wells Fargo officials to present Hall with an ornate Colt revolver.[8]

Andy's messenger duties took him frequently to Globe, a mining camp and county seat of Gila County. He knew personally three of Globe's townsmen, Curtis B. Hawley and a pair of brothers, Cicero and Lafayette Grime. Hawley hailed from Utah, where he had operated a sawmill and a mine in Coalville and a foundry in Salt Lake City. He became quite wealthy, but then he lost all his money speculating in risky mining ventures. In 1875, he was shot and wounded in a dispute over a coal mine. A Salt Lake City newspaperman wrote of him, "At one time he was looked upon by acquaintances as a good sort of man, but wild speculation and drink seemed to take him down." In 1881, Hawley abandoned his wife and three children and left for Arizona. He settled in Globe, where he sold wood and charcoal to the copper mines and became friendly with Cicero and Lafayette Grime. The Grime brothers were recent arrivals from California. Cicero had been a photographer in Mendocino and San Luis Obispo counties. He came to Globe in 1880 with his wife, Sylvia, and three small children, and opened a photography studio. He was joined by his diminutive younger brother, Lafayette, known as "Little Grime," who worked as a miner and millhand.[9]

In 1882, Lafayette Grime joined a local volunteer militia unit, the Globe Rangers, which had been formed in response to the threat of Apache raids. That July, Lafayette and two of the Rangers were ambushed by Apaches and barely escaped with their lives. Meanwhile, Cicero Grime had formed a company to build a wagon road from Pinal to Riverside (now Kelvin), on the Gila River. He submitted the low bid to the county board of supervisors but lost the contract because he was unable to obtain a performance bond. Then the Grime brothers met Hawley at his house in Globe and proposed a new venture: constructing a toll bridge at the lower end of town. Hawley had a better idea, which he called the "Indian racket." He told the Grime boys, "We might rob the stage and lay it to the Indians."

"I think that would be easy to do," responded Cicero. "No one would be suspicioned." Hawley later explained, "I was informed by them that young [Lafayette] Grime had had experience in that business before in Northern California."[10]

On August 19, 1882, Lafayette Grime rode south from Globe to scout a place for a holdup. At that time, there was no wagon road from Globe to Florence. Instead, a pack trail led south eleven miles to the stagecoach depot in Pioneer Pass, 5,900 feet high in the Pinal Mountains. From there, a stage road went the rest of the way into Florence.

Lafayette found an ideal spot four and a half miles south of Globe. The road made a sharp turn around a pile of boulders at a place that would become known as Six Shooter Canyon. There he concealed a hatchet and a pick, then rode back to Globe. The next day, Hawley and the Grime brothers rode out to the holdup spot. On the way, they cut the telegraph line into Globe. Then, while Hawley and Lafayette Grime set up an ambush, Cicero Grime rode up the trail to Pioneer Pass, where he loitered about the stage station, waiting for the arrival of Wells Fargo's express.

Meanwhile, Andy Hall was on his way from the railroad depot in Casa Grande, riding the mail buckboard and carrying an express box containing a five-thousand-dollar payroll for the Mack Morris Mine. Andy's buckboard pulled into the Pioneer Pass station at midday. Hall and Frank Porter, who ran the pack train into Globe, began transferring the mail from the buckboard onto the mules. Cicero Grime stepped forward to help Porter lift the express box onto the back of one of the mules. He noted that Hall was armed with a six-shooter and a shotgun that appeared to be unloaded. Then Grime swung into his saddle and quickly rode off to tell his partners that the Wells Fargo box was heavy with coin. Hall suspected nothing amiss. While Andy ate his lunch, Porter loaded the rest of the mail pouches onto his six mules. Then he and Hall mounted horses and started down the trail, leading the mules behind them.

By this time, Cicero Grime had galloped up to the ambush site and called out to his partners, "The treasure box feels heavy. The packer has no arms and Hall has got an old gun with no cartridges and a pistol."

Cicero raced back to Globe so that he would not be suspected. Soon the pack train came into sight. Curtis Hawley was concealed in the rocks above the trail, armed with a Henry rifle, while Lafayette Grime was below him, carrying a .50-caliber Springfield rifle, known as a "needle gun" due to its long firing pin. Grime had borrowed the rifle a day earlier from Dan Lacey, captain of the Globe Rangers. As the lead mule approached, they unloosed a fusillade of shots, killing the animal. Then they turned their fire on Hall and Porter, who galloped for cover. The unarmed Porter yelled, "Andy, I'll go to the ranch, get a gun, and return!"

"Frank, I'll stay with you, old boy," Hall shouted back. "Don't run!"

As rifle fire rained down on him, Andy exclaimed, "There is more than one, and we better get out of this!"

Hawley emptied his sixteen-shot Henry rifle as Grime pounded away with his needle gun. One bullet tore into Andy Hall's thigh, making a flesh wound. Porter, hanging on to his horse for dear life, raced off toward a ranch house two miles distant. Andy charged his animal up a side canyon, dismounted, and climbed a hill to get a look at his attackers. Grime, unseen by Hall, ran onto the trail and used his hatchet to cut the Wells Fargo box from the dead mule. He quickly pried open the strongbox, removed the gold coin and a pocket watch, and stuffed them into a pair of saddlebags. Then he joined Hawley, who berated him for leaving the mail, insisting, "We might get several thousand dollars out of the registered mail."

But Grime refused to go back to the mules, and the two started off on foot. Hall, who could not see them from his perch on the hill, thought that his attackers were Apaches. He managed to pry the bullet out of his leg and bandaged the wound with strips torn from his shirt. Then he descended the hill to the ambush site and found footprints in the ground, which was soft from recent rains. Despite his wound, he started out on foot, tracing the robbers' muddy tracks across the rough terrain.

Meanwhile, Hawley and Grime had walked about a mile when a rider approached. The horseman, Dr. W. F. Vail, a Globe druggist and prospector, was on his way to his mine. He had heard the gunfire and thought that robbers were shooting at him. He recognized Hawley and Grime, having seen them in Globe, but he did not know their names. Lafayette Grime later recalled, "I told him he better rush on into town, and he said that he did not want to go in alone for it might be Indians." At that, the unsuspecting Dr. Vail dismounted and walked across a ridge with the two bandits. Then he remounted and started off toward Globe. Hawley recognized that Vail was the only witness who

Cicero Grime, one of the stage-robbing gang who killed Andy Hall. [*Author's collection*]

could place them at the robbery site. He levered a round into his rifle and told Grime, "We will have to kill him."

Hawley fired twice and Grime once. The heavy slugs tore Vail out of his saddle and he dropped to the ground, desperately wounded. The two robbers left him, continued up a small canyon, and stopped to rest on a ridge above Russell Gulch. Soon they spotted Andy Hall limping toward them. He had followed the tracks and the sound of gunfire. Lafayette Grime shouldered his rifle and fired, and Andy dived for cover into a thicket of bear grass. He still thought the raiders were Apaches, but after peeking through the grass, he was relieved to see Hawley and Grime, forty feet distant.

"Hold on," he called out. "I thought you fellows were Indians. There are some back yonder and they shot me in the leg. See, here's the bullet," and he stepped forward and showed them the slug that he had removed from his thigh.

"And we thought you were an Indian too," replied Grime, lying.

"Let's get away from here and get into town as quick as possible," Hall responded.

Andy kept his revolver in his hand as they started toward Globe. He began to grow suspicious when Grime shouldered the heavy saddlebags. Hall made sure that Hawley and Grime walked next to him or in front. Said Hawley later, "When I saw him eyeing those saddlebags I knew damn well he knew what they contained and was only watching for a chance to shoot us both." After walking almost two miles, they stopped to rest atop a ridge. Hawley managed to work himself behind Hall, then quickly raised his rifle and shot the Wells Fargo man in the back. Andy ran about ten steps, then turned and opened fire with his six-gun. He traded fire with the two outlaws, firing five rounds at them, but they riddled him with rifle bullets. As he lay dying on the ground, Grime stepped forward and finished him off with a .50-caliber slug. Then the killers fled to Globe.[11]

By this time, Frank Porter had galloped into Globe and raised the alarm. Andy Hall's body was soon discovered near the trail, his six-gun in his right hand. It was the same ornate Colt revolver presented to him by Wells Fargo. Dr. Vail was also found, close to death. Before he died, he said that his killers were white men, one big and one small, and both were from Globe. News of the double murders spread like wildfire. Heavy rewards were offered by Wells Fargo and the Gila County board of supervisors. Sheriff Pete Gabriel, a crack lawman, rode into Globe to help in the investigation. He learned from Dan Lacey, the captain of the Globe Rangers, that the day before the murders he had loaned a Springfield rifle to one of his men, Lafayette Grime. When Grime returned the rifle, Lacy noticed that it had been fired and had recent dents in the stock. Captain Lacey also said that when the Rangers had been called out to help in the manhunt, young Grime failed to appear. In the past, he had always been first to report for duty. Sheriff Gabriel and Lacey went to Globe's gunsmith shop to compare empty cartridges found at the ambush site with those used in the borrowed rifle. Cicero Grime happened to be inside the shop, and Gabriel thought that he "seemed uneasy and looked guilty."

As they stepped out of the shop, Gabriel remarked to the captain, "That man is guilty. Who is he?" When told it was Lafayette's brother, Gabriel set out with Captain Lacey and several companions in search of Lafayette Grime. They found him working in a mill in Wheatfields, twelve miles north of Globe. Gabriel, who was unknown to Grime, exclaimed loudly to the other men present, "That's the man! Put the handcuffs on him. I was on the hill and saw him shoot at Hall three times."

A shocked Grime blurted out, "No, I didn't. I only shot at him twice."

Thoroughly duped, Lafayette now had no choice but to make a full confession. He admitted that he and Hawley had slain the two men and had been assisted by Cicero; they had buried the stolen gold at the head of Russell Gulch. Gabriel left Grime under guard at the mill, then rode into Globe. He could not find Cicero Grime, but he quietly arrested Hawley at his house. To avoid a lynching, he and his little posse started for Florence with Hawley and Grime. By this time, W. W. Lowther, sheriff at Globe, learned of the arrests and raced after Gabriel's posse. Lowther demanded that Sheriff Gabriel turn the prisoners over to him. Gabriel refused, declaring that the killers would be lynched if they were taken back to Globe. After a heated debate over who had proper jurisdiction, Gabriel finally relented.

Sheriff Lowther lodged Lafayette Grime and Curtis Hawley in the Globe jail, where they were joined by Cicero Grime. Pete Gabriel's fears were well grounded. That night, August 23, 1882, a huge mob took the prisoners from Sheriff Lowther. One of the vigilante leaders was J. J. Vosburgh, Globe's Wells Fargo agent. He sent a wire to John Valentine in San Francisco, advising that the bandits had been caught. He asked, "Will you pay the reward to our men if they turn them over to our citizens to hang them in front of the express office to a tree?" Valentine promptly responded, "The rewards are matters of no consequence to us, but I suggest that your citizens let the law take its course." Then Lafayette Grime and Curtis Hawley led Vosburgh and thirty citizens to Russell Gulch, where they dug up the gold and returned to

Globe. At 2:00 A.M. the next day, August 24, the mob, with Vosburgh in the lead, took Grime and Hawley to a large sycamore tree on Broad Street. Then, in one of the Southwest's most famous lynchings, the vigilantes looped ropes around their necks and strung them up.

The mob took pity on Cicero Grime because his wife and children were known to most of them and because he was not one of the actual killers. He pled guilty to robbery and was sentenced to twenty-one years in the territorial prison in Yuma. There he feigned insanity and officers transferred him to the California insane asylum in Stockton, which then housed inmates from Arizona. In September 1883, Grime escaped and was never recaptured. Wells Fargo officials paid the reward to Sheriff Gabriel and his possemen. Gabriel used one-third of his share to pay for Andy Hall's tombstone and a fence to enclose the burial plot.[12]

Over the years, time and the elements removed all trace of Pete Gabriel's tribute to his brave friend. Today Andy Hall's remains lie in an unmarked grave in the Globe city cemetery. Nothing more than weeds mark the final resting place of the first Wells Fargo shotgun messenger to be murdered in the line of duty.[13]

II

THE MAN WHO CAPTURED BLACK BART

Harry N. Morse

Wisps of November fog drifted down Montgomery Street as the distinguished, nattily dressed bon vivant turned onto Bush Street and started up the sloping sidewalk. He looked like any other successful businessman hurrying along in the hustle and bustle of downtown San Francisco. Throngs of pedestrians pressed in as delivery wagons, buggies, and hacks rattled along the stone-paved streets. Swinging his gold-headed walking stick and tipping his derby hat to the ladies, the man stepped briskly toward the doorway of Thomas Ware's tobacco shop. He never suspected that in the next moment his long career as the West's most wanted gentleman bandit was about to end.

Charles E. Boles, better known as Black Bart, was the most prolific—and infamous—stagecoach robber in American history. Between 1875 and 1883, he held up twenty-nine coaches on the lonely stage roads of Northern California. On two occasions, he left bits of clever doggerel behind, goading Wells Fargo's men to capture him. He became renowned as the "Poet Highwayman." The story of how the company's intrepid chief detective, James B. Hume, tracked down the wily bandit and arrested him in San Francisco is one of the best known of the

American West. But there is a problem with that tale: It just isn't true. Jim Hume did not capture Black Bart. That honor belongs to Harry N. Morse, one of the great sheriffs and detectives of the Old West.[1]

Henry Nicholson Morse hailed from New York City. In 1849, at the age of fourteen, he joined a ship's crew and worked his way "around the Horn" to California and the mining camps of its great Gold Rush. For years, he drifted from one job to another: gold miner, wagon driver, hotelkeeper, butcher, expressman, and grocer. A strong supporter of the Union during the Civil War, he helped organize a California militia unit, the Oakland Guard, and rose to become its captain. In 1863, he was appointed a deputy provost marshal, and later that year he won election as sheriff of Alameda County, across the bay from San Francisco. At the age of twenty-eight, one of the youngest of all California sheriffs, he finally found his calling.

At first, the rookie sheriff was decidedly ineffective. The eastern portion of his county, the Amador and Livermore valleys, was infested with desperadoes, both Anglo and Hispanic. The bandidos contemptuously called the beardless young officer "El Muchacho," "the boy." For two years, he did almost nothing to take on the brazen gangs of robbers and cattle thieves. But in 1866, having acquired skill as a horseman and deadly accuracy with rifle and revolver, he began to go after them with a vengeance. He encountered the notorious outlaw Narciso Bojorques and shot and wounded him in a close-quarters pistol duel. In 1867, he tracked down and killed a murderer, Narato Ponce, in a wild gunfight at the outlaw's hideout. A year later, he trailed the killer Joe Newell for twelve hundred miles on horseback and captured him near Los Angeles. In 1870, following a months-long investigation, he ran down an infamous robber and murderer, Jesus Tejada, high in the Coast Range. A year later, Morse trapped the bandit chieftain Juan Soto and shot him to death in the most renowned outlaw-lawman gunfight of the California frontier. No longer was the young lawman El Muchacho. The bandidos gave him a new nickname: "El Diablo," "the devil."

During his fourteen years as sheriff, Harry Morse captured scores

Harry Morse, the great
California sheriff and detective,
in 1885. [*Author's collection*]

of bandits and livestock thieves throughout central California. While most lawmen of that era rarely left their bailiwicks, he thought nothing of trailing outlaws far beyond the boundaries of Alameda County. He paid both informants and manhunting expenses from his own pocket, and grateful legislators had the state reimburse him. That led the governor to appoint Morse as head of a state-funded posse to track down Tiburcio Vásquez, the most notorious California outlaw since the Gold Rush. During the spring of 1874, Morse and his men tracked Vásquez for sixty-one days and 2,720 miles, until they finally located him in what is now West Hollywood. Using Morse's information, Los Angeles lawmen raided Vásquez's hideout and shot and captured him. In 1875, he died on the gallows in San Jose.[2]

In 1878, Morse left the sheriff's office and founded his own detective agency in San Francisco. He quickly became the most prominent private investigator on the West Coast. In addition to a myriad of routine matters, Morse handled two of the most significant cases of graft in the city's history. He cracked the Dupont Street Frauds case in 1879, implicating San Francisco's mayor in corruption. Then he smashed the Harkins Opium Ring, resulting in the prosecution of a corrupt federal magistrate in 1883. Thus it was only natural that Wells Fargo's Jim Hume asked him that summer to try his hand at capturing Black Bart.

For eight years, an elusive lone highwayman had been robbing stages throughout Northern California. He first appeared on the morning of July 26, 1875, on Funk Hill near Copperopolis, in the Sierra Nevada foothills. As a stage was climbing the hill, he stepped into the roadway. He wore a linen duster and a flour-sack mask, topped by a white hat. In his hands was a double-barreled shotgun.

"Please throw down the box," the road agent ordered in a deep, hollow voice.

As the jehu reached for the strongbox, the bandit boomed, "If he dares to shoot, give him a solid volley, boys!"

Glancing at the roadside brush, the reinsman saw what he thought were several rifle barrels pointed at him. At the robber's next demand he threw out the mailbags. A terrified female passenger threw her purse out of the stagecoach. The highwayman picked it up and handed it back to her. Bowing politely, he reassured her: "I don't want your money, only the express box and mail."

Then he ordered the coach on. Soon a second stage appeared and the bandit again demanded the express box. When the driver said he wasn't carrying one, the robber let the coach proceed. Later it turned out that the rifle barrels were merely sticks pointing from the brush, and the robber had been alone. The modus operandi the highwayman used, and the disguise he wore, would be replicated many times in the years to come. Later that year, the same road agent stopped a coach in Yuba County, in the Northern Mines, and the following year he pulled but one job, in Siskiyou County, far to the north. On August 3, 1877, he held up a stage near Fort Ross, on the Sonoma County coast, and left behind in the shattered express box a short verse that has become famous in the annals of American crime:

I've labored long and hard for bread,
For honor and for riches,
But on my corns too long you've tread,
You fine haired sons of bitches.

It was signed "Black Bart, the Po8."[3]

A full year passed before the bandit reappeared. After robbing the Quincy to Oroville stage on July 25, 1878, he left a longer bit of doggerel with the same signature. Although he never left behind any other verse, ever after he was known as Black Bart, the Poet Highwayman. The lone bandit continued to stop coaches with near-monotonous regularity: one in 1877, four in 1878, three in 1879, and five each in 1880, 1881, and 1882. He plagued stage routes from the Pacific Coast to the Sierra Nevada, and from the Oregon border to Sonora, in the Southern Mines. He was polite, gentlemanly, and never robbed the passengers. He was careful never to rob a coach with a shotgun messenger; hence he never made a big haul in any of his holdups. He violated that rule but once, in 1882, when he made the mistake of tangling with Wells Fargo messenger George Hackett on the La Porte to Marysville route. Not only did Bart fail to secure the eighteen-thousand-dollar treasure in the express box; he received a scarred forehead from a blast of buckshot from Hackett's shotgun.

Jim Hume and other lawmen worked tirelessly to capture Black Bart. They learned that he was an extraordinary cross-country walker, able to walk fifty miles with little rest. In an era when wanted men were often identified by their horses, Bart never rode one. His robberies were always in isolated mountain regions, where he could easily disappear on foot. He broke down his sawed-off shotgun and carried it out of sight in his blanket roll. Although Hume flooded Northern California with wanted posters, again and again Black Bart slipped away. In 1883, he robbed three more stages. Bart's twenty-eighth holdup took place on June 23, 1883, at the foot of the Morrow Grade near Jackson, in the foothills of the Sierra Nevada. Hume was thor-

Charles E. Boles, better known as Black Bart. He was America's most prolific stage robber. [*Author's collection*]

oughly frustrated and decided he needed a detective to work specifically on the Black Bart case. He chose Harry Morse.[4]

The veteran lawman began his investigation by going to Jackson and spending several days looking into the latest holdup. Then he met with Wells Fargo detectives Hume, John Thacker, and Charles Aull, as well as with the Calaveras County sheriff, Ben K. Thorn. From them, he learned a great deal about Bart, his holdups, and his methods. During the next four months Morse worked on the case off and on but made no progress. Then, on November 3, 1883, Bart struck again. He held up stage driver Reason E. McConnell, later a noted Wells Fargo shotgun messenger, on Funk Hill, the site of his first holdup, in 1875. After Bart cracked open the iron safe, McConnell and a young hunter, Jimmy Rolleri, fired several shots and put the bandit to flight.

He escaped with $4,500 in gold. A posse found Black Bart's camp and recovered his derby hat, sacks of food, a leather opera-glass case, three dirty linen cuffs, and some buckshot tied up in a handkerchief. Sheriff Thorn found an old hunter, Thomas Martin, who lived a mile from Funk Hill and had spoken with a man who matched Black Bart's description. Wells Fargo's John Thacker arrived to investigate. He carefully inspected the handkerchief and found that it bore the laundry mark "F.X.O.7." It was evident that the mark came from a populous city like Stockton, Sacramento, or even San Francisco, because small-town launderers did not need such marks to identify their customers' clothing.[5]

Thacker delivered the evidence to Jim Hume in San Francisco. Hume kept the hat, cuffs, and opera-glass case so that he could work on identifying them. He met with Morse in his office on November 7, four days after the robbery, and handed him the handkerchief. Recalled Morse, "I knew I had a job before me, as there were ninety-one laundries in the city." He methodically began visiting every laundry, showing each proprietor the handkerchief. On November 12, the fifth day of his search, Morse visited the Ferguson & Biggy California Laundry on Stevenson Street. The co-owner, Phineas Ferguson, checked his books and identified the laundry mark as that of a customer named C. E. Bolton. He explained that Bolton's laundry was dropped off and picked up at Thomas C. Ware's tobacco shop at 316 Bush Street.[6]

Morse immediately walked to Ware's shop on Bush Street, situated a few doors above Montgomery Street. To avoid tipping off his quarry, he announced simply that he was looking for C. E. Bolton. The unsuspecting Ware replied, "Why, certainly. I know Mr. Bolton well. He is in the city now; just arrived from his mine two days ago, and if you will call later you will probably meet him here, for he is an old acquaintance of mine and makes this his headquarters when he is in the city."

Morse said later that he asked Ware about Bolton. "The laundry-man said Bolton was a mining man who often visited his mines, although he [Ware] did not know where they were situated. Sometimes he would be gone a week and sometimes a month. I assumed as a pretext that I wanted to consult with him on some mining matter, and not being certain that he was the Bolton I was looking for, I wished he would describe him." The description Ware provided matched that of the stage robber perfectly. Ware said that Bolton roomed nearby at the Webb House at 37 Second Street.

Morse left and assigned one of his operatives to watch the Webb House. An hour later, Morse returned to the tobacco shop, intending to take Ware into his confidence. Ware explained later that Morse asked "if he could have a little private talk with me if I could spare a few minutes from my business. I consented, and we started down the street together." They had only taken a few steps when Ware exclaimed, "Why, here comes Bolton now. I'll introduce you to him."

Morse quickly eyed Bolton. "He was elegantly dressed and came sauntering along carrying a little cane. He wore a natty little derby hat, a diamond pin, a large diamond ring on his little finger, and a heavy gold watch and chain. He was about five feet, eight inches in height, straight as an arrow, broad shouldered, with deep sunken, bright blue eyes, high cheek bones, and a large, handsome grey mustache and imperial; the rest of his face was shaven clean. One would have taken him for a gentleman who had made a fortune and was enjoying it, rather than a highwayman."

Ware started to introduce Bolton, then turned to Morse and said, "I don't know your name, sir."

"Hamilton is my name," responded Morse. The two shook hands and Morse asked if he was Mr. Bolton, the mining man.

"Yes, I am," he replied.

Morse said that he had some ore samples in his office, and asked if Bolton could spare a few minutes to look them over. "Certainly," Bolton replied.[7]

The two walked a few doors down to Montgomery Street, then turned left and strolled several blocks to the Wells Fargo building at California and Sansome. They went upstairs, where Morse introduced Bolton to Jim Hume. The Wells Fargo detective asked him to take a seat, then questioned him about his business. Hume asked where his mine was located, and he replied that it was in Nevada, on the California line. Hume pressed for more details, and Bolton was unable to state the name of the mine or exactly where it was located. He began to sweat profusely, and declared, "I am a gentleman and don't know who you are. I want to know what all this inquiry is about."

"You shall know presently," Hume told him quietly. At that point, Morse noticed that there was a dime-size piece of skin missing from Bolton's right hand. He recalled that one of the packages found at the robbery site had had blood on it.

"How did you get that?" Morse asked, pointing to his hand. Bolton became angry and exclaimed, "If it is your business, I will tell you that I struck it on the car rail."

"No, you didn't," interjected Hume. "You got that when you broke open our box a little while ago."

As Bolton turned pale, Hume asked, "If you will tell me where you were on the 1st, 2nd, 3rd, 4th, and 5th days of November, I'll keep the telegraph offices open all night in order to verify your statement and if you will not do that I am going to take you down and lock you up."

"Take me down and lock me up," declared Bolton defiantly.

Hume summoned police captain Appleton W. Stone, head of the city prison. When Stone arrived, the three lawmen bundled Bolton into a hack and drove to the Webb House. They searched Bolton's room and found a large trunk, two valises, and several men's suits. In a pocket Morse found a handkerchief bearing the same laundry mark. Inside the trunk they found shirts, cuffs, and collars, all with the identical mark. There was also a letter with handwriting that matched that of one of the poems written by Black Bart.

On being shown the laundry marks, Bolton declared, "I am not the only one whose things bear this mark. Others have their washing done at the same place. Somebody may have stolen the handkerchief from me, or I may have lost it and someone else found it."

When the detectives pointed out that the handkerchief had been found at the scene of the last stagecoach holdup, he exclaimed, "Do you take me for a stage robber? I never harmed anybody in all my life, and this is the first time that my character has ever been brought into question."

Next the detectives found a flyleaf from a Bible, with an inscription to Charles E. Boles from his wife, dated 1865. This was their first clue as to Black Bart's real name. They took him to the city prison and booked him for the night. In the morning, Morse, Stone, and Thacker took him to Stockton, first wiring Sheriff Thorn to meet them at the depot with Thomas Martin, the hunter. "Bart seemed full of fun all the way going up," Morse later said, "and showed no desire to escape. He was not ironed, and his jaunty appearance warded off any suspicion of his identity."

When they stepped off the train in Stockton, Thorn and Martin were on the platform waiting for them. Martin spotted the prisoner in the crowd of a hundred people and cried out, "That's the man! That's him!"

They took him to the photo gallery of John P. Spooner. Said Morse, "At first he strongly objected, saying we had no right to do it, and he had done nothing, but finally he submitted and sat quietly." As Boles sat in a chair, he motioned toward the camera and asked with a laugh, "Will that thing go off? I would like to go off myself."

Spooner took five now-famous images of the bandit: two of him standing, holding his little cane, and three bust views. The officers were joined by Sheriff Tom Cunningham, and all five posed for a group photograph, today the best-known image of pioneer California lawmen. Then they took Boles to the county jail and locked him up for the night. In the morning, the officers took him on the railroad to Milton, where Reason McConnell was waiting. He could not identify the suspect but stated that his voice was the same as that of the robber. A large crowd appeared to see the notorious highwayman, who realized that his days of anonymity were over. He told Morse, "The whole town has turned out to meet me. I guess they'll know me when they see me again."

Morse, Stone, and Thorn put Boles into a buggy and drove twenty-two miles to San Andreas, the Calaveras County seat. Recalled Morse, "The whole population of the town—men, woman, and children—had turned out, and it was amusing to hear the remarks as they mistook

Harry Morse and fellow lawmen celebrate the capture of Black Bart in 1883. *Left to right:* Sheriff Tom Cunningham, San Francisco Police Captain Appleton W. Stone, Sheriff Ben Thorn, Wells Fargo Detective John N. Thacker, and Harry Morse. [*Author's collection*]

the natty looking prisoner for an officer and some one of us for the culprit." It was evening when Morse took Boles into the jailor's office to interview him. "I had written down all the facts we had gathered in connection with the case," said the detective. "These I carefully read to him, explaining what bearing they would have at the trial. He would often break off and go into other subjects." After five and a half hours of grilling and verbal sparring, Boles finally said, "I don't admit that I committed this robbery, but what benefit would it be to the man who did, to acknowledge it?"

Morse knew he had finally broken through. He explained that if the case went to trial, evidence would be submitted showing that he had committed numerous stage robberies. However, if Boles pled guilty and returned the stolen treasure, a judge might go easy on him. Boles then asked, "Suppose the man that did commit the robberies should do this. Would it not be possible for him to get clear altogether?"

Morse truthfully replied that this would be impossible, and that if he was convicted of all the stage holdups, he could receive a life term in prison. At that, Boles exclaimed, "I want you to understand I am not going to San Quentin. I'll die first!"

Morse called in Thorn and Stone, and after a few minutes of discussion about the stolen loot, Boles suddenly announced, "Well, let us go after it."

The detective later recalled that "in a few minutes we were in a buggy driving in the moonlight toward the place where Bart had hidden his treasures. They were in the stump of a hollow tree, buried in leaves. On the way Bart told me of his doings. He said that he had been about mills and stage offices, learning when bullion was to be shipped and when the stage was to carry money." After recovering about four thousand dollars in gold amalgam, they returned Boles to his jail cell in San Andreas. Then Morse sent a telegram to Leonard F. Rowell, Wells Fargo's division superintendent in San Francisco: "Black Bart throws up the sponge. Stone, Thorn, and myself have recovered all the stolen treasure. Inform Thacker."[8]

Two days later, on November 17, 1884, Boles plead guilty to a single count of robbery and received a six-year term in San Quentin. Newspapers outdid themselves in reporting the story, publishing reams of fact and fiction about the notorious highwayman. It turned out that Charles E. Boles had been born in England about 1829. His family came to the United States when he was two, settling in Jefferson County, New York. In 1850, he and a brother joined the California Gold Rush. He returned east in 1854, married, and settled in Decatur, Illinois. Boles served with distinction in the Union army during the Civil War, fighting in numerous engagements and suffering severe wounds in 1864.

After being mustered out at war's end, he joined the gold rush to Montana, leaving behind three daughters and an infant son. They never saw him again.

He drifted through the mining camps of Montana, Idaho, and Utah, and eventually returned to California. He sent letters to his wife, always promising to return home. She eked out a living as a seamstress and raised their children alone in near poverty. By 1875, Boles was living in San Francisco, where he posed as a mine owner. He was a gentleman, only associated with respectable people, and even befriended several police detectives. Because he did not drink, gamble, or consort with prostitutes, his true calling was never suspected. On his early release from San Quentin in 1888, having received credits for good behavior, he was shadowed by detectives, but they lost him within a month. Following three stage holdups by a lone highwayman later that year, Jim Hume announced that Boles was the prime suspect. However, despite a huge manhunt, he was never found, and his ultimate fate remains a great mystery of the Old West.[9]

Harry Morse's capture of Black Bart was one of his most outstanding feats and brought him national attention. His detective agency prospered and he went on to handle some of the most important cases of the era: the 1895 trial of San Francisco sex killer Theodore Durrant, known as the "Beast in the Belfry"; the Selby Smelter robbery of 1901, one of America's biggest gold thefts; and the 1905 death by poisoning of Jane Stanford, cofounder of Stanford University. When he died at his grand home in Oakland in 1912, he was widely eulogized as one of the greatest peace officers of the American West.

12

TRUE GRIT

Mike Tovey

On an isolated stretch of Highway 88 in California's picturesque Mother Lode country rests a lonely stone marker on the roadside. Its brass plaque, visible only up close, depicts the bas-relief of a six-horse stagecoach, and its inscription honors the "brave, intrepid, self-sacrificing and loyal Wells Fargo messengers and stage drivers of California." This simple monument marks the final episode of the adventurous life of one of the company's most famous shotgun guards.

Martin Michael Tovey was a Canadian, born in Perth, Ontario, on February 4, 1842, to Michael Tovey and Katherine Tierney. His parents were from Irish families who had emigrated to Canada. They raised a large brood of twelve children, including Mike's twin brother, Peter. In 1848, the Toveys came to the United States, settling first in Iowa, then in Illinois. In the late 1850s, they moved west to Nebraska Territory, establishing a farm near Fort Calhoun. At the outbreak of the Civil War, Peter Tovey went to Iowa and enlisted in the Union army, while Mike drifted west and became a pony rider for Ben Holladay's Overland Mail & Express Company. This grueling work, replete with the dangers of weather, Indians, and road agents, honed his wits and his endurance. It also brought him to the attention of Wells Fargo, and

Mike Tovey, Wells Fargo shotgun messenger, in the late 1870s. [*Author's collection*]

in 1871, he signed on as a shotgun messenger on the perilous route from the railhead at Corinne, Utah, to Helena, Montana.[1]

Mike Tovey quickly exhibited a dauntless courage that matched his powerful physique: He stood over six feet tall and weighed two hundred pounds. A friend recalled that he was modest and never boastful. "Brave men don't talk much, and Tovey would rather sit and tell you a funny story than blow about himself." Despite his new occupation, Tovey's first recorded encounter with an outlaw did not involve a stage holdup. In the spring of 1874, a pair of notorious horse thieves, William Butler and Charles Slater, were released from the Montana territorial prison. The two worked honestly for a few months in Helena, but in August they stole a herd of horses and mules and fled to Slater's home in Malad City, Idaho. Mike Tovey and a local sheriff got on their trail and caught up with them near Malad City. When Tovey ordered the pair to surrender, Butler jerked his six-gun and fired four rounds, "just trimming Mike's hair," according to a witness. Tovey did not even shoot back; he simply covered Butler "with the muzzle end of one of those short shotguns the W.F. boys carry." Butler and Slater immediately surrendered and were jailed in Malad City. Butler was handed a ten-year term for the stealing and shooting, while Slater got two years in the Idaho prison.[2]

During his years in Montana, Tovey's companions were shotgun messengers John X. Beidler, Aaron Y. Ross, Shotgun Jimmy Brown, Eugene Blair, and John Brent. In 1875, he was sent to Nevada to guard Wells Fargo's express on the stage routes from Virginia City to Pioche, and from Carson City to Bodie, California. Bodie was known as much for its violence as for its gold. According to a popular 1879 story, a little girl, on learning that her family was moving to the boomtown, cried out, "Good-bye God, we are going to Bodie in the morning." The *Bodie Free Press*, however, insisted that she actually said, "Good! By God, we're going to Bodie." While there, Tovey rode with Wells Fargo messenger Bob Paul, former sheriff of Calaveras County and later one of Arizona's most celebrated lawmen. The two became good friends. In 1877, company officials sent Tovey to Ogden, Utah, to protect gold shipments on stagecoaches from Montana. He arrived during the Nez Perce War, and in August he had a dangerous encounter with the Indians. His coach was accompanied by several mounted cavalrymen near Pleasant Valley stage station in Idaho. Suddenly, a band of armed Nez Perce arose from the brush and ordered them to go back. The soldiers were outnumbered and returned with the coach to Pleasant Valley. Tovey borrowed a saddle horse at the station and carried the express through alone. He reported "a good many Indians in sight, but that they had done no damage except rifling Hole in the Rock station." He also found the body of a dead Indian.[3]

In 1879, Tovey was sent back to Bodie, where his closest companions were the formidable shotgun messengers Aaron Y. Ross and Henry C. Ward. While riding the Bodie stage, Mike had one of his most memorable adventures. The story began that winter on a sheep ranch near Lincoln, in the foothills of Placer County, California. Two hired hands worked at the ranch: William C. Jones, alias Frank Dow,

The notorious stage robber Milt Sharp.
[*Author's collection*]

an ex-convict, and Milton Anthony Sharp. The latter, born in Missouri in 1846, had led an honest life, having gone west in 1866 and working as a miner in California and Nevada. Sharp was a gentleman who did not smoke or drink, but he had lost all his earnings gambling in risky mining stocks. Now Jones convinced him they could make a haul by robbing stages.

On May 15, 1880, they stopped a coach near Auburn, lined up the passengers, and stripped them of money and valuables. Then they crossed the Sierra Nevada, and three weeks later, on June 8, held up a stage from Carson City to Aurora near Sweetwater Summit. This spot, 6,800 feet high in Nevada's Sweetwater Mountains, was about forty miles north of Bodie. The two highwaymen robbed the passengers and took three thousand dollars from the Wells Fargo box. A week later, on June 15, Sharp and Jones halted another coach at the same spot, looting the strongbox of three hundred dollars. Jim Hume investigated the two holdups, and when Paiute Indians took to the trail, the two bandits fled back to California. On August 6, they held up yet another stage near Auburn, again robbing the passengers at gunpoint. They spared no one, even taking a gold pocket watch from a Catholic priest. Finally, they used a hammer and chisel to break open the iron pony safe, which netted them fifteen hundred dollars.[4]

Now Sharp and Jones returned to Nevada to continue their robbery spree. On August 30, they tried to stop the Bodie coach near Coal Valley stage station. The driver ignored their demand to halt, and as he whipped up his team, they fired a shot that narrowly missed him. Three days later, on September 2, Sharp and Jones halted the Carson City–bound stage from Candelaria, fifty miles southeast of Bodie, and escaped with the Wells Fargo box. By this time, due to the spate of holdups, Wells Fargo officials had assigned Tovey, John Brent, Aaron Ross, and another messenger, Tom Woodruff, to guard the Bodie stages. Woodruff was only a temporary guard, while his brother Hank was a respected Wells Fargo messenger. According to Aaron Ross, Mike Tovey and Tom Woodruff rode a southbound coach from Carson City, headed for Bodie. The stage stopped at Genoa, thirteen miles south of Carson City, where they met Ross and Brent. Ross told Tovey, "It is pretty near time for them fellows to come out on the road again—the robbers—pretty near time for them to be coming back." Ross, who disliked Tom Woodruff, claimed that he tried to convince Tovey not to take Woodruff with him. Ross said to Tovey, "Maybe I better go back with you and send Woodruff . . . to come back down with Brent."[5]

But Tovey had faith in Woodruff and declined Ross's offer. He and Woodruff arrived in Bodie without incident. At five o'clock in the evening on September 3, one day after the most recent holdup, they boarded the northbound stage for Carson City. Late that night, they met the down stage. The driver and his eight passengers excitedly reported that they had been held up seven miles north of Aurora, scene of the prior robberies. The bandits, wielding rifles, had emerged from the darkness, and one ordered, "Throw up your hands God damn quick or I'll blow your damn brains out."

Then the jehu and passengers were lined up while one of the desperadoes broke open the Wells Fargo box. There was very little in it, and his partner exclaimed, "Is that all? Shall we go through the passengers?"

"No," the other highwayman responded. "I don't like to rob passengers."

They allowed the stage to proceed. After three hours of travel, the driver and passengers met the northbound stage, and they told Tovey and Woodruff about the holdup. Though Mike thought that the highwaymen were probably long gone, he decided to proceed with caution. As they reached a spot five miles from the holdup site, Tovey spotted footprints in the light of the headlamps. He got down with a lantern to inspect them, then climbed aboard. Each half mile or so he stopped to check the tracks, which were heading northward. Finally, at about 3:00 A.M. the coach arrived at the holdup site. Tovey and H. A. Billings, division agent for the stage line, were riding with the driver, while Woodruff was inside the coach with several passengers. Tovey again swung down and walked forward, following the tracks. Suddenly, a voice called out from the blackness, "You son of a bitch, you thought you'd sneak up on us, did you?"

"Don't shoot. I'll go back and get the box," Tovey cried, feigning fear.

"Go back, you whelp, and if you make a move we'll murder every mother's son of you."

The voice belonged to Jones, and he raised his rifle and fired twice. The first bullet whined by Tovey and struck one of the lead horses in the head, killing the animal instantly. The second passed between the driver and Billings. Tovey dived for cover under the coach, then whispered to Billings, "Hand down that gun."

Billings tossed him his shotgun, at the same time jumping down from the box. Tovey and Billings, joined by Woodruff, took cover behind the stage. At that, Jones yelled, "If you fellows fire a gun, we will murder every son of a bitch of you!"

"Nobody is firing any guns," Tovey called back as he cocked the hammers of his shotgun. "What's the matter with you? If you want anything, come along."

William C. Jones, alias Frank Dow.
He was shot and killed by Mike Tovey
in 1880. [*Author's collection*]

Jones then stepped forward into the light of the headlamps. Tovey
called in a loud voice to the driver, "Throw down the box, quick, and
let's get out of this!"

At the same time, he crouched and rested the barrel of his shotgun
on top of the rear wheel. Just as Jones passed the body of the fallen
leader, Tovey fired one barrel. The heavy load of buckshot tore into
Jones's face and neck, killing him instantly. Milt Sharp, armed with a
six-shooter, opened fire, and Tovey staggered as a bullet tore into his
right arm, shattering the bone below the elbow. He dropped his shotgun, drew his six-gun with his left hand, and fired back. By this time,
Billings and Woodruff had gotten their guns into play and sent a volley of shots toward Sharp. They saw him stagger and thought they had
hit him. Woodruff chased after Sharp into a stand of willow trees but
lost him in the dark and ran back to the stage.

Tovey was bleeding heavily, so Woodruff and Billings carried him
to a house a short distance down the road, while the unarmed reinsman calmed his team and unhitched the dead horse. Suddenly he
heard a voice say, "Throw down the box." Sharp had returned to finish

the robbery. The driver tossed down the Wells Fargo box, and Sharp quickly chopped it open with a hatchet and took out $750 in cash. The bandit could not see Jones's body, because it lay under the team, and he asked which way his partner had gone. The driver, fearing for his life, said he didn't know. Sharp, his gun in one hand and his loot in the other, vanished into the darkness as he continually called out, "Partner, where are you?"[6]

Mike Tovey was loaded into a buggy for the jolting sixty-mile trip to Carson City, where his wound was treated. Soon he was up and about, his arm heavily bandaged. Jim Hume, who was on a case in Utah, rushed to Bodie to investigate. He concluded that Tom Woodruff had "scrambled behind the stage and let off both barrels" but that he "couldn't shoot straight." According to Hume, both Woodruff and the wounded Tovey had heard Sharp chopping open the express box. Tovey had begged Woodruff to go back and tackle the bandit. "The fellow 'funked,' however," declared Hume, "and couldn't be induced to go a step, although Tovey swore at him and taunted him with cowardice." Aaron Ross said in his memoirs that Woodruff had put up only a token resistance and later gave as an excuse that the barrels of his shotgun were crooked. According to Ross, John Valentine instructed him to investigate Woodruff's account. Ross had a Bodie gunsmith inspect the shotgun and found it to be in good working order. He then reported to Valentine that "the man was crooked instead of the gun." Ross's story was false, for Woodruff had pursued Sharp on foot, and he could not possibly have been in league with the two bandits, who had already held up seven stagecoaches without anyone's complicity.[7]

Hume met Aaron Ross and John Brent at the holdup scene. They found that a local rancher, John Rogers, and several other men had buried the dead highwayman. The three Wells Fargo men dug up the body. Hume wiped the dirt and blood from his face but did not recognize him. There was no money in his pockets, but they found something much more helpful: a San Francisco bank book in the name of W. C. Jones. It listed his address as a Minna Street boardinghouse in

Wells Fargo's Aaron Y. Ross stands next to a stagecoach at the site of the holdup and shootout between Mike Tovey and the bandits Milt Sharp and William C. Jones. [*Bobby McDearmon collection*]

San Francisco and showed that he had deposited one thousand dollars in his account. Hume sent a telegram to the city police, and two detectives searched the room, finding a watch and other items stolen in the holdups. They also discovered photographs of the dead robber and quickly identified him as ex-convict William C. Jones, alias Frank Dow.

The detectives staked out the room. On September 14, ten days after the fatal holdup, a roughly dressed stranger, carrying a blanket roll, walked in. They threw him to the floor and relieved him of two Colt revolvers and a bowie knife. He wore a money belt holding sixteen hundred dollars, and sewn into the lining of his coat was another eight hundred. In his pockets were 150 shares of mining stock. The officers grilled their captive and he soon admitted he was Milton Anthony Sharp. Jim Hume soon arrived in San Francisco and took Sharp back to Nevada to stand trial. He was tried in Aurora, convicted of robbery, and sentenced to twenty years in the Nevada State Prison.[8]

While behind bars, Sharp admitted his guilt and revealed that Jones had had about eighteen hundred dollars in large bills in his pockets when Tovey killed him. This was the type of currency taken from several of the looted express boxes. Wells Fargo men investigated the missing cash and focused on John Rogers, the rancher who had buried the body, who was a well-known Nevada pioneer. They learned that after the holdup he had tried to exchange some large bills. Under questioning, Rogers admitted that he had taken two hundred dollars from Jones's body, and then offered to repay that sum. However, Wells Fargo officials refused the offer and filed a lawsuit against him in Dayton, Nevada, for the full eighteen hundred dollars. The case came to trial in 1885 and a jury ruled in favor of the small rancher and against the big corporation.[9]

Meanwhile, Mike Tovey's wound healed quickly, and by November 1880, Wells Fargo officials ordered him back to Montana. Like the other veteran messengers, he was sent wherever he was most needed. In the spring of 1882, Tovey found himself in Arizona Territory, guarding treasure shipments out of Bisbee. The following year, he was back in the mining country of eastern California and western Nevada. In December 1883, a stage driver, Louis Schalten, reported that his coach had been held up and the treasure box stolen near Bishop, California, on the east side of the Sierra Nevada. Tovey and Wells Fargo's John Thacker investigated and arrested the driver and two accomplices. Schalten admitted that they had stolen the box, and the three were sent to San Quentin. On October 8, 1884, David Francis, a notorious stage and train robber, escaped from the Nevada State Prison. Francis fled south, but Tovey and a local sheriff got on his trail and a week later captured him at Soda Springs, near Hawthorne, Nevada.[10]

Hawthorne was then a freighting and staging stop with a few saloons and businesses, situated on the busy wagon road running to the wild silver towns of Candelaria and Belleville. Mike Tovey was still in Hawthorne that winter when he had trouble with Bill Withrow, a noted gunman. There had been bad blood between the two for several years. Withrow was a saloonkeeper who had worked off and on as a special shotgun messenger for Wells Fargo on the Bodie to Carson

City road. He was a tough character; in 1880, he had shot and killed a gambler, Charles Slade, in Bodie. The next year, Withrow had served briefly as a Bodie policeman, then drifted to Tombstone, Arizona, where he'd acted as a police officer in the spring of 1881. Soon thereafter, he had returned to Nevada and ran a saloon in Belleville. On November 14, 1881, the northbound stage to Carson City had stopped in Belleville. Just as it pulled out, Withrow had stepped from his saloon and fired two shots into the air. A few miles outside of town, the coach was held up by three highwaymen. Two of the passengers were prostitutes, and they recognized the bandit leader as Jesse Pearson, alias Pierce. The robbers were quickly captured.

Tovey believed that Withrow had fired the shots to alert the bandits of the stage's departure. Later, he accused Withrow of trying to spirit away the two women to keep them from testifying. Pearson was convicted of the stage robbery, but Mike's charge against Withrow was never proved. Withrow moved to Hawthorne, opened a saloon, and nursed a deep grudge against Tovey. On the night of December 20, 1884, Mike was drinking with friends in a Hawthorne saloon when he casually remarked that he "was the last man in the world to pick a quarrel, but a good man when he got into one."

Withrow heard of the statement and took it as a challenge. The next evening, he walked up to Tovey in a saloon and said, "You said last night that you were a good man. Are you as good a man now?"

Mike laughed and replied that he "felt about as good." Without another word, Withrow jerked his six-gun and fired two shots, hitting Tovey in the right thigh and left hip. Tovey seized his assailant and the two fell to the floor. Bystanders overpowered Withrow and disarmed him, while others carried the heavily bleeding shotgun messenger into a drugstore. The tough-as-nails Tovey quickly recovered, and five months later Withrow was brought to trial for attempted murder. When the jury acquitted Bill Withrow, Tovey's many friends threatened to lynch him if he ever returned to Hawthorne.[11]

In 1887, Mike Tovey was sent to California, where he rode the stage routes of Amador and Calaveras counties in the Sierra Nevada foothills.

Mike Tovey, wearing a bearskin coat that was typical winter wear for stage drivers and shotgun messengers. [*Author's collection*]

Two years later, Milt Sharp fled the Nevada State Prison. Following his escape, Wells Fargo officials received a letter, purportedly written by Sharp, warning them to retire Tovey or he would be killed. Later, Mike received a letter, again signed by Sharp, warning him to leave California or "take the same medicine dealt out to poor Jones." The veteran messenger ignored the threats. Then, at seven o'clock on the morning of April 30, 1892, he boarded a stage in San Andreas, bound for Sheep Ranch, in the mountains sixteen miles east. The Wells Fargo box held four thousand dollars in gold coin, the payroll for the Sheep Ranch Mine. The coach was a canvas-topped mud wagon, like a huge buggy, with three seats. The front seat held Tovey and the whip, seventeen-year-old Alphonso "Babe" Raggio, whose eldest brother owned the stage line. The second seat was occupied by Johannah Rodesino, age fifteen, and her sister, Louisa, fourteen, daughters of a prominent mining and mercantile family. The girls had attended a party in San Andreas and were on their way home to El Dorado, now called Mountain Ranch. The rear seat held two more female passengers.[12]

The stage rattled out of town and slowly made the five miles to Willow Creek, about halfway to Mountain Ranch. Suddenly, a masked bandit arose from behind a large boulder above the stage road. Without a word of warning, he fired a single blast from his shotgun. Two buckshot struck young Raggio in the right shoulder and two more in his breast, piercing his right lung. He reeled in his seat, and as blood poured from his mouth, he gasped, "They have killed me, Tovey, look out for the horses."

At the same time, another buckshot tore into Mike's right arm and several more struck Johannah Rodesino in the chest and head. She fell forward onto the floor of the stage. Tovey thought she was unhurt and had merely fainted. Raggio was desperately wounded and about to fall from the coach. The big messenger, with a herculean effort, seized him with his good arm and dragged him back into his seat. Raggio was bleeding heavily, and he moaned, "I'm about done."

By now, the terrified horses had burst into a full gallop. Tovey seized the reins and brought them under control. Once they had reached a safe distance, he stopped the coach, lifted Raggio down, and placed him on one of the rear seats. Then he checked on Johannah Rodesino and was stunned to find her dead. She had been instantly killed. Her sister had been saved when three buckshot missed and struck the seat next to her.[13]

This cold-blooded murder of an innocent girl created a public furor. Sheriff Ben Thorn, at the head of a 150-man posse, scoured the mountains and gorges but came up dry. One of Thorn's deputies managed to track the killer three miles and found a giant powder cartridge that he had dropped, indicating that the desperado had planned to blow open the stage safe. Heavy rains washed away the rest of the tracks. It turned out that Tovey had only a flesh wound, while doctors thought Babe Raggio would die. He eventually recovered, but he carried two buckshot for the rest of his life. Jim Hume immediately suspected that Milt Sharp was the culprit, but he changed his mind after conferring with Wells Fargo's route agent James C. Tice, who had gone to the scene to investigate personally. Although the Rodesino family offered a two-thousand-dollar reward, the culprit was not captured.[14]

This was the third time Tovey had been shot and wounded. He was soon back on the box, assigned to the stage route between Ione and Jackson, in Amador County. The railroad terminal was in Ione, and from there stages connected with towns in the foothill mining country. Tovey, to protect passengers from an accidental discharge of his shotgun, was in the habit of unloading it during stage stops and whenever passengers rode on top of his coach. And just as he had done in Nevada, he would occasionally get down from the box and walk ahead of the stage, especially if he saw anything suspicious. On the night of February 16, 1893, Tovey was aboard the stage from Ione to Jackson with a large mine payroll in the strongbox. They reached the base of the Morrow Grade, about four miles from Jackson. This had been the scene of Black Bart's second-to-last stage robbery, in 1883. Mike considered it a likely spot for another holdup, so he got down and walked ahead of the coach. He soon bumped into a length of barbed wire, stripped from a fence and stretched chest-high across the road. Though he was armed with a six-shooter, he ran back to the stage and fetched his shotgun. Tovey searched the area, but the culprits had fled.[15]

Three months later, he received another letter signed "Sharp," saying that he "had better leave Wells Fargo service and get out of the state, otherwise he would apt to be killed." This time, Tovey took the threat seriously, telling a friend in Ione that he expected to be killed—as he put it, "to be taken off at any time on account of trouble in Nevada in 1880." A few weeks after that, on the afternoon of June 15, 1893, he boarded the stage in Ione, bound for Jackson. At the reins of the six-horse team was Tovey's good friend, Dewitt C. "Clint" Radcliff, a veteran of seventeen years on the box. Radcliff had been held up several times, most notably on the Morrow Grade by Black Bart in 1883. Inside the coach were four passengers, including two woman and a boy, and a fifth rode on top with the driver and messenger.

It was five-thirty when the stage reached a lonely spot on the Morrow Grade, five miles west of Jackson. Several of the passengers heard a sudden shout for the stage to halt, but Radcliff made out nothing over the rumbling of his coach. A split second later, gunfire shattered the evening stillness. A lone bandit stood behind a three-foot high rock pasture fence on the right side of the road, working the lever of his .44 Winchester rifle. His first bullet struck Mike Tovey in the ride side, fracturing one rib and rupturing his aorta. The Wells Fargo man started to fall from the stage, and Radcliff yanked him upright. At the same time, Radcliff tried to control his team, which lunged forward into a run, crazed by the explosion. The bandit fired again, and the slug grazed Radcliff's shoulder and slammed into Tovey's body. The horses continued to run, and the desperado shot twice more, wounding the off wheel and off swing horses in their right flanks.

By the time Radcliff managed to halt the coach three hundred yards down the road, Mike Tovey was dead. As the killer walked slowly toward a thicket, several farmers, ricking hay in a field, came running. Moments later, a buggy driven by C. A. Swain pulled up. The women were outside the coach, screaming in terror, the child was crying, and Radcliff was unhitching the wounded animals from the team. Swain spotted the outlaw escaping, two hundred yards distant, and grabbed Tovey's shotgun from the stage. Not knowing the messenger's habits, he later explained, "On attempting to use it I found there were no cartridges in it, a fact I cannot understand, and we were obliged to go through Tovey's pockets to find them." Then they loaded the dead guard inside the stage. Radcliff raced to Jackson and Swain to Ione to spread the alarm.[16]

Mike Tovey's funeral took place before a crowd of hundreds in Jackson. He had never married, and his brothers and sisters, scattered about Montana, Nebraska, and Oklahoma, were sent the sad news.

Bill Evans, who was sentenced to life in San Quentin for the murder of Mike Tovey. [*California State Archives*]

The veteran messenger was laid to rest in Jackson's city cemetery. Wells Fargo paid for his marker, which read, "He was shot and instantly killed by a robber who attempted to hold up the stage on which he was traveling as guard. Erected as a tribute of respect by his employers." Meanwhile, Sheriff Ben Thorn, as he had done a year before, organized a huge manhunt. Guards were placed on all roads and bridges, and Wells Fargo's Jim Hume, John Thacker, and James Tice quickly arrived to help, but the search soon fizzled out.[17]

Once again, Milt Sharp was suspected. Charles Aull, former Wells Fargo detective and now warden of Folsom Prison, insisted that Sharp had killed Tovey in revenge. Clint Radcliff doubted that, saying, "I don't go much on the theory that the man wanted Tovey and not the box. In that case he wouldn't have shot the horses." Three months later, Sharp was captured in Red Bluff, in Northern California, after being recognized by an ex-convict. He managed to prove that he had led an honest life since his escape, and provided alibis from his employers showing that he could not have been at the murder scene. Jim Hume believed Sharp and helped get him a parole in 1894.[18]

Meanwhile, Sheriff Thorn was convinced, due to the similarity of the two attacks, that the same man had murdered Mike Tovey and Johannah Rodesino. He picked up Bill Evans, an inveterate thief and three-time loser. Evans had been working as a hired hand on a farm in Calaveras County. Thorn used questionable techniques on Evans, including plying him with opium and whiskey, to obtain a confession. On August 1, Evans made a detailed statement, saying, "I did not know Messenger Tovey and did not want to kill him. I wanted to stop the stage and secure the treasure." Within a few days, however, Evans retracted his confession, insisting that it had been coerced.[19]

Although the confession was thrown out of court by the trial judge, Sheriff Thorn put together a strong circumstantial case. Clint Radcliff identified Evans, a witness had seen him hiding in the grass near the scene a day previous to the shooting, and Evans had made incriminating statements to others about the murders of both Mike Tovey and Johannah Rodesino. A jury convicted Evans of first-degree murder and he was sentenced to life in San Quentin. Jim Hume and John Thacker were convinced that Thorn had railroaded him into prison. Despite leading a campaign in the press, they were unable to prove his innocence. When Evans was finally paroled in 1909, it was due to his age and his good conduct in prison. In the end, though doubts remain about his guilt, Bill Evans remains the strongest suspect in the murder of Mike Tovey.[20]

The ever-modest Tovey left behind no memoirs and no written record, but to this day he is one of the most famous of all shotgun messengers. As Wells Fargo official James Otey Bradford commented in 1893, "He regarded the treasure box at his feet as a sacred trust and the company knew that no robber would ever get a dollar of its money from Mike Tovey as long as the breath of life was in him. His vigilance, intrepidity, and fidelity made him a representative without a peer of the shotgun messenger." But it was Mike's friend Clint Radcliff who paid him the simplest but most fitting of tributes: "Tovey was true grit."[21]

13

VIGILANTE VENGEANCE

Buck Montgomery

The steady tramp of feet rattled through the midnight streets of Redding, California. Forty strong, the men marched abreast in military formation. Each was masked and carried a rifle, revolver, or shotgun. As they moved ghostlike through the blackness, the flicker of their torches cast eerie shadows against the brick and wood-frame buildings. They strode into the courthouse square, determined to wreak vigilante vengeance on the outlaws who had murdered a valiant Wells Fargo messenger. For more than a century, Buck Montgomery's death, and the violent fate of his killers, has been detailed in countless newspapers, magazines, and books. Yet almost nothing has been written about his life.

Amos Buchanan Montgomery was born in Missouri on September 5, 1856, one of eleven children of Andrew J. Montgomery and Elizabeth Anderson Montgomery. They took their large brood overland by covered wagons to California in 1859. The following year, they settled briefly in Yolo County, just west of Sacramento, then crossed the rugged mountains of the Coast Range to Mendocino County. Situated on the North Coast, Mendocino County was then an isolated frontier, peopled by four thousand whites and more than twelve thou-

Buck Montgomery, Wells Fargo
shotgun messenger and manhunter.
[*Author's collection*]

sand Indians. Many of its early settlers were hardy pioneer families
from Missouri. At first, Andrew Montgomery raised livestock and
farmed near Ukiah, but in the early 1860s, he homesteaded 647 acres
near Orrs Springs, in the mountains west of Ukiah. Dotted with vir-
gin groves of coast redwoods, his ranch is now Montgomery Woods
State Natural Reserve and features some of the tallest trees in the
world. With too many redwoods and not enough grass, it was poor
land for stock raising, and Montgomery soon sold out and moved his
family back to Ukiah.[1]

His son Buchanan attended school through the early 1870s, then
worked as a cowboy and farmhand. Recalled a newspaperman who
knew him, "'Buck' as he was familiarly called, was a true mountaineer.
He was a crack shot, and when a boy few excelled him in bringing
down deer, bear, panther, and the other wild game that roamed the
frontier." Buck Montgomery grew into a tall, handsome young man,
standing six two, rugged and powerful. When he was twenty-two, the
stage robber Charles E. Boles, alias Black Bart, struck near his home.

On October 2, 1878, at a spot about ten miles north of Ukiah, Bart pulled his seventh stagecoach holdup. His spoils were so paltry—just forty dollars and a gold watch—that the next day he robbed another coach from Covelo to Ukiah, this time getting about four hundred dollars.[2]

Jim Hume, Wells Fargo's chief special officer, immediately went to Ukiah and interviewed the robbery victims. He later reported that he had hired five men to try to locate the road agent. One of the victims, Henry B. Muir, recalled years later, "He asked me the name of a good reliable mountaineer I could send for that [bandit]. I spoke right up and says, 'Buck Montgomery.'" Explained Muir, "He was a hunter, he was observant and had endurance, and he could keep his own counsel." Hume offered to pay Buck to track the highwayman, but Montgomery protested that he had "never done that kind of work before." But he soon relented, and accompanied Hume to the site of the last holdup. Muir said that for a week young Montgomery had trailed Black Bart south to Suisun Bay, a distance of 130 miles. Black Bart never rode a horse and regularly eluded lawmen on foot. This manhunt marked the first time that Montgomery saw duty for Wells Fargo.[3]

The next year, he reportedly took part in the manhunt for the Mendocino Outlaws, a band of robbers who murdered two possemen on the coast. In 1880, Buck settled in Round Valley, in the northern part of Mendocino County, and in January 1882, he married nineteen-year-old Jennie Miller, a pretty brunette. Later that year, he moved back to Ukiah and leased a dairy ranch just north of town. He and his bride promptly produced two sons, Orrie, born at the end of 1882, and Grover, in 1884. He and his brother Alex then ran a stock ranch, but it failed. In 1886, Buck was appointed postmaster of Calpella, just north of Ukiah. But this work proved too tame for him. In January 1888, Black Bart was released from San Quentin. Jim Hume believed that he returned to the road, for several new stage holdups bore all of Bart's earmarks. Two stagecoach robberies, allegedly by Bart, took place in Mendocino County. The first was on November 20, 1888, when the Eureka to Ukiah stage was stopped near Willits, and the second soon after, on December 4, when the Mendocino to Cazadero coach was halted. In both instances it had been a lone robber, and once again Wells Fargo called on Buck Montgomery to hunt Black Bart.[4]

W. P. Thomas, undersheriff of Mendocino County, later said that Jim Hume came to Ukiah immediately after the first holdup and explained that, due to the modus operandi of the lone highwayman, Black Bart was the prime suspect. Thomas called on Montgomery, whom he termed "the best mountaineer I ever knew." Buck, no longer postmaster, was running another dairy near Ukiah. He rode to the holdup scene near Willits and tracked the road agent into the Coast Range. The bandit's trail was frequently wiped out by bear tracks, but each time Montgomery stuck to the scent. For ten days, he painstakingly followed the tracks, which eventually led him more than a hundred miles to Arbuckle, on the Southern Pacific Railroad in the Sacramento Valley. Buck believed that the road agent had boarded a train two days before he got there.

Montgomery returned to Ukiah and met with Undersheriff Thomas, who in turn had him write out a detailed report and mail it to Hume. In response, Hume sent Thomas a letter with a check for payment to Montgomery, and wrote, "That's the finest report that's

Jim Neafus, captured by Buck Montgomery. [*California State Archives*]

come into the Wells Fargo office since I have been here. Tell Mr. Montgomery to come and see us the first time he comes to San Francisco." Soon after this, Wells Fargo officials hired Buck as a part-time shotgun messenger on the stages out of Ukiah. As was customary, he also acted as a special officer investigating robberies of the company's express.[5]

For many years, the cattle king of Round Valley was George E. White, a notorious scoundrel whose retinue of hired gunmen intimidated, and in some cases murdered, anyone who dared oppose him. In the late 1880s, White and his young wife became embroiled in a bitter divorce in San Francisco. White employed every kind of fraud and perjury in a desperate effort to prevail. In June 1889, he asked his old friend Jim Neafus, a notorious Indian fighter and mountaineer, to steal a letter from San Francisco that contained important evidence and was being sent north by stage. Neafus consented, but he quickly realized that because he was illiterate, he would not know which letter to steal. He enlisted the help of twenty-seven-year-old Johnnie Asbill, the educated half-Indian son of another pioneer family.

At nine o'clock on the night of June 19, 1889, three miles south of Bell Springs, Neafus and Asbill stopped the northbound mail stage, a two-horse buckboard with a driver but no shotgun messenger. This spot was located on the old stage road that ran from Mendocino north to Humboldt County. The robbers covered the jehu with Winchesters and demanded the Wells Fargo box, but there wasn't one on board. Then they ordered the driver to throw out the mail pouch. They cut open the bag and scattered letters all over the roadway, taking only the mail from San Francisco. Then they handed the pouch back, waved the buckboard on, and mounted up and rode off. To confuse pursuers, Neafus had shod their horses with mule shoes nailed on backward.

Buck Montgomery was notified of the holdup and he rode to the scene, arriving at six o'clock the next evening. Unfazed by Neafus's ruse, he spent several days following the backward tracks down Bell Springs Creek to the Eel River, then across the mountains to the

Johnnie Asbill, stage robber.
[*California State Archives*]

mouth of Hulls Creek, north of Round Valley. There he found Jim
Neafus, Johnnie Asbill, and the latter's uncle, Pierce Asbill, herding a
flock of sheep. As Buck spoke to the trio, he spotted a band of horses
nearby, and the four men took a few minutes to round them up. They
drove the horses into a pole corral, where Montgomery noticed that
two of them left backward hoofprints. He dismounted and lifted one
animal's foot to inspect the shoe.

"Well, I'll be damned," exclaimed Neafus in feigned surprise.
"What goddam fool done that, you reckon?"

"Jim," replied Buck, "it was no damned fool who put them shoes
on, but some damned fool who left them on."

Montgomery arrested both road agents and took them to jail in
Ukiah five days after he had started his manhunt. The pair were quickly
convicted of assault with intent to commit robbery and sentenced to two
years in prison. They entered San Quentin on July 11, just three weeks
after the stage holdup.[6]

Buck was still extremely restless. In July 1890, he secured an appointment as the night-watch policeman for the town of Ukiah. Only
six weeks later, he acquired some land in Oregon and announced that

he was moving north. But he soon changed his mind. He was still in Ukiah on the morning of October 12, 1890, when a lone bandit held up a stage on Robber's Ridge, five miles south of Willits. The highwayman ordered the driver to throw down the Wells Fargo box, then demanded the mail sacks. When the whip told him they were in the rear boot, the robber began cutting the leather straps that held them in. The reinsman, seeing his chance, jerked out a pistol and exchanged shots with the bandit. The terrified stage team broke into a run and soon was far from Robber's Ridge.

Two miles on, the coach reached Angle's ranch, where the jehu found Alex Montgomery, Buck's brother. Alex and several other men rode to Robber's Ridge and found the broken express box and the empty mail pouches. When the stage arrived in Ukiah, Buck Montgomery, Wells Fargo messenger Henry C. Ward, and a local constable promptly left for the holdup site. The Montgomery brothers, Ward, and the constable tracked the highwayman while Sheriff Jeremiah M. "Doc" Standley, one of California's best manhunters, investigated the holdup. Learning that a stranger had stayed the previous night at a hotel in Willits, he suspected that the man had come from San Francisco. Standley returned to Ukiah, then boarded the evening train for San Francisco. When the train stopped in Cloverdale, he spotted a young man on the depot platform who matched the description of the fugitive. The sheriff clapped him in irons and bundled him onto a Ukiah-bound freight train. He turned out to be twenty-one-year-old George W. Cummings. He pled guilty to mail robbery in U.S. District Court and was handed a ten-year term in San Quentin, which then held federal prisoners.[7]

Wells Fargo's Jim Hume, John Thacker, and Henry Ward all thought highly of Montgomery. Thacker in particular became his close friend, once saying, "Buck was one of the best men I ever knew. He was a crack shot, quick as lightning, and a man of iron nerve." Thus an express messenger's job should have been Buck's for the asking. But in January 1891, perhaps to placate his wife, he tried yet another safer and more domestic occupation by buying the Elite Restaurant in Ukiah.

That venture lasted only a few months. Finally in May of that year, he signed on as full-time shotgun messenger for Wells Fargo on the stage route between Weaverville and Redding, 250 miles north of Ukiah. This was a rich mining region where coaches brought gold shipments to the railroad depot in Redding. As a result, since 1887, sixteen stages had been held up on the roads leading into Redding. As related in chapter 3, Buck's friend Henry Ward, the veteran messenger, had shot it out with the notorious Ham White on the Weaverville-Redding route in March 1891. Ward, who had been badly wounded in an 1886 holdup, was given lighter duties and Montgomery took over his job. He moved his wife and sons to Redding and made it his new home.[8]

Meanwhile, Buck Montgomery was on a collision course with a desperado named John D. Ruggles. Born in 1860, he was the spoiled son of a prosperous farmer, Lyman Ruggles, who lived near Wood-land, north of Sacramento. In 1875, the elder Ruggles moved his family south to Tulare County, in the lower San Joaquin Valley, where he acquired several farms. John, the eldest of six children, was indulged by his parents and became a heavy drinker, a regular patron of bordel-los, and a petty thief. In the fall of 1878, when Ruggles was eighteen,

John D. Ruggles, stage robber and desperado.
[*Author's collection*]

he went to Stockton and found work as a hostler. He quickly squandered his earnings in the town's bagnios, then pulled two minor street holdups to replenish his coffers. His second robbery, on Halloween night that year, was of a youthful couple out for a stroll on a downtown sidewalk. Unfortunately for Ruggles, the young man was packing a pistol. Ruggles, after stealing the girl's ring, tried to flee but caught a bullet in the back. The two youths exchanged eight ineffectual shots at close range. Ruggles, badly wounded, staggered into the police station and surrendered.

He quickly recovered, pled guilty, and got a seven-year jolt in San Quentin. His father promptly started a campaign for a governor's pardon. He had doctors write letters claiming that John had a sexual addiction and had "practiced self-abuse for two or more years." This supposedly impaired his mind and rendered him "almost [an] imbecile" at the time of the holdup. The doctors, of course, did not explain how sexual compulsions could cause someone to commit two armed robberies. In the end, Lyman Ruggles's money and influence won out, and in February 1880, his son received a full pardon. It was such leniency that caused Wells Fargo's Jim Hume to complain frequently about "gross abuses of the pardoning power."[9]

For a time, John Ruggles seemed to reform. In 1883, he purchased a quarter section of cropland near his father's farm. In 1886, he married Ida Henderson, and the following year they had a baby girl. But the marriage was not a happy one. John Ruggles wanted easy cash and a fast life. He constantly borrowed money and his farm became deeply mortgaged. He blamed his father for all his problems, later writing to his siblings, "A few dirty dollars dealt out to me once in a while didn't help me at all. I would sooner be an outlaw or dead than to always be begging a man for a few dollars. I have always been a sucker of the first rank. Pa could have kept me out of the 'pen' with $250, but he let me go to hell and that blasted all my future life and after that [he] roped me into a marriage with a woman I knew nothing of at all."[10]

When Ida died in 1889, John Ruggles must have thought he had won his freedom. He abandoned his heavily mortgaged farm, left his

two-year-old daughter with his aunt, and went north to Shasta and Siskiyou counties. He spent much of his time hunting and became well
acquainted with the Klamath and Trinity mountain ranges. Meanwhile,
his brother Charlie, ten years younger, went to work at the Iron Mountain Mine, near Redding. There his closest friend was a miner known as
"Arizona Pete." Redding citizens later suspected that Arizona Pete and
the Ruggles brothers had pulled some of the many highway robberies
in the region. John Ruggles did later admit that he led his brother into
crime. He said that he wrote to Charlie at the mine and convinced him
to meet him in San Francisco, where they spent the winter of 1891–
1892. While there, John told his brother that he had "a good scheme to
make lots of money easily."[11]

The brothers boarded a northbound train in Oakland, arriving in
Redding on May 7, 1892. On the evening of May 9, they took up a position on the wagon road west of town, but they were not prepared. "The
stage came fifteen minutes too soon," John explained later. The following evening, now ready, they stopped the coach from Weaverville a mile
west of Redding. They wore long linen dusters, masks, and sacks tied
around their feet to conceal their footprints. One of the brothers stood
in the road with a shotgun. The passengers spotted a second bandit in a
clump of roadside willows, a pistol in his hand. Buck Montgomery was
not aboard the stage because the Wells Fargo box contained nothing of
value. The Ruggles boys told the whip, John Boyce, to throw down the
strongbox, then ordered him to drive on. After breaking open the express box, they hiked seven miles into the mountains in the dark. A
posse from Redding hunted the bandits, without any luck. "All went
well," John later said, "except we got nothing but a damn passbook for
our trouble."[12]

Four days later, the Ruggles boys struck again. On May 14, the
stage left Weaverville for Redding. John Boyce was again at the reins,
and next to him rode Buck Montgomery. The two Wells Fargo boxes
held $3,375, which included $675 in coin and the rest in gold bullion.
The coach stopped in Shasta and picked up a lone passenger, George
Suhr. He climbed up on top next to Boyce, while Buck took a seat

Charlie Ruggles, brother of John.
[*Author's collection*]

inside the coach, his shotgun resting across his knees. It was shortly after five in the evening when Boyce urged his four-horse team up a long grade called the Blue Cut, a mile east of Shasta and five miles from Redding. Just as they reached the top of the grade a shotgun-wielding man with a red bandanna mask appeared in front of them and yelled, "Stop, stop!"

The bandit was Charlie Ruggles. Boyce pulled up his horses and Charlie called to Suhr, "Passenger, hold up your hands!"

Suhr complied and the robber ordered Boyce, "Throw out those boxes."

As Boyce was tossing down the strongboxes, John Ruggles, standing at the side of the coach, spotted Buck Montgomery shoving his shotgun barrel outside the coach toward Charlie. John, armed with a pair of .44 Colt revolvers, fired one shot. A split second later, Buck blasted both barrels into Charlie Ruggles. The bandit dropped to his knees, struck by thirteen buckshot in his face, neck, and upper chest. One buckshot tore out two of his teeth and lodged in his neck. Charlie raised his own shotgun and pulled the triggers. Fifteen buckshot slammed into Boyce's legs and three more into Suhr's right calf. At the same time, John Ruggles kept firing his pistols, putting two .44 slugs into the messenger's back. Buck never saw the man who shot him. The terrified horses bolted and the coach careened down the grade.[13]

George Suhr grabbed the reins and brought the team under control. A Redding doctor and his wife, who were headed to Shasta in a buggy, met the stage. The doctor took over the stage from Suhr while his wife raced back to Redding to raise the alarm. The coach continued on two miles to the Middle Creek Hotel, where the three wounded men were unloaded and taken inside. Soon another doctor and a crowd of citizens, including Buck's wife, Jennie, and his young sons, arrived from Redding. A newspaper reporter wrote that he found the Wells Fargo man on his deathbed in the hotel, "with his wife wringing her hands and nearly crazed by the tragedy." Surgeons could not save him, and Buck died at nine o'clock that night.[14]

Meanwhile, Charlie Ruggles had staggered away from the holdup scene, soaked in blood. John followed him, carrying an ax and the two strongboxes. Charlie gasped, "Go, you have got me done for."

"Not much," replied John, but Charlie stumbled to the bottom of a gulch and fell facedown in the water. John rolled him over. "Oh, what an awful sight," he said later. "His head literally shot full of holes and the blood just running all over his clothes." Thinking that his brother had but a short time to live, John broke open the boxes, stuffed the gold into a sack, and fled.

Within a few hours after the holdup, a huge manhunt swung into action. Lawmen, citizens, a company of the National Guard, and even teenage boys with shotguns, all spurred on by heavy rewards, scoured the woods. At 2:00 P.M. the next day, three teenagers found Charlie in a canyon near Shasta. Though half dead, he managed to gasp that he was one of the robbers and that his partner had left him. He refused to state his actual name. Charlie was taken to jail in Redding in a spring wagon. With good medical treatment, he quickly began to recover. Jennie Montgomery, on the other hand, was overcome with grief. She took her dead husband home to Ukiah, where he was laid to rest in what is now known as the Russian River Cemetery.[15]

Look Out for Stage Robber and Murderer!

$1100 REWARD

For the Arrest and Conviction of

JOHN D. RUGGLES,

Who was principally concerned in the robbing of the stage near Redding, May 14th, and the murder of Messenger Montgomery.

DESCRIPTION.

He is thirty-two years of age; 5 feet 11½ inches high, weight 175 pounds; born in California; light or florid complexion, long features; heavy, light brown moustache (now colored black), light brown hair, dark blue eyes; long features, high forehead, square chin; wears number 8 or 9 shoes and 7¼ hat; when last seen wore a black felt hat; has large scar on right side of neck caused by burn; has large brown mole below shoulder-blade; scar on breast-bone; gunshot wound on leg; large, bony hands, calloused from work; restless and uneasy, looking around out of corners of eyes, looking sharply right and left when talking to you; most always has mouth open; smokes cigarettes and makes them; has a habit of clearing his throat every little while, caused by being an inveterate cigarette smoker; does not drink to any extent; folds his arms across his breast when talking to any one, and generally standing or leaning against something; at time of robbery wore a dark coat, spring-bottom bluish pants, with welt-seam along the sides; he carried two 44 cal. Colt bronze pistols.

He was sent to San Quentin November 16th, 1878, from San Joaquin County, for a term of seven years, for robbery, and was pardoned and restored to citizenship February 26th, 1880.

He lived many years with his parents near Woodland, Yolo County. He owns a quarter section of improved land in Tulare County, near Traver, mortgaged to the Sacramento Bank for $4,500, and is well known in that county. For two or three years past has spent considerable time, summers, hunting in Shasta and Siskiyou Counties, and is proficient in the use of all kinds of firearms. He is an extraordinary footman, and can outtravel a horse on mountains; is a thorough mountaineer.

In the robbery, 14th instant, he took from the Express Box 79½ ozs. of quicksilvered gold from Weaverville, about 880 fine, and valued at $1,300; also, 96½ ozs. gold amalgam, about 730 fine, and valued at $1,400; also about $675 in coin. Total, $3,375.

In addition to the $600 standing reward offered by the State and Wells, Fargo & Company for the arrest and conviction of this class of offenders, Governor Markham has offered $500. If arrested, wire Sheriff Green, Redding, Shasta County, Cal., or the undersigned. His conviction certain.

J. B. HUME,
J. N. THACKER,
SPECIAL OFFICERS WELLS, FARGO & Co.

SAN FRANCISCO, CAL., May 21, 1892.

Wells Fargo reward poster for John Ruggles. [*Author's collection*]

Wells Fargo Detective John Thacker went to Redding and interviewed the prisoner, but he still would not reveal his true name. Finally, on May 20, Charlie confessed his identity and Thacker wired Lyman Ruggles the bad news. Rewards totaling eleven hundred dollars were now offered for John Ruggles, but he managed to evade capture for a month. On June 19, he went briefly to the home of his uncle in Woodland, and the family notified local officers. The next day, Deputy Sheriff David Wyckoff, a boyhood schoolmate, spotted John in a Woodland restaurant. When Ruggles reached for his pistol, Wyckoff shot him in the neck. The deputy searched him and found around his waist a money belt holding $595 in gold coin, as well as a boastful letter to his brothers. "I am on the watch, you bet," he wrote, "and unless the cops jump right on top of me, I don't think they will get me without one or two of them being sent over the long road." Of the dead Wells Fargo man, he said, "Montgomery's soul, if he had any, is in hell and I put him there and am glad of it."[16]

Jim Hume went to Woodland and interrogated John Ruggles, whose wound turned out to be a minor one. He admitted that he had hidden the stolen gold but refused to reveal the location. On June 23, John Thacker and Deputy Wyckoff took Ruggles to Redding by train. A large, peaceful crowd gathered at the depot to get a glimpse of him. By this time, Charlie Ruggles had recovered from his wounds. At the jail, the two brothers grasped hands and John exclaimed, "Charlie, I thought you would die." Then John broke down in tears, and Charlie told him not to say anything else.[17]

The Ruggles boys were both quite handsome, and in time-honored fashion, a number of misguided young women began to lionize them. During the next month, several girls sent notes, novels, flowers, fruits, cakes, and candies to their jail cells. This infuriated Buck's friends. Then, on July 23, the *Redding Free Press* reported, "We learn that the defense of the Ruggles case will endeavor to show that Buck Montgomery was implicated in the robbery of Wells, Fargo & Co., or, in other words, that he was a partner with the Ruggles boys, and with them planned the robbery. The defense will endeavor to establish the fact that Buck Montgomery was seen in conversation with John Ruggles prior to the robbery. Our readers will at once ask the question on reading the above why it was that John Ruggles killed Montgomery. The defense will try to show that John Ruggles killed Buck because he thought that he had played him false and because Buck had shot Charlie Ruggles. Of course, all this in the way of a defense is the worst kind of bosh, but they hope to get a juror or two who will believe it."[18]

This story was the final straw. Buck Montgomery had been hugely popular in Redding, and Wells Fargo officials considered him scrupulously honest, which, of course, was why they had trusted him as a messenger. That night, a band of vigilantes began making careful plans to avenge Buck's death. At 2:00 A.M., July 24, forty masked men marched in military formation to the courthouse square. After placing sentries around the jail, they awoke the jailor, George Albro, and demanded the cell keys. Albro said they were locked in a safe in the sheriff's office. The sheriff was home asleep and the undersheriff was out of town, and they were the only ones who knew the combination to the safe. The mob, however, was well prepared. They drilled a hole in the safe, poured in blasting powder, and made two tries to blow the door open. When that failed, they produced sledgehammers, cracked it open, and removed the keys.

The Ruggles boys, awakened by the noise, knew what was coming and hastily pulled on their shirts and trousers. The vigilantes ordered jailor Albro, whom they had blindfolded, to open John's cell. Recalled Albro, "As I opened the door the man holding my left arm was exposed. John sent him crashing to the floor with a blow from a table leg. No one ever knew how he obtained it. As the crowd pushed into the cell I could hear Ruggles hitting with the table leg, but he was in such close quarters that it didn't have much effect."

The lynch mob overpowered John, and he pleaded, "Gentlemen, be lenient with my brother, he is innocent of this crime." The vigilantes paid no attention and slipped a pair of handcuffs on him. Said Albro, "John shouted and swore until the mob put a rope gag in his mouth." Then one of the men declared, "Let's get the other one out."

They opened Charlie Ruggles's cell and took him outside. The brothers, in their stocking feet, were marched two blocks from the courthouse to a blacksmith shop near the railroad tracks. There a block and tackle hanging from a crossbeam was suspended high between two pine trees, used by the blacksmith to hoist wagons from their running

The lynching of the Ruggles boys, the murderers of Buck Montgomery, in 1892. Charlie is at left, John at right. [*Author's collection*]

gear. The mob bound the brothers hand and foot, dropped nooses over their necks, and affixed them to the hoist. Then one of the vigilante leaders said, "If you want to make a statement, now is the time, and be damned quick about it."

John Ruggles, nodding toward his brother, replied, "Gentlemen, spare him."

One of the lynchers spoke up and asked John if he been involved in two recent robbery-murders in Calaveras and Siskiyou counties.

"I know nothing of the affairs," he replied.

Next he was asked to reveal where he had buried the stolen treasure. "Spare Charlie and I will tell you," he said.

"Never mind the treasure," said one of the mob. "Tell us if you want to. If not, say what you have to say quick."

But John Ruggles refused to utter another word. The lynchers pulled on the crossbeam rope and hoisted them four feet up. The brothers slowly strangled to death. The bodies were left hanging until nine that morning. A local photographer took two images before the coroner cut them down. Thus ended one of the most famous lynchings of the Old West.[19]

Jim Hume, on hearing the news, told a reporter, "Wells Fargo & Company loses $3,000 by this premature execution, for John Ruggles told me in Woodland that he had bullion to that amount buried somewhere, promising at the same time that he would tell me later where his treasure is cached. He would probably have told it right there had I held out any inducements for him to do so, but I would not make that man any promises if the amount were ten times $3,000, and so his secret probably died with him." Over the years, many searched for the treasure, but it was never found. Its value today would be about $200,000.[20]

Buck Montgomery left a more lasting legacy. His son Orrie, perhaps remembering the efforts of Redding doctors to save his father's life, attended medical school and became a noted surgeon in San Francisco. Buck's brother Alex joined the Wells Fargo service in 1894, taking over Buck's old job in Redding. Alex Montgomery served more than twenty years in Nevada and California and was still a shotgun messenger in 1918, when Wells Fargo ceased its express business. He died in 1944, long after the days of stage robbers had faded into history.[21]

14

❦

DOUBLE-BARRELED DEATH

Billy Hendricks

Billy Hendricks cradled his shotgun on his lap as the big Concord coach lurched and rattled down the grade outside of Angels Camp in the foothills of the Sierra Nevada. For weeks, the highways and byways of Calaveras County, California, had been plagued by a gang of stage robbers, and the young express guard strained his eyes for the slightest movement in the roadside scrub oak. There was a fortune in gold in the Wells Fargo strongbox, and Hendricks was determined that no highwaymen would take it. The passengers chattered nervously about the recent robberies, much to the distress of two teenage girls aboard. Their wildest imaginations could not have prepared them for the terror that awaited. And Billy Hendricks had no way of knowing that more than fifty years later he would be recalled as the last living Wells Fargo shotgun messenger who killed a stage robber in the line of duty.

William Nathaniel Hendricks was born on August 31, 1868, in Calaveras County, the youngest of three children of William and Christina Hendricks. He grew up in the gold-mining town of Jenny Lind, where his father served as a deputy under the eminent pioneer sheriff, Ben K. Thorn. Like most boys in the mining country, Billy grew up hunting

Wells Fargo shotgun messenger Billy Hendricks, posing with his shotgun the day after he killed John Keener. [*Author's collection*]

with firearms and became a dead shot. As a young man, he drove stagecoaches, which led him, in 1893, to a job as special guard for Wells Fargo. The company found him trustworthy and capable. He was not a regular shotgun messenger, but instead was assigned to protect gold shipments whenever necessary. Since the 1860s, Calaveras County had seen many stage holdups, and they were still common in the 1890s. From the railhead in Milton, a narrow-gauge track led to Stockton, thirty miles west. Stagecoaches carried gold from the mines in the Sierra Nevada foothills to the depot in Milton. These stages were the favorite target of highwaymen.[1]

During Billy Hendricks's idyllic boyhood in the mining region of the 1870s, two youths from Visalia, 160 miles to the south, took a decidedly different path. The Keener and Dowdle families came to California from Missouri, via Texas, in a large wagon train in 1858. First arriving in Los Angeles, they later settled in Tulare County, where they raised cattle. John Levi Keener was born in 1860 and grew up in

Visalia with five siblings. His parents died when he was four and relatives took him in. His childhood friend was William E. "Doc" Dowdle, born in Visalia in 1863. The Keeners and Dowdles were close,
having experienced many hardships together on the Overland Trail. The
Dowdle family moved to Arizona Territory in 1877 and established a
cattle ranch near Tucson. John Keener went with them and worked as
their ranch hand. The Dowdles prospered, and one son became county
recorder in Tucson, and a daughter married a California banker.[2]

Doc Dowdle and John Keener, on the other hand, were a wild and
hard-drinking pair. In 1883, Keener was tried and acquitted of destroying a mining company's pipeline in Pima County. The Dowdles
paid for his lawyer, and upon his release, he left Arizona and returned
to Visalia. Doc Dowdle later married and had a child but neglected his
family. In 1889, he was a suspect in the Wham Paymaster Robbery,
one of the bloodiest and most celebrated crimes in Arizona's violent
history. A large band of desperadoes led by a prominent Mormon, Gilbert Webb, ambushed a U.S. Army payroll wagon, shooting and
wounding eight African-American Buffalo Soldiers who were escort-
ing a $28,000 payroll. A massive manhunt resulted in numerous arrests.
In a sensational trial, Webb and six accomplices were acquitted, despite overwhelming evidence of their guilt. Dowdle was an associate of
the gang, but no solid proof against him surfaced. He was, however,
certainly capable of robbery. On January 6, 1894, Dowdle and two of
the Wham robbers, Jake Felshaw and Leslie Webb (son of ringleader
Gilbert Webb) took part in a stage holdup on the road between Solomonville and Bowie in southeastern Arizona. Felshaw pulled the robbery, while Dowdle and Webb were accessories. They split the $3,300
taken from the U.S. mail. Felshaw and Webb were arrested and later
sent to prison, while Dowdle escaped by train to California.[3]

Doc Dowdle appeared in Visalia on January 11, 1894, just five days
after the holdup. He told people his name was Kirkland, but when
several old Visalians recognized him, he admitted that he had been in
trouble in Arizona. Dowdle was flush with robbery loot and enjoyed
flashing his roll of greenbacks in the saloons and gambling houses of

The notorious stage robber William E. "Doc" Dowdle. [*California State Archives*]

Spanishtown, Visalia's red-light district. He quickly met up with John Keener, who had managed to stay out of trouble in Visalia. The worst that could be said of Keener was that he liked to drink and gamble, and habitually lost every dollar he earned. His brothers warned him "to have nothing to do with Dowdle, as he would get him into trouble." Keener paid no heed. In a few weeks, Dowdle's money was gone and he and Keener got work cutting wood in a lumber camp in the Sierra Nevada foothills. It wasn't long before Dowdle convinced Keener that there were easier ways to make money. Keener was enthusiastic about robbing a stage and tried to convince Dan McCall, a fellow woodcutter, to go along, but he declined. McCall's decision did him little good, for two years later he was shot dead in an attempted train robbery near Visalia.[4]

About the first of March 1894, Keener and Dowdle left the lumber camp and headed north for the mining region in Calaveras County. On March 7, they stationed themselves on the stage road between Milton and Angels Camp. The latter town had been made famous by Mark Twain in his 1865 short story, "The Celebrated Jumping Frog of

Calaveras County." At 5:00 P.M., two stages loaded with passengers crawled up the Bear Mountain Grade, ten miles from Milton. Dowdle and Keener, masked and brandishing double-barreled shotguns, called for the drivers to halt. They ordered the whip on the first coach to throw down the Wells Fargo box, which proved to hold no money. Keener and Dowdle satisfied themselves with relieving the passengers of their jewelry and pocket change, then waved the two stages on. A short time later, a third stage pulled up, carrying extra passengers for whom there had been no room in the first two coaches. As there was no Wells Fargo box aboard, the two road agents again robbed the passengers before allowing the stage to proceed.[5]

A manhunt for the robbers was spearheaded by Sheriff Ben Thorn, but no trace of them could be found. John Keener was inspired by his first experience with stage robbing. While Dowdle kept out of sight, he loitered about Angels Camp, picking up information on the stagecoaches and express shipments. Five weeks later, on April 16, as driver Fred Wesson's Milton-bound coach was making a hard uphill pull near Altaville, a mile from Angels Camp, one of the outlaws stepped from the roadside brush and ordered the coach to halt. His partner was probably covering him from the roadside timber. Wesson ignored the command and started to whip up his team.

"Stop, I tell you!" the bandit roared, and leveled his shotgun at Wesson's head.

The jehu wisely halted his coach, and the bandit ordered the seven passengers out and lined them up. He forced Wesson to unhitch the horses and run them up the road. This coach held a pony safe under one seat, secured to the floor with iron straps. The highwayman produced a cold chisel and a hammer and quickly cut the straps. Two more blows knocked off the padlock and the bandit scooped up packages containing two thousand dollars. Then he sat down on the side of the road and carefully opened each money packet. He acted so casually, the passengers believed he had a partner watching them from the brush.

Fred Wesson became impatient and called out, "Ain't you through yet?"

"I'll tell you when I'm through!" exclaimed the road agent. Finally, he tossed the bills and coin into a sack and jokingly told the passengers, "I guess I haven't time to count this now. If I had I'd give you fellows $20 apiece."

He ordered Wesson to hitch up the team and the passengers clambered back into the coach. As Wesson started up the horses, the desperado called out gaily, "Good-bye, Fred. I will see you in Angels in a day or so, and we will take a drink on this."[6]

A posse was soon on the scene. They found no trace of the robbers but discovered seven hundred dollars of the stolen money buried nearby. For Keener and Dowdle, this second holdup proved more successful. They had done their homework, robbing a cash-full Wells Fargo safe and even learning the name of the stage driver. Doc Dowdle then returned to Visalia, where he rounded up Amos Bierer, a twenty-five-year-old laborer and friend of Keener's. Dowdle convinced Bierer to join them in what Bierer later referred to as "the holdup game." On April 25, the two left Visalia and set off for Angels Camp in search of John Keener, who was busy planning a third job. Bierer was not made of the same hard stuff as Keener and Dowdle, and while he agreed to assist them, he was too timid to take part in the actual holdup.[7]

On May 2, Keener and Dowdle took up positions on Funk Hill, three miles east of Copperopolis on the Sonora-Milton stage route. They were probably unaware that the spot they had selected was the scene of Black Bart's first stage robbery, in 1875, as well as his last, in 1883. At 6:00 P.M., the ill-fated Fred Wesson hove into sight, urging his horses up Funk Hill. While Dowdle took cover by the side of the road, Keener stepped out with his shotgun shouldered and ordered Wesson to get down from his seat. The bandit lined up the passengers next to the stage and ordered Wesson to unhitch the team. He then blew open the iron Wells Fargo safe inside the coach with a stick of dynamite. The explosion shattered the interior of the stage and tore open the strongbox. To Keener's chagrin, it was empty. His only booty was a solitary express package.

Postmortem photo of John Keener, 1894.
[*Author's collection*]

The disappointed desperado had Wesson hitch up his horses. When the passengers were in their seats, he called out, "Drive on, and don't look back for five miles. The first one that looks back will die."[8]

Once again, the holdup men vanished. One passenger reported having seen a second robber hiding off the road, and a merchant, L. S. Bar, gave a detailed description of the first bandit to a San Francisco newspaper. Wells Fargo detective John N. Thacker arrived to investigate, but he had no success. Just five days later, the highwaymen struck again. On May 7, Keener stopped Fred Wesson's down stage on Carmen Hill, about midway between Angels Camp and Milton. As in the other holdups, Dowdle was probably covering him from the brush. Keener wore a black cap pulled down over his ears, and a black handkerchief concealed his face; his clothes were covered with old sacks. Nonetheless, Fred Wesson recognized his voice. "It's rubbing it in a little too strong to be held up twice in one week," the driver exclaimed. "I guess I had better give up this job to you fellows."

"It is getting to be hard times and a man has got to do something," replied the outlaw. He then ordered the passengers from the coach. It was a new one, a replacement for the damaged stage, and Wesson did not fancy having another coach blown up. He offered to unbolt the Wells Fargo box from the stagecoach floor. Keener agreed, and as the driver worked on the box, the robber reassured the occupants, "I never rob passengers or kill those who obey me."

Keener had read the newspaper accounts of the prior holdup, and he asked the jehu whether Bar, who had reported his description, was aboard. Wesson told him no, and tossed the heavy strongbox out of the coach. The highwayman then returned the express package he had taken in the last holdup. Attached to it was a note—reminiscent of Black Bart's—that reflected the robber's sense of humor: "Some advice to Mr. Bar, and other good detectives beside, is to let me rob and let your notions slide."[9]

John Thacker, with local officers, again investigated but could find no trace of the bandits. Due to the rash of holdups, Thacker had assigned veteran messenger Reason E. McConnell, whose usual duty was the Angels-Milton route, to the Sonora-Milton stage. He placed Billy Hendricks on the Angels-Milton stage. For the past year, Hendricks had been driving stage and riding as a special guard whenever Wells Fargo needed him. Thacker later told a newspaperman, "We run a messenger now whenever there is any treasure on a stage, and we will see that hereafter all the money they get they will have to fight for."[10]

At 9:30 A.M. on May 19, 1894, the Milton-bound stage rumbled out of Angels Camp with Fred Wesson once again at the ribbons. Hendricks had given up his customary seat alongside the driver to a lady passenger, Lillie Stowell. Five more passengers were inside the Concord coach, among them T. T. Hume, a businessman from Murphys. Two teenage girls, Maria Bunney and Ella Bray, shared the center seat with the rawboned frame of messenger Hendricks, his eyes alertly focused on the roadside chaparral, his sawed-off shotgun resting across his knees. Inside the Wells Fargo strongbox was fifteen thousand dollars in gold bullion from the Utica Mine of Angels Camp.

"Keep your eye out for stage robbers," Wesson warned his passengers.

At 10:30 A.M., the stage pulled into Elkhorn station, thirteen miles

John Keener lies dead where he was killed by Billy Hendricks while attempting to rob the Angels Camp stage. His six-shooter is in his hand and his shotgun and hat are nearby. [*Author's collection*]

from Milton, where the horses were changed. The passengers kept up a stream of talk about the recent stage holdups, and Maria Bunney and Ella Bray became increasingly fearful. The proximity of Hendricks's shotgun did nothing to calm their nerves, and at Elkhorn the girls moved to the rear seat, with Hume taking their place next to the messenger. Fred Wesson cracked his whip and the heavy coach lurched forward and passed Carmen Hill. This was the site of the most recent robbery, and once again the talk turned to stage holdups. When one of the passengers remarked that this spot was a good place for a holdup, Hendricks replied with a grin, "I guess I'll make it interesting for anybody who attempts to stop the stage."

For the two frightened girls, highwaymen no doubt seemed to be lurking behind every mesquite bush and scrub oak. It was eleven o'clock when the coach reached the foot of a grade a quarter mile west of the Salt Spring Valley road. Suddenly, Lillie Stowell clutched Wesson's arm and cried out, "There's a man in the bushes!"

At that, John Keener, thirty feet distant, stood up from behind an old tree stump on the right side of the road, his shotgun at full cock. "I saw a man rise up out of the tall grass and weeds," Hendricks said later. "He was wearing a flour sack over his head in which eye holes had been cut, and he wore a linen duster to hide his clothing. I did not hear a command to halt. I knew the man was a stage robber, and so I let him have it." Hendricks lunged forward in his seat, thrust his shotgun out the stage window, and squeezed one trigger. Sixteen buckshot slammed into Keener's right side and head. The outlaw dropped to one knee and his shotgun discharged into the air. "My first shot spun him around, just as he was bringing his shotgun to his shoulder. He fell to the ground, and I thought he started to crawl away, so I shot him again and he quit quivering," Hendricks later said.

"Fly, Fred, fly!" shrieked Lillie Stowell, and Wesson laid the lash on his team. At the same instant, Doc Dowdle, concealed behind a tree on the opposite side of the road, unloosed his shotgun at the fleeing coach. A charge of buckshot tore into the stage, striking Maria Bunney in her neck and forehead.

"Drive on, Fred!" shouted Hendricks just as Dowdle fired again. The shot went through the stagecoach, wounding Hume in the shoulder. Wesson whipped up his team into a dead run. "I expected to be dashed to pieces every minute," recalled Lillie Stowell. "It was the wildest ride I ever want to take, rounding curves on a rough mountain road, the stage threatening every second to upset."

The team, spooked by the gunfire, thundered on, and for a mile the coach careened wildly as Wesson fought to control his horses. Recalled passenger Hume, "The horses were running away and I think this alarmed the passengers as much as the shooting. Miss Bunney attempted to get out of the stage and the guard and myself had all we could do to keep her from leaping through the window."

With Ella Bray screamed in terror and blood spurting from her friend's forehead, the stagecoach sped onward to a nearby ranch, where the wounded girl was carried inside. "Her face was a mess," said Hendricks later. "A buckshot hit her forehead above the right eye and entered her head at the right side of her nose. The bullet passed downward and lodged near the left ear." A doctor was summoned, and although Maria's injuries at first appeared to be fatal, she eventually recovered, as did the wounded Hume.[11]

The bloody holdup attempt created a sensation. Major newspapers in California ran long front-page stories about the affair. John Keener's body was photographed on the spot where he fell, and also at the undertaker's. Near his corpse, riddled with thirty-two buckshot, were found a hammer, chisel, and three sticks of dynamite. It was not long before he was fully identified. Visalia lawmen notified Sheriff Thorn that Keener had left town with Dowdle, supposedly on a mining trip, and that Dowdle had later departed with Amos Bierer. They provided detailed descriptions of the missing desperadoes.

Sheriff Thorn organized a huge manhunt for Keener's partners. Billy Hendricks and Reason McConnell joined the posses. Although the countryside was thoroughly scoured, no trace of the missing bandits could be found. Finally, nine days later, on the night of May 28, a ranch hand found a delirious stranger moaning in agony behind an old shed on the Ed Moore ranch, near Copperopolis. The man was half crazed from starvation and exposure, and a local constable was summoned and immediately recognized him as the fugitive Dowdle. Two weeks later, one of Sheriff Thorn's deputies captured Amos Bierer on a ranch near Angels Camp.[12]

The two outlaws were lodged in the county jail at San Andreas. Sheriff Thorn, an expert at "sweating" criminals, worked hard on the pair, but for two weeks they steadfastly denied their guilt. Finally, a plea bargain was arranged, and Dowdle and Bierer confessed to the last holdup. They pled guilty in exchange for prison terms of fourteen years each for assault with intent to commit robbery. Bierer admitted that he had helped plan the last holdup and claimed that he had warned Keener "that there would probably be a messenger aboard and Keener said that if there was he would dump him. He said he would as soon kill him as not." Dowdle acknowledged that it was he who had fired into the fleeing stage. He added, "After Messenger Hendricks had shot down

Amos Bierer, partner of John Keener and Doc Dowdle. [*California State Archives*]

Keener and the stage had driven off, Keener called to me and told me that he could not live. He asked me to take his pistol and kill him, which I refused to do. Keener said, 'Then you get away.' I left and after getting away 200 or 300 yards I heard a shot from Keener's pistol. I think he killed himself."[13]

But those who examined Keener's body stated that they saw only buckshot wounds, so it seems unlikely that he committed suicide. Keener's body was buried in Calaveras County, and Dowdle and Bierer were shipped off to Folsom Prison. In November, Dowdle was sent to Arizona to testify against Jake Felshaw and Leslie Webb in their trial for the January stage robbery. Dowdle's family used their money and political influence to lobby for a pardon, and in 1903 both Dowdle and Bierer were released from prison. Dowdle became foreman of a large Arizona cattle ranch but lived less than three years, dying of illness in January 1906.[14]

Billy Hendricks became a local hero. Wells Fargo presented him with an inscribed gold pocket watch and the state of California paid a three-hundred-dollar reward for killing the stage robber. Company officials promoted him to full-time shotgun messenger. "And, as I recall, I got a raise in wages, too," said Hendricks later. But his biggest reward was a bride, for three months after the holdup, he married eighteen-year-old Gertrude Hibbitt.[15]

Yet not everyone thought Hendricks was a hero. Jack Morley, a part-time Wells Fargo guard and later a constable in Murphys, thought that Hendricks should not have opened fire. In later years, Morley told writers and reporters that he had been hired as a shotgun messenger only because he had told Wells Fargo officials that he would never put passengers in danger by shooting first. He claimed that Hendricks had violated company policy, declaring, "Wells Fargo never hired Hendricks again." That was hardly true, for Billy Hendricks continued to ride for Wells Fargo for several years.[16]

At seven-thirty on the evening of March 26, 1895, Hendricks was aboard a stage from Angels Camp to Valley Springs. At a spot not far from San Andreas, he spotted a man wearing a white sack mask rising from behind a brush fence. As the robber yelled "Halt!" Hendricks fired both barrels of his shotgun. The driver "laid on the leather" and the stage raced off to safety. At daylight, officers went to the scene but found no trace of the bandit. When the driver and two passengers reported that they had not seen the man or heard his shout, it began to appear that Hendricks was seeing things and was becoming trigger-happy. However, several days later, a man from Tuolumne County came forward and reported that he had driven his buggy along the road half an hour before the stage. At the same spot, he saw a masked man stand up from behind the brush fence. He gave the buggy a quick look, then crouched down out of sight. It was evident that he had been on the lookout for the stagecoach.[17]

Wells Fargo was taking no chances and began running two messengers whenever it sent a large treasure shipment from Angels Camp. Three months later, on June 27, Billy Hendricks and Reason McConnell delivered a fifty-thousand-dollar payroll to the Utica Mine. "No highwayman had the nerve to tackle this outfit," declared one newspaper. The two shotgun messengers regularly teamed up to protect gold shipments. Hendricks was also assigned to guard Wells Fargo's express on the narrow-gauge railroad from Valley Springs to Lodi. Criminals steered clear of him. On one occasion in 1896, a wanted thief spotted Hendricks on the train, recognized him as the noted messenger, and jumped from the moving cars, narrowly escaping a broken neck.[18]

By 1900, Hendricks had left Wells Fargo's employ to work as a saloonkeeper in Angels Camp. When his marriage got rocky, he and Gertrude divorced. In 1908, he remarried, this time to Venie Chancellor, who had an eight-year-old son. During the following decades, he followed employment more suited to his skills—as a guard in Calaveras County gold mines. He and Venie later divorced. Billy Hendricks lived out his days in Angels Camp, a popular figure on the streets of the old mining town. He died on October 7, 1948, at the age of eighty, one of the last of his breed.[19]

PART THREE

THE TRAIN ROBBERY ERA

✦

15

"I AIN'T AFRAID OF ANY MAN"

Aaron Y. Ross

Aaron Ross, a veteran shotgun messenger of proven courage, was nonetheless terrified of Wells Fargo car number 5. It was one of the original express cars on the Central Pacific Railroad after the transcontinental route was completed in 1869. Three years later, in October 1872, the car was in a deadly accident when an eastbound train descended the summit of the Sierra Nevada into Truckee, California. The brakes failed and the train careened off the tracks, killing four of the crew, including two Wells Fargo messengers. One of them, Howard Van Wormer, was found dead inside car number 5, his head crushed. For years thereafter, company messengers insisted that the car was haunted. They told many stories: Van Wormer's bloodstains were still on the floor, strange noises were heard at night, and boxes of freight moved about on their own. One expressman even claimed that a corpse's head and torso arose from a coffin in transit, called out his name, and vanished. The messengers were greatly relieved when car number 5 was sent to the Sacramento rail shops in 1882 to be rebuilt. They thought that the repairs would also cleanse it of its ghostly spirit.[1]

The car soon returned to service. Aaron Ross was aboard car number 5 late one night in September 1884, sleeping in his cot, when a loud crash awakened him. Thinking that a freight box had fallen, he checked the car but found everything in order. A few days later, at the identical spot on the railroad, it happened again. This continued for the next two weeks, each time when the train passed the same place. Explained Ross, "By this time I was a good deal mystified, but I concluded to pay no attention to the noises, thinking that some time the cause would be clear to me." Then one night he was awakened by an even louder crash and sprang from his cot. "At the other end of the car, standing at my desk, with pen in hand, was the shadowy figure of a man," declared Ross. "The train was in regular motion, and the doors were all locked and barred on the inside. I was wondering how anybody could get in, and at the same time reaching for my rifle, which lay beside the bed. Suddenly the figure disappeared. I looked around, found nothing, gave the thing up as a mystery, and kept it to myself. Two or three nights after this I saw the same thing half a dozen times during the night. Every time I opened my eyes there would be a man always at my desk writing. Well, I was getting uneasy, nervous, and fidgety, and I made up my mind that I wouldn't stand it any longer. So I put in a requisition for a new car. I ain't afraid of any man that ever walked, but I can't fight devils, and I know old No. 5 has a devil in her."[2]

Aaron Yerxa Ross came from Old Town, Maine, where he was born on March 22, 1829. He grew into a large, powerful young man, standing six three and weighing 230 pounds. Ross was loud, humorous, and flamboyant. In August 1856, at the age of twenty-seven, he left for California by steamer via the Isthmus of Panama, in search of wealth and adventure. He arrived in San Francisco after a thirty-day voyage, purchased mining supplies, and went to Murphys Camp in Calaveras County. There he spent four years working as a gold miner and soon picked up the frontiersman's penchant for telling tall tales of his adventures.[3]

Not long after his arrival in the mining region, Ross was hired as one of twenty-five men to guard a water flume at Cave City, near Murphys. Calaveras County had a complex system of seventeen different ditch and flume systems, 325 miles long. The flumes and ditches were operated by

Wells Fargo shotgun messenger
Aaron Y. Ross with his arm bandaged
from gunshot wounds received in the
Montello train robbery of 1883.
[*Author's collection*]

companies that supplied water to the mines and hydraulic-powered
stamp mills. Problems arose when they siphoned creeks and rivers dry
and angry miners, who needed moving water to operate their sluice
boxes, destroyed the flumes. As Ross told the story, he and the other
guards "held a water ditch from 350 armed men. . . . Our men were entrenched behind a ditch and desultory firing was continued throughout
the night. Only two men were killed, both on the other side, but a great
many were wounded." According to Ross, "We were snugly ensconced
behind a huge rock, and were discovered by an Irishman, who crept
around to the back of us. My colleague, who was an old man, raised his
pistol to cover and capture him, when the weapon was accidentally discharged, and our opponent, who was very close, had the entire top of his
head blown off." Though occasional violence flared over water flumes, no
such fight as Ross described took place in Calaveras County during the
late 1850s.[4]

In 1860, Aaron Ross traveled north to The Dalles in Oregon, and
two years later he drifted into the gold camp of Idaho City. He spent

three years there, mining and logging. In 1865, he joined the gold rush to Montana Territory. He recalled, "At one time I was paid $100 a day for defending a water ditch on a mining claim in Montana. I was unmolested during seven days, after which time I left. Three men who succeeded me were beaten almost to death by a party of one hundred miners, who were determined to have the water." Ross said that on one occasion, while acting as a ditch guard, he was fired at and caught a bullet in the wrist. In Fort Benton, he obtained steadier, but not safer, work as a stage driver for Wells Fargo.[5]

In 1866, the company had bought out Ben Holladay's Overland Mail and established stagecoach service in Montana Territory between Fort Benton and Helena. Fort Benton, an important transportation hub, was the upper navigation point for steamers on the Missouri River. From Fort Benton, a wagon road ran six hundred miles west to Walla Walla, Washington. In October 1868, Aaron Ross began driving Wells Fargo's stagecoaches out of the river port. He had numerous encounters with Indians. And like many westerners, his view of Native Americans was far from enlightened. He said that he soon took part in the lynching of an Indian. "The Indians killed two night herders on [a] bull train out on the prairie, and they come into town and told what they had done. Some of the men, cowboys and settlers, had one Injun named Crotaw in jail but could not get hold of him as he had a big knife and stood them off; so they came down to the stable and wanted me to come up and get him. I went up and went into the jail with the other fellows and he came at me with a knife, and I took hold of him, ketched him by the hand and took the knife away and throwed him and held him until the rest got hold of him and then I let go. They took him out and hung him, and then we went around town and caught two more, and someone shot and killed them." Ross explained what they did with the bodies: "We put a rope on them and dragged them down to the river and throwed them in and let them go; made 'good Injuns' out of them."[6]

On another occasion, Ross was getting ready to drive his stage out of Fort Benton. He stepped inside a gambling house and told one of his passengers that the coach was about to leave. The saloonkeeper, named Carson, did not want to lose a customer and ordered Ross to get out. This led to hot words, and Carson shot him in the left thigh. Explained Ross, "As he fired I grappled with him, and, although he was a heavy fighter of great repute, I used him so badly during the tussle that he never molested me again."[7]

On September 1, 1869, six miles north of Malad City, Idaho, four bandits stopped a stage bound from Helena to Corinne, Utah. They escaped with two Wells Fargo boxes holding $25,000 in bullion. Five days later, the same gang held up a coach ten miles from Malad City, this time taking $30,000 in gold from Wells Fargo. Because the amount stolen was so large, the company offered a reward of $10,000 for the bandits or one quarter of any loot recovered. On September 9, a five-man posse led by "Curly Dan" Robbins, a famed stage driver and division agent for the Gilmer & Salisbury line, trapped two of the outlaws in a mountain canyon. In a pitched gun battle, they killed one highwayman named Pryor and wounded another, Frank Long. Curly Dan was badly wounded by a bullet in the stomach. The possemen recovered most of the stolen gold and were entitled to the reward.[8]

Wells Fargo officials assigned Aaron Ross to deliver an eighteen-hundred-dollar share of the bounty to one of the posse, a man named Blackburn. As Ross later said, "He lived in Marsh Valley. He was a Mormon and had quit the church; had two wives, and was supposed to be a hard man, which he was, a hard man to fool with." Ross drove his stage up to the front of Blackburn's house. Blackburn stepped outside with a gun in his hands and demanded, "What do you want?"

"I want to come in and pay you," replied Ross. He handed Blackburn a voucher, and after he signed it, Ross handed over the cash. Ross offered to count it, but Blackburn said that was not necessary. Then he turned to one of his wives and exclaimed, "Sally, it pays better to kill a man for Wells Fargo than it ever did to kill a man for Brigham Young!"[9]

Wells Fargo's agent in Helena, Richard T. Gillespie, was impressed with the burly stage driver. Recalled Ross, "Dick Gillespie recommended me as guard. They thought a man coming from the state of Maine would not make a fight, and Dick said he would recommend me. He told [Assistant Superintendent] Brastow that if he thought there were any better than I was for them to send me out with some money and to try to take it away from me. Gillespie said they need not be afraid because I was 'the hardest son of a bitch that ever struck the road.'" He started as a shotgun messenger in 1872. According to Ross, soon afterward his coach was attacked at midnight by Indians between Fort Benton and Sun River, Montana. As twenty-five warriors swooped down, the jehu lashed his team into a gallop. Ross opened fire with his shotgun and two six-shooters, killing three of the war party.[10]

Ross recalled that his first encounter with stage robbers took place near the gold camp of Silver Star. He said he was riding with John Featherstone, a noted Montana vigilante, lawman, and Wells Fargo messenger. "When we got there they had a rope across the road and bags and sacks around some bushes, with sticks sticking out like guns," Ross said. "When the team hit this rope they commenced to kick, broke the rope and started to run. The road agents hollered at us, and we shot into the brush as near as we could to the sound. I shot both barrels at once and it nearly lifted me off the seat. We thought we killed one and wounded one." Yet Ross's story is simply untrue. This holdup attempt did indeed take place—on September 14, 1872—but Featherstone was the only messenger on board, guarding $100,000 in gold. The stage ran into the rope, the highwaymen called for a halt, and Featherstone yelled back, "Halt yourselves, you sons of bitches!" Then he opened fire and put the bandits to flight. Aaron Ross wasn't there and had nothing to do with it.[11]

Despite his penchant for wild tales, Aaron Ross proved a highly capable shotgun messenger. In 1874, a passenger who rode on his stage remarked, "When we heard that Ross was going we knew we were on a treasure coach, and all the stories of robberies by road agents, besides stories of a great many robberies that had never occurred, came through our minds, and we felt some trepidation; but when we saw the magnificent proportions of Ross and his shotgun—a regular road agent gun—and his brace of pistols, we felt a little easier, and we went ahead, never fearing but that we would arrive at our destination all right." He described the big messenger's rollicking sense of humor and declared, "Ross is the life of the party—the life of the stage line."[12]

The following year, Aaron Ross married thirty-year-old Mary Ann Covington West. She had been one of nine wives of Chauncey Walker West, a prominent Mormon pioneer, who had died in 1870. Though Aaron was a Roman Catholic and she a Mormon, they began a happy forty-five-year union. They made their home in Ogden with her young son from her prior marriage. At that time, Ross was assigned to guard express shipments on the Central Pacific Railroad between Ogden and Reno, Nevada. Despite the fact that he was now married, Wells Fargo officials continued to send him, like unwed messengers, to remote mining frontiers. In August 1877, his fellow messenger and friend from Montana, Eugene Blair, was surprised to meet him in Eureka, Nevada. Ross had been dispatched there to assist Blair in guarding treasure on the road between Eureka and Pioche. At that time, the hunt for Philadelphia child kidnapping victim Charley Ross was much in the news. "Little Charley" Ross had been abducted in America's first kidnapping for ransom and was never found. Blair, who had not seen his fellow messenger in several years, joked that "Charley Ross has been found and he is now a messenger for Wells Fargo & Co. . . . under the assumed name of Aaron Ross." Ever after, Ross was affectionately nicknamed "Lost Charley."[13]

Because of the frequency of stage robberies, during the next four years Aaron was sent repeatedly to Eureka, Pioche, and Bodie. He spent as much time at home in Ogden as possible, and during those years his wife presented him with two girls and a boy. By 1882, he was reassigned to railroad duty so that he could be with his family in Ogden. On the evening of March 15, 1882, Ross was sorting packages in his express car near the train depot. At the same time, an Ogden policeman tried to arrest an armed burglar, George Cole, at the Union

Frank Hawley lies wounded after his capture in 1883.
[*Author's collection*]

Pacific Railroad baggage office. Cole fled through the rail yard, with officers and citizens in pursuit. Numerous shots were exchanged in a running gunfight, but no one was hit. The gunfire alerted Aaron inside his express coach. He peered outside, spotted Cole ducking under a freight car, and raced forward to seize him. Cole thrust his six-shooter into the doughty messenger's stomach and pulled the trigger. To Ross's everlasting relief, the gun misfired. He dragged Cole out from under the car. The burglar tried to resist, but he had no chance. A newspaper-man reported that "the man got his face badly disfigured." Ross turned him over to the police.[14]

Aaron Ross was destined to encounter even more dangerous free-booters. That summer, a gang led by Frank Hawley, a twenty-six-year-old desperado, was busy robbing stages in southern Idaho and northeastern Nevada. On July 25, 1882, Hawley, with David Francis, a thirty-four-year-old Kentuckian, and two young cowboys, Billy Adams and Jack King, stopped a coach bound from Kelton, Utah, to Albion, Idaho. The spot they chose was near the Clear Creek bridge in Idaho, about thirty-five miles north of Kelton. A woman passenger, who had spotted the outlaws riding adjacent to the stage road, later said, "They reached the bridge before we did, crossed it, dismounted, and awaited the approach of the stage. They had six horses, two of them pack animals." She described the desperadoes: "The party were young men, none over thirty years of age, and were well mounted, and armed with knives, revolvers, and rifles." The highwaymen ordered the male passengers out of the coach, taking seven hundred dollars from one, but did not bother the woman. After finding the Wells Fargo box empty, they galloped away.[15]

Five days later, Hawley and his comrades held up a four-horse stage at a spot twelve miles south of the first robbery. There was one woman aboard, and once again the bandits allowed her to remain in the coach while they lined up six men and relieved them of their gold watches and eleven hundred dollars in cash. They opened the mail sacks, the Wells Fargo box, and also the passengers' trunks, taking jewelry and other valuables. Then the outlaws told the stage driver, "We will be fair with you and divide the horses evenly. You take two and we will take two." After unhitching the lead horses from the team, the bandits escaped south into Nevada.[16]

On August 14, Frank Hawley and David Francis stopped a coach from Wells to Cherry Creek, in northeastern Nevada. This time, there were no passengers and they got only forty dollars from the Wells Fargo box. Ten days later, two of the same gang held up yet another stagecoach on this route but got little of value. By this time, Wells Fargo's special officer John Thacker was hunting the bandits. On August 21, at Parker Station, about ninety miles south of Cherry Creek, he found a suspicious hard case near the stage barn, carrying three six-shooters in his gun belt. Thacker and three possemen placed him under arrest. Then they spotted another stranger behind the barn, getting his horse shod. While one of Thacker's posse covered him with a shotgun, the detective recalled the robbers' frequent orders that stage passengers hold up their hands. Thacker said politely, "Now, my dear fellow, as it has become a fashionable custom to throw up hands, please elevate yours." The pair proved to be Billy Adams and Jack King. They confessed to the two Idaho holdups but denied any guilt of the Nevada robberies. Thacker took them to Boise, where both received life terms in prison.[17]

Frank Hawley and David Francis were hiding out near Parker Station and managed to avoid Thacker. The two bandits soon met Ormus B. Nay, a Mormon with a wife and four young children, who eked out a living as a farmhand, peddler, and charcoal burner for local mines. Nay's wife, Louisa, recalled that he first encountered Hawley and Francis at Pleasant Valley, a few miles from Parker Station, in October. However, a desperado who rode with Hawley later insisted that Nay had previously participated with them in several robberies in southern Utah. Ormus Nay agreed to join a new gang organized by Hawley and Francis. Nay, in turn, recruited nineteen-year-old Sylvester Earl, a younger brother of his wife, Louisa. Earl was a cowhand, and his friend Erastus "Ras" Anderson, also nineteen, joined up as well. On December 20, 1882, they raided the general store of John Devine in Deep Creek, Utah, near the Nevada line. The outlaws looted the store, broke open the safe, and escaped with booty and a band of horses.[18]

Fearful settlers sent a message to the governor of Utah Territory advising that the outlaws were "encamped in the mountains defying attempts to capture them." The governor declined a request to dispatch a troop of cavalry, and instead conferred with Utah's U.S. marshal. It turned out that the bandits made their headquarters in a stone stockade in the isolated Swasey Mountains, about forty-five miles northwest of Deseret, Utah. One end of the stockade was dug into the side of a steep canyon and the rest was built of rock, with portholes for defense. It had formerly been the hideout of Ben Tasker, one of Utah's most notorious outlaws. A month passed and still the authorities took no action against the desperadoes. Wire reports announced, "The gang of robbers . . . have fortified themselves in the mountains,

David Francis, stage and train robber. [*Author's collection*]

and are making raids on the neighboring settlements. The sheriff of the county is afraid to attack them, and they appear to be having their own way."[19]

Now Hawley and Francis began planning their most ambitious robbery. At this time, train holdups were rare. There had been only three in the far west: two in Nevada in 1870 and an attempted robbery in California in 1881. On the night of January 21, 1883, the gang rode up to Montello, Nevada, a water stop on the Central Pacific Railroad about five miles from the Utah border. The band consisted of Hawley, Francis, Nay, Earl, Anderson, and a hard case named John Brently, who several years earlier had ridden with Hawley and Nay in southern Utah. They broke into the section house and gagged and bound five Chinese railroad hands. Then they captured four white section bosses and locked them in the water-tank building. At 1:00 A.M., the eastbound passenger train approached and one of the masked bandits flagged it down with a red signal lantern. When the train stopped, the

Ormus B. Nay, the Utah bandit and stage robber.
[*Author's collection*]

outlaws quickly captured the conductor and the crew, herded them into the section house, and tied them up with the rest.

Aaron Ross happened to be on duty in the Wells Fargo car. At the last stop, he had loaded the express and checked his waybills. He then had climbed into his cot and gone to sleep. He awoke to a loud rapping on the side door and thought it was the Wells Fargo agent at the next stop. As Ross slid the door open, a robber covered him with a gun and ordered, "Hop out. We are going through you."

Though the safe held only six hundred dollars, Ross had no intention of surrendering. He slammed the door shut and closed the latch. A bandit on the other side of the car called out, "Open up the door and jump out. We are going to rob the train."

"Just wait until I get my boots on," replied Ross.

"Never mind your boots," snapped the bandit. "Hop right out here and we will get through with you and then you can get your boots on."

Ross quickly pulled on his boots, crouched behind his messenger's kit trunk, threw blankets on top of it, unlimbered his shotgun and six-shooter, and made ready for a fight.

"Open up or we'll burn you out and murder you!" the outlaws yelled.

Ross's answer was a blast of buckshot, which tore a hole through the car's one-inch redwood wall. For several minutes, there was silence. Then one of the robbers asked plaintively, "Ain't you going to open the door and come out?"

Ross made no reply. Five of the gang took positions around the car, and all fired simultaneously. One bullet struck Ross in his left hand, another his hip, and a third grazed his stomach. The gunfire put out the lamp in the express car. The messenger was bleeding but unfazed. When he heard two of the bandits scramble onto the roof of the car, he fired twice, and they leaped for cover. Now Ross heard the westbound train approaching. The outlaws ordered the engineer to back the train onto a side track. Then they covered the westbound engineer with their guns and told him to pull out, which he did with alacrity.

The outlaws returned to Ross's car and John Brently climbed on the roof. Ross heard him and aimed carefully at the ceiling. He fired another blast, which tore through the wood planking. Brently tumbled to the platform, desperately wounded. The gang was undeterred. They took coal picks from the engine and tried to batter open the doors. When that didn't work, they fired another fusillade into the car, but Ross was well protected by a barricade of trunks and boxes. The bandits forced the brakeman to uncouple the express car from the mail and baggage coach, which was between the locomotive and the Wells Fargo car. They had the engineer pull forward, then into reverse. The mail car slammed into the express car, knocking both side doors open. Ross sprang forward and closed them quickly. The outlaws repeated the process, but again Ross outwitted them by closing and latching the doors.

Next the gang began searching for wood to set fire to the express car. They went to the engine but found that it burned coal, not wood. Frustrated, they held a council in front of the mail car. The outlaws thought that they were opposed by two shotgun messengers. Three unarmed clerks in the mail car overheard one of the robbers say, "Before we shot the light out I saw two of 'em in the car."

The bandit leader, probably Hawley, responded, "It don't make any difference if it's one or two. He's a plucky son of a bitch."

The gang was unable to find enough wood to start a fire, and one of them called to Ross, "Ain't you going to hop out?"

He made no reply, and again the robbers had the engineer crash the baggage car into the express car. But by now the engine was low on steam and the impact was slight. They asked the conductor how long before the next train arrived, and he told them thirty minutes. At that, they draped Bentley onto a horse and rode off into the blackness. The attack had lasted about two hours. The train continued on to Ogden, where a large crowd, alerted by the telegraph, greeted the heroic messenger and counted forty bullet holes in the express car's walls. Doctors treated Ross's wounds and he quickly recovered.[20]

Meanwhile, the robbers fled south to their fortified hideout. Along the way, John Brently died of his wounds, and his comrades buried him. Then they raided two isolated ranches, taking rifles, revolvers, ammunition, and fresh horses. Detective Sam Deal of the Central Pacific Railroad was in Elko, Nevada, when he got word of the holdup. He quickly formed a posse, raced to the scene by special train, and cut the gang's sign in the fresh snow, leading south through the high desert. John Thacker rushed by rail from California to Deseret, Utah, where he joined local lawmen. Early on the morning of January 24, three days after the holdup, Thacker and his posse rode northeast toward the Swasey Mountains, hoping to locate the outlaws' stockade. The weather was numbingly cold, twenty degrees below zero. The possemen were spurred on by rewards of $1,250 for each of the band.

Late that afternoon, as Thacker's men approached Swasey Spring, at the southeastern tip of the Swasey Mountains, they spotted two riders in the distance. They were Frank Hawley and Ormus Nay. At a range of 150 yards, the officers ordered them to halt. The outlaws leaped from their saddles, taking cover behind their horses, and opened

Sylvester Earl, *left,* and Erastus "Ras" Anderson, *right,* both nineteen and the youngest of the Montello train robbers. [*Author's collection*]

fire. Thacker and the lawmen opened up with a volley of rifle shots, which killed both animals. After a blistering exchange of gunfire, Nay caught bullets in his right shoulder and one leg. Hawley took a slug in each of his legs. Both surrendered. The posse loaded the wounded outlaws into a wagon and sent them back to Deseret. Then Thacker and the rest rode two miles north and made camp for the night.

Early the next morning, Sam Deal and his posse rode into the camp from the north. At daybreak, the combined posses located the stockade seven miles from Swasey Spring. It was occupied by the rest of the gang: David Francis, Sylvester Earl, and Ras Anderson. Faced by overwhelming odds, the three promptly surrendered. The outlaws quickly admitted guilt in the Deep Springs raid and the Montello holdup. They had clothes and horses stolen at Deep Springs. The three robbers were jailed, while Hawley and Nay were hospitalized in Salt Lake City. Three weeks later, when the wounded men were well enough to travel, all five were put under guard on an eastbound train to stand trial in Nevada. Aaron Ross met the train at the Ogden depot so he could get a look at the desperadoes who had tried to rob him. After exchanging

The gold pocket watch presented to Aaron Ross by Wells Fargo "for his courageous and successful defence of the express car against highway robbers at Montello, Nev., January 23, 1883." [*Courtesy of Robert J. Chandler*]

cordial greetings, Ross held up his bandaged hand and said, "You see what you gave me?"

At that, Frank Hawley exclaimed, "Well, I got it afterwards, so we're even."

The robbers all pled guilty to the Montello train holdup. Because of their youth, Sylvester Earl and Ras Anderson received twelve years each. Frank Hawley, David Francis, and Ormus Nay got fourteen years apiece in the Nevada State Prison. Aaron Ross was the hero of the hour. His fellow Wells Fargo men gave him an embellished Colt revolver. And, as he later recalled, "Wells Fargo presented me with a gold watch and chain valued at $650 and a $1,000 check; and Mrs. Ross presented me with a girl baby. She was named after the station, Montello." His daughter was Henrietta Montella Ross, and his express car became known as Fort Ross. Ever after, Wells Fargo men called the plucky messenger "Hold-the-Fort Ross."[21]

By now a celebrity, he continued as a shotgun messenger for another thirty-three years. Hale and hearty well into old age, "Dad" Ross regularly made the run between Ogden and San Francisco. As late as 1912, when he was eighty-three, he guarded $500,000 in silver bullion from San Francisco to New York City. The arrival of the rugged pioneer was greeted with much interest. Reporters interviewed Ross, and photographers had him pose with Wells Fargo express boxes, holding his Winchester rifle. He expressed amazement at New York's tall buildings and teeming streets, which were so far removed from the scenes of his early life on the frontier. He finally retired from Wells Fargo in February 1916, with a pension of fifty dollars a month. Despite his retirement, for two more years he continued to make occasional trips as a shotgun messenger to Kansas City. In old age, Ross remained much in demand and on several occasions drove stagecoaches in parades in Utah and California.[22]

Aaron Ross enjoyed his celebrity and never lost his penchant for spinning yarns of his adventures. But the older he got, the wilder his

Aaron Ross with his Winchester rifle and Wells Fargo strongbox in New York City in 1912. [*Tom Martin's collection*]

stories became. As early as 1888, he told newspapermen that he had shot all of the bandits at Montello. He later claimed that he and Wells Fargo messenger Johnny Brent once killed a road agent in a Montana holdup, but Brent himself said that his coaches were never attacked by highwaymen. Ross also asserted that he and Mike Tovey were aboard the stage when driver Charley Phelps was slain by bandits in Portneuf Canyon, Idaho, in 1873. In fact, it was Joe Pinkham who shot it out with the killers; Ross and Tovey were not there. Ross even claimed that it was he who shot and killed Big Jack Davis during the holdup of the Eureka-Tybo stage in Nevada in 1877. In fact, as we have seen, Davis was slain by Shotgun Jimmy Brown, and Ross had no involvement whatsoever. Ross alleged that when stage robber Milton Sharp broke out of jail in Aurora, Nevada, he tracked the fugitive down and captured him. However, that feat was accomplished by a local policeman, not by Ross. Even more incredible was Ross's story that he had captured Black Bart in Sacramento, when, of course, Bart was nabbed by Harry Morse in San Francisco.[23]

Ross's bogus yarns were unfortunate. Instead of sticking to embellishment of his own feats, like John X. Beidler had done, he went much further and attempted to hijack other men's valor. Nonetheless, he deserves great credit for serving Wells Fargo with courage and dedication for almost fifty years. Aaron Ross died in his Ogden home on April 3, 1922, surrounded by his family. As one journalist observed, "Ross bore the record of having guarded the treasures carried by his company during the past half century without losing a cent." Added the *New York Times*, "The old man who passed away quietly at ninety-three lived and moved and had his being in some of the roughest spots of the rough west."[24]

16

TRAIN ROBBERS' NEMESIS

John N. Thacker

A huge throng, brandishing rifles, shotguns, lanterns, and torches, surrounded Molly Evans's rustic wood-frame farmhouse in Visalia, California. Wrathful shouts crackled the night air as Wells Fargo detective John Thacker stepped out of the house to face the mob. As he did so, an armed vigilante yelled to the crowd, "Burn up the barn!"

"Let's shoot through the house!" another shouted, to the terror of Mrs. Evans, whose children were in their beds.

"So we will!" cried the others, and the mob began to surge through the front gate, led by a man with a gun.

John Thacker stepped in front of the leader and rammed the muzzle of his sawed-off shotgun against the man's temple.

"Drop your gun quick," the Wells Fargo officer ordered. "If you make a motion to fire through that house I'll blow your damned brains out."

The man wisely obeyed. Thacker's prompt action took the fight out of the mob, and its members rapidly melted away. Though John Thacker was the nemesis of stage and train robbers, he would not stand for mistreatment of women and children, even if they were the family of a bandit and murderer. The raw courage he showed on that warm summer night in Visalia was emblematic of his thirty-two years in the saddle for Wells Fargo.[1]

John Nelson Thacker came from Miller County, Missouri, where he was born on November 1, 1837, the son of Joel and Mariah Brumley Thacker. He and his twin brother, James, were the eldest of twelve children, eight of them twins. Reflecting the high infant mortality rate of the era, four died in childhood. In the spring of 1853, when John was fifteen, his father took the family west by wagon train to California. John and Jim took turns driving one of the teams of oxen. They encountered many hardships and adventures: some of their livestock drowned in a river crossing, several horses were trampled to death in a buffalo stampede, their prize ox, Old Bob, was stolen by Indians, and they narrowly escaped dying from thirst when crossing Nevada's barren desert. But the journey hardened John Thacker and turned him into a rugged frontiersman. After five months on the Overland Trail, the family arrived safely at Oregon Bar, on the Yuba River in California's Northern Mines.[2]

While their father ran a general store in Oregon Bar, John and Jim Thacker hefted shovels and picks in the Yuba River mines. When the diggings played out, they drifted on to other gold camps, then joined the 1859 rush to the Comstock Lode in Virginia City, Nevada. Finally tiring of mining, in 1861 the twins settled in Humboldt County, in northern Nevada. John Thacker acquired a ranch on the Humboldt River and opened a hotel, while his brother ran a saloon. Their father and brothers later joined them and the family became prominent in business and social affairs. In November 1868, John Thacker won election as sheriff of Humboldt County and served a two-year term. His bailiwick was a vast territory covering sixteen thousand square miles, an area twice the size of Massachusetts. He captured several murderers and established a reputation as a manhunter and detective.[3]

Thacker ran for reelection in 1870 but lost. He returned to ranching and acted as foreman for John Sutherland, a cattle baron from Fresno, California, who ran large herds of horses in Nevada. In 1873, John went to Marysville and married Sarah Eliza Hurley, the twenty-one-

John N. Thacker, about 1870.
[*William B. Secrest collection*]

year-old daughter of a family he had known in Yuba County. The next year, their first son, Eugene, was born on the Sutherland ranch in Fresno County. Then, in 1875, Thacker was hired by Wells Fargo to investigate an express robbery in California. For the next six years, he divided his time between his Humboldt River ranch and sleuthing for the company on a case-by-case basis.[4]

His first important Wells Fargo investigation began on November 10, 1875, when three highwaymen robbed a stage just south of Boise, Idaho, taking seven thousand dollars in gold and greenbacks. Local lawmen were unable to solve the crime, and in April 1876, Wells Fargo officials sent in John Thacker. He made several trips to Boise and then to Silver City, where he focused on a miner named John "Crooked Neck" Lee, whom Idaho officers had long suspected. After Thacker offered him immunity, Lee turned state's evidence and made a full confession. He admitted that he had robbed the stage with George Bouldin and John Souder. The driver, Charles Downey, had tipped them off to the bullion shipment, and some of the stolen gold was melted down by James Trask, an assayer in Silver City.

Thacker and the local sheriff searched Trask's assay office. They dug up the earth floor in the building's basement and found fifteen hundred dollars in gold that had been melted down from the stolen coins. Next they searched Bouldin's house and discovered thirteen hundred dollars in gold coin hidden in his mattress. After lodging Lee, Trask, and Bouldin in jail, they picked up Souder at his camp on Trout Creek. Thacker believed that Souder was the brains of the outfit. Finally, they arrested the stage driver, Downey, who confessed and led the officers to a spot on the Snake River where he had hidden five hundred dollars of the loot. But getting convictions in court would prove difficult. After several trials, juries convicted only Bouldin and Downey. Both were sentenced to terms in the state prison in Boise. Wells Fargo officials were nonetheless highly pleased with Thacker's work and they began to assign him cases in Nevada and California on a regular basis.[5]

During the late 1870s, a silver rush began to Arizona Territory. Wells Fargo rapidly expanded its operations to Tombstone as well as many of the other new mining camps. Stage robbers were quick to follow. Jim Hume, Wells Fargo's chief detective, disliked the long trip by train and stagecoach to Arizona and despised the desert heat. As a result, Bob Paul, a noted lawman of the California Gold Rush who had become one of the company's most trusted shotgun messengers, was sent into Arizona as a Wells Fargo detective. Paul's extraordinary abilities resulted in his winning the office of Pima County sheriff in Tucson in April 1881. Wells Fargo officials promptly appointed John Thacker as his full-time replacement.[6]

During the next twenty-six years, Thacker would investigate scores of stage and train robberies, pursuing bandits and thieves all over the West. Two of them pulled California's first successful train robbery, which also happened to be one of America's most ingenious. They were Hoadley L. Gorton and his brother George, the sons of Hiram P. Gorton, a prosperous farmer. The Gortons were natives of Mantua, Ohio, where George was born in 1862 and Hoadley two years later. In 1878, their mother died, and the following year Hiram Gorton remarried and moved west to Lenexa, Kansas, where he acquired a new farm. Soon afterward, Hoadley left home and drifted south to New Orleans, where he enlisted in the navy at the age of seventeen. He was discharged three years later, in 1885, then met up with his brother George, and the pair landed in California in 1887. George got work running a steam-powered sawmill in Boulder Creek, in the Santa Cruz Mountains, and Hoadley drove a hay wagon for a feed store in Alameda, across the bay from San Francisco.[7]

According to Thacker, Hoadley then "worked as a flunky in a San Francisco restaurant" until he tired of it. In September 1888, George joined Hoadley in San Francisco. A month later, the brothers drifted north to Sonoma County, where they cut trees and chopped wood for a fruit grower on the Russian River. Then, on the first of December, they borrowed a pair of muzzle-loading shotguns and disappeared. Three days later, on the evening of December 4, 1888, the Gorton boys stopped the eastbound stage from the coastal town of Mendocino at a wooded spot nine miles from Cazadero, in Sonoma County. Only one bandit was visible to the reinsman and passengers, and he demanded the Wells Fargo box and the mail pouch.

One of the passengers, later described as a "dignified elderly lady," was hard of hearing and could not understand why they had been stopped. A male passenger, figuring that bandits would not rob an old woman, tried to hide his pocketbook in her stocking. She was shocked, and, as a reporter later explained, "for a few minutes there was something of a sensation in that vehicle." The Gortons, however, had no interest in the passengers and waved the stage on. They then disappeared, leaving behind the looted strongbox and mail pouch. Jim Hume investigated and erroneously concluded that the robber was Black Bart, who had been released from San Quentin earlier that year. Hume's reasoning was that the highwayman's MO was the same as Black Bart's: He seemed to have acted alone, he did not rob the passengers, and Bart had robbed a stage on the same route in 1877, famously leaving his first poem at the scene.[8]

Hoadley L. Gorton, the Clipper Gap train robber. [*Author's collection*]

John Thacker and local officers learned that two young strangers had worked for the Russian River fruit grower, borrowed the shotguns, and vanished just before the stage robbery. They searched the strangers' vacant cabin and found that a batch of papers had recently been burned in the fireplace. They had left behind one clue: a postal card bearing the name George Gorton. Thacker interviewed some local boys, who said that one of the men "had talked a great deal about Black Bart's feats." The officers then checked the voting registries for each county in Northern California. A George Gorton had registered to vote in Boulder Creek in August. Thacker issued a reward circular for them, giving their descriptions and advising law officers that they were suspected of the holdup. But despite his efforts, he could not locate the stage robbers.[9]

Three weeks later, on Christmas Eve, the Gortons swung aboard a Central Pacific train when it stopped for water at Clipper Gap, on the transcontinental railroad in the Sierra Nevada. The express car was in charge of Wells Fargo messenger Robert Johnston and his helper, Emery Carpenter. It had two doors, front and rear, and a sliding door on each side, with glass windows in the doors. The expressmen did not wear revolvers, but a rack holding several loaded shotguns was on the right-hand side of the car, opposite the Wells Fargo safe. The Gorton boys each carried a six-gun, a rope ladder, and an ax. As the train pulled out, they climbed to the roof of the Wells Fargo car and fastened the rope ladders to the edges of the roof on each side of the car. They dropped the ladders over the side of the car and climbed down to the door windows.

Johnston was working at his desk, at the left rear of the car, while Carpenter was near the side door on the right, sorting packages for delivery to the Colfax depot. Suddenly, one of the Gorton brothers, dangling from the side of the lurching train, smashed open the right door's window with his ax. He thrust a six-gun inside, inches from Carpenter's head.

"Throw up your hands!" the robber barked, and Carpenter instantly complied. As a startled Johnston turned from his desk, he heard the crash of shattering glass from the opposite door. He turned again, in time to see the muzzle of a revolver pointed through the broken window, aimed directly at his head. Johnston twisted quickly toward the shotgun rack, six feet from his desk.

"If you move you're as good as dead!" exclaimed the bandit, and Johnston realized he had no chance to resist. The desperado ordered him to raise one hand and open the side door with his other. He did so, and the holdup man sprang inside the express car. Then the other robber smashed the window near the end of the right door, reached inside, unhooked the door, and jumped in. Hoadley Gorton was unmasked; George wore a neckerchief, concealing the lower half of his face.

The Gortons ordered Johnston and Carpenter to the rear end of the car. While one brother guarded the expressmen, the other looted the open safe. He removed money packets containing five thousand dollars and some watches and jewelry but overlooked a canvas bag on the floor, which held ten thousand dollars in gold coin. Then they forced

Johnston and Carpenter to kneel and face the back door. One of the brothers ordered, "Now don't look around this way at your peril. We will be back here shortly to see you again."

One of the Gortons climbed on top of the express car and recovered the rope ladders. Then, as the train lumbered up the steep grade at fifteen miles an hour, the bandits jumped down from the platform and vanished into the night. Johnston and Carpenter did not know that, and fearing that the robbers were still aboard, they did not pull the lever to activate the air brakes. When the train reached the next stop, New England Mills (now Weimar), a hobo leaped from the baggage car and told the engineer that he had seen the Wells Fargo car being robbed. The train crew promptly sent word of the robbery over the telegraph line.[10]

On Christmas Day, John Thacker, Jim Hume, and a small army of railroad detectives and local lawmen rushed to the scene. Thacker later aptly described the robbery as "one of the most unique and daring train robberies known in criminal history." The newspapers had a field day with the story. The *San Francisco Chronicle* quoted an "old railroad man" who declared, "It is nonsense to talk about any one being able to clamber on top of a railroad car, and move about as these robbers must have done, without being heard by those inside. . . . Then the idea that they could fasten rope ladders on top of the car and climb down to the side door without being heard seems to me utterly preposterous. . . . Besides this, it looks strange indeed that one man, hanging to a swinging rope on the outside of a moving car, should be able to cover two men through a small window." The *Chronicle* asserted that Johnston and Carpenter had either colluded with the robbers or were cowards.[11]

A reporter for the *Sacramento Daily Union* interviewed Robert Johnston and wrote, "He feels very keenly some of the comments of the press on the robbery and the insinuations that the messengers may have been in collusion with the robbers." Thacker and Hume, on the other hand, had utmost faith in the two expressmen. Johnston was a veteran messenger, and Carpenter, though a new employee, would later have a long career with the company as a route agent. Railroad

John Thacker's folding Burgess shotgun. It could be folded in half and carried in a leather case. [*Author's collection*]

detectives searched the area where the robbers had jumped from the train. Heavy winter rains had wiped out all footprints, but in the brush they found two rolled-up rope ladders with iron rungs. This was strong evidence that Johnston and Carpenter were telling the truth.[12]

Thacker and Hume made an intensive investigation. A few weeks later, they found a man who admitted that Hoadley and George Gorton had stayed with him in his cabin four miles from New England Mills. He said that the brothers had the iron rungs for their ladders made by a blacksmith in Grass Valley, and that he had bought the rope and loaned them an ax. He was angry at the brothers, complaining that they had given him only thirty dollars for his help. Four days after the robbery, they had left on an eastbound train. Thacker learned that the Gortons were from Lenexa, Kansas, and he had U.S. Post Office inspectors issue a wanted notice for the brothers and circulate it in Kansas. In February 1889, a Lenexa constable spotted Hoadley, who had come to town to visit his father. He notified a postal inspector, who followed Gorton by train to Kansas City, where the fugitive was arrested on February 15.[13]

Based on Jim Hume's belief that the wanted robber was Black Bart, the *Kansas City Times* trumpeted the headline BLACK BART, THE LONE HIGHWAYMAN TAKEN. The story was picked up by wire services and printed nationwide. Meanwhile, Gorton posted bond and returned to his father's farm. There he was rearrested a week later and turned over to John Thacker. The Wells Fargo detective told newspapermen, "He is as much like Black Bart as a bird's nest is like a mile post." He took

Wells Fargo detective John Thacker, about 1890. [*Author's collection*]

Gorton back to California and jailed him in San Francisco. Under questioning, Gorton stoutly maintained his innocence. He was tried in federal court for robbing the mails in the Sonoma stage holdup, but a jury acquitted him when a key witness could not be found. Thacker immediately rearrested Gorton and took him to the Wells Fargo office in Sacramento. There, Robert Johnston positively identified him as one of the Clipper Gap robbers. Thacker took Gorton to Auburn, where in July he was tried and convicted of the train robbery and sentenced to ten years in San Quentin.[14]

Two weeks later, Thacker visited Gorton in San Quentin. The detective later explained to reporters, "I called on Gorton at the prison and he made a full confession. He expressed the desire that the matter be mentioned in the papers, because the two express messengers, Johnson and Carpenter, were treated so badly in the published accounts at the time of the robbery." Gorton admitted both the stage robbery and the Clipper Gap holdup, and that his brother George was his partner in crime. Said Thacker, "Gorton tells me he had been a thief and robber for ten years, and had stolen large sums of money, but spent it as fast as he got it." Despite Thacker's efforts to find him, George Gorton disappeared and was never brought to justice.[15]

By this time, an epidemic of train holdups swept the country, and John Thacker was at the forefront of many manhunts. He played a key role in the case of Chris Evans and John Sontag, who held up six trains in California, Wisconsin, and Nebraska. Thacker laid the plans that resulted in the ambush and capture of both outlaws, and even protected Evans's wife and children from that vengeful lynch mob in Visalia on August 8, 1892. He helped lead the dragnets for such noted train robbers as Kid Thompson and Alva Johnson in Los Angeles County and Burt Alvord and Billy Stiles in Arizona, and took part in the Southwest manhunts for the Black Jack Ketchum band, the High Five gang, and the "Bronco Bill" Walters gang.

One of his most successful bandit pursuits had its origins on the night of September 4, 1897, when robbers tried to halt a Southern Pacific train at Morrano Switch, fifteen miles south of Stockton, California. The desperadoes placed a huge pile of railroad ties on the track and set them afire. The engineer managed to stop in time, but when a pistol-toting brakeman jumped down from the cars, the would-be bandits lost their nerve and fled. Tom Cunningham, famed sheriff of San Joaquin County, started work on the case with his deputies. A few days later, a Stockton youth, George Cook, went to the sheriff and revealed that the culprits were a pair of young hard cases, George Williams and George Schlagel. Cook had been rooming with Williams, who asked him to join them in a second holdup. Cook refused and Williams threatened to kill him if he told anyone.

Sheriff Cunningham knew them both well. George Williams was very bright; he had invented a railroad car coupler and a type of smokeless gunpowder. But he also had a wild streak. Cunningham had arrested him as a teenager in 1892 for robbing a railroad depot and sent him to the state reformatory for two years. There Williams met George Schlagel, and upon their release they went to Williams's family home in San Joaquin County. Soon afterward, Schlagel stole a horse, but Cunningham tracked him down and had him sent to San Quentin for three years. When his term expired, he immediately rejoined Williams.

Cunningham learned that the pair were rooming at a boarding-house in Stockton and instructed his deputies to shadow them. On the evening of September 8, four days after the first holdup attempt, the deputy sheriffs spotted Williams and Schlagel heading out of town in the company of a third, unidentified man. Cunningham ordered two of his deputies to board the next southbound train, while he started south in a buggy.

Meanwhile, Williams and Schlagel, with their partner, who turned out to be an ex-con named James Roup, set up another blazing pile of railroad ties at Morrano Switch. The Southern Pacific train approached from the north at nine o'clock and stopped safely. The two deputy sheriffs, carrying sawed-off shotguns, climbed down from the coaches and walked up the tracks toward the bonfire. As they approached, the three outlaws, armed with a Winchester rifle, a shotgun, and a six-shooter, opened up with a volley of gunshots. The lawmen jumped for cover and returned fire. A stray bullet from the desperadoes' guns wounded a tramp riding atop one of the cars. While the officers kept up their fire, Williams, Schlagel, and Roup fled on foot toward the San Joaquin River. The deputies tried to follow them but soon lost them in the blackness.[16]

At daybreak, Sheriff Cunningham organized a manhunt, and John Thacker arrived the next day to help out. The two were old friends, having worked together many times, most notably on the Black Bart case fourteen years earlier. Thacker and Cunningham were joined by two Southern Pacific detectives, and the railroad offered a fourteen-hundred-dollar reward. The lawmen got word that Williams and Schlagel had held up a woodchopper near the San Joaquin River and stole all his provisions. Thacker and Cunningham quickly cut the outlaws' trail. Despite that the fact that both officers were almost sixty years of age, they had the energy and endurance of much younger men. They began a re-lentless pursuit, and for the next six days barely stopped to sleep or eat.

George Williams, one of the Morrano Switch holdup men. [*California State Archives*]

They believed that George Williams would not be easy to catch, for he knew the river bottoms like the back of his hand.

Thacker and Cunningham trailed the footprints of the two young outlaws south along the San Joaquin River. The mark made by Williams's left boot was a peculiar one, which Cunningham later called "a guide to us throughout our search." The tracks continued south into Stanislaus County, where Thacker and Cunningham were joined by Sheriff Richard Purvis. Although today the San Joaquin River bottom is irrigated cropland, at that time it was a vast, isolated marsh choked with dense thickets of tules, willows, and scrub oak. Thus the officers often lost the trail and were forced to double back over and over to cut the bandits' sign. They warned the occupants of the remote farmhouses and woodchoppers' camps to be on the lookout for the fugitives.

On the night of September 12, they learned that the outlaws had visited a religious camp meeting on the river, where they had been fed supper. Thacker and the two sheriffs soon arrived at the camp, but

Williams and Schlagel fled west toward Modesto, with the officers several hours behind. The desperadoes brazenly walked into Modesto, where they read newspaper reports of the train holdup. The next day, after searching both sides of the river, the officers got word that a rancher's wife had spotted the two fugitives near Carpenter's Ferry, four miles north of Crow's Landing. Driving a buggy, Thacker, Cunningham, and Purvis searched the bottomland around Crow's Landing without success. They spent the night with a farmer near Hills Ferry. At daybreak, September 15, suspecting that the fugitives might have spotted the buggy, they exchanged it for the farmer's wagon. Then they recruited three local men to join their little posse.

Again the officers found the print left by Williams's left boot, which led them to a camp the outlaws had made the previous night. Despite searching both sides of the river, they could not find any further tracks. As they recrossed the river, the farmer ran toward them, yelling that he had just spotted two men crawling out of a nearby haystack. Thacker and Cunningham immediately divided the posse. Thacker and one man started on foot toward the haystack to track the outlaws. At the same time, one posseman guarded the side of the field, and Cunningham and Purvis raced their wagon around to a gate on the opposite side of the field. The outlaws spotted them and made a run for the river bottom. Cunningham and Purvis tried to pursue them in the wagon but were halted by a barbed-wire fence. They had no tools to cut the wire, so they jumped out of the wagon and raced across the fields on foot.

The chase after the fugitives took them two miles farther. Thacker and his posseman followed the trail of broken brush along the river, then followed the road that paralleled the stream. Suddenly, they spotted Williams and Schlagel jumping over a fence just in front of them. As the outlaws ran onto the road, Thacker unlimbered his gun and shouted, "Throw up your hands!"

Schlagel immediately dropped his shotgun and shot his hands skyward. Williams, however, raised his Winchester and started to turn away, only to see a shotgun-wielding Cunningham approaching from the adjacent field.

George Schlagel, captured
by John Thacker in 1897.
[*California State Archives*]

"Drop the gun, Williams," Cunningham ordered, and the young desperado wisely complied. Williams and Schlagel insisted that they were merely out hunting and had had nothing to do with the train holdup. However, the jury who heard Williams's case a month later found him guilty of attempted train wrecking and sentenced him to life imprisonment. The next day, Schlagel pled guilty and admitted that the third man was James Roup. Schlagel also received a life sentence. A few months later, Sheriff Cunningham found Roup; he was handed a life term for an unrelated crime. Both Thacker and Cunningham received much newspaper praise for their exploit.[17]

As John's close friend and boss Jim Hume slowed down, Thacker found himself increasingly in charge of Wells Fargo's detective force. By the 1890s, the company employed several full- and part-time detectives. When Hume died in 1904, Thacker succeeded him as chief special officer. As late as 1905, Thacker organized the manhunt of the killers of Wells Fargo shotgun messenger Dan Haskell in an attempt to rob the Redding stage. He retired from Wells Fargo on his seventieth birthday, November 1, 1907, with a pension of fifty-two dollars a month. It was small recompense for a dangerous career that took him to every frontier of the Old West.[18]

Thacker spent his remaining years quietly, dividing his time between his old ranch in Nevada and his suburban home in Oakland, California. He suffered a stroke and died in Oakland on January 3, 1913. Newspapers remembered him as the lawman "who struck terror to the hearts of the stage and train robbers in California, Nevada, and Arizona" and who "probably captured more desperadoes than any officer in the west."[19]

A California journalist gave him his finest tribute: "Some of the newspapers in eulogizing John N. Thacker, the veteran Wells Fargo detective, for his grit and bravery use the term that he has 'notches on his gun.' Thacker has been an officer and detective in this state and Nevada for over thirty years and it is to his credit that there is not a notch on his gun. In his career of hunting and capturing criminals he has exercised intelligence, courage and suasion and has not resorted to killing his fellow-being either for glory or money reward."[20]

17

"DIE, DAMN YOU!"

J. Ernest Smith

Near El Paso, on a clear fall night in 1887, a Wells Fargo messenger shot and killed two bandits in a train holdup that was trumpeted in newspaper headlines throughout the nation. For a time, he was a heroic figure, his name a household word. A humble man who never sought notoriety, he then slipped into quiet obscurity. And when he died many years later, few recalled who he was or what he had done. It is high time that this wrong be undone.

J. Ernest Smith hailed from Greenville, Illinois, where he was born on March 16, 1853. His father, John M. Smith, a veteran of the Mexican War, claimed to have been one of the soldiers who captured the cork prosthetic leg of Gen. Antonio López de Santa Anna following the Battle of Cerro Gordo in Mexico in 1847. The elder Smith took his family to Texas in 1874 and settled in Texarkana. His son, J. Ernest, grew into a mild-mannered young man. A journalist once described him as "modest and pleasant," with blue eyes, light-colored hair, and a florid complexion. Smith was friendly and talkative, so garrulous that his friends nicknamed him "Windy." By 1880, he was married, had a baby daughter, and was working as a grocery clerk in Texarkana. The marriage ended either with his wife's death or a divorce, and in 1883,

Smith hired on as a messenger for Wells Fargo on the railroad between Jefferson and McKinney, Texas. Later he was assigned to the route between San Antonio and El Paso.[1]

El Paso, a dusty adobe village on the Rio Grande, was the stomping ground for outlaws, desperadoes, and gunfighters, whose bloody exploits gave the town its well-deserved nickname, "Hell Paso." As early as 1877, the El Paso Salt War pitted local Mexican-Americans against a gang of American gunfighters from New Mexico. The town boomed after the 1881 arrival of the railroad. Its two-gun city marshal, Dallas Stoudenmire, rode herd on the rowdies who patronized the many saloons, gambling parlors, dance halls, and bordellos. Stoudenmire won the 1881 "Four Dead in Five Seconds" shootout, in which he killed three men, one of them an innocent bystander. A resulting vendetta led to Stoudenmire's death in a gunfight the next year. He was followed as city marshal by the former Texas Ranger sergeant James B. Gillett, who eschewed Stoudenmire's proclivity for killing. Later, during the 1890s, El Paso would host such gunmen as John Wesley Hardin, John Selman, George Scarborough, Bass Outlaw, Pat Garrett, Jeff Milton, and many others.

Windy Smith came to know El Paso well. His first four years with the company proved uneventful, but that changed in 1887. A gang of robbers had been operating in El Paso for more than a year. Two of its leaders were Jack "Kid" Smith and John "Dick" Maier, both former railroad brakemen. In January 1886, Kid Smith and the notorious desperado "Cowboy Bob" Rennick robbed and killed a merchant across the border in Paso del Norte (now Ciudad Juarez). In July, Kid Smith, Cowboy Bob, and a third robber raided the celebrated Gem Saloon in El Paso and shot and wounded three patrons. On March 15, 1887, Smith gunned down an El Paso police officer, wounding him seriously. The next day, Smith, Maier, and a fellow bandit, George Green, left for Tucson, where they intended to pull Arizona's first train robbery.

On the night of April 27, they stopped a Southern Pacific train in the Cienega Creek wash, seventeen miles east of Tucson. They riddled the express car with bullets, but Wells Fargo messenger Charles F.

J. Ernest Smith, Wells Fargo messenger, in 1887. [*Author's collection*]

Smith (no relation to Windy Smith) refused to open up. Finally, when the bandits threatened to blow him up with dynamite, he came out. Unknown to the robbers, he had hidden $3,500 in the stove. Smith and Maier, using their railroad experience, uncoupled the mail and express coaches from the rest of the train, climbed onto the locomotive, and drove toward Tucson, leaving the train crew and passengers behind. After taking $6,000 from the mail and the express, but missing the money in the stove, they abandoned the train and vanished.

News of the daring holdup was published throughout the country, and messenger Smith received kudos for his stove ruse. Wells Fargo and the Southern Pacific offered rewards of one thousand dollars each for the robbers, to no avail. Three months later, Kid Smith and Dick Maier returned to Tucson. On the night of August 10, 1887, using track torpedoes and a red signal lantern, they stopped another Southern Pacific train a mile east of the spot where they had held up the first train. Once again the Wells Fargo messenger was Charles F. Smith, and once again he refused to open up. When Smith and Maier blasted a hole in a side door with a stick of dynamite, the messenger finally relented. As he clambered down from the express car, one of the masked bandits recognized him from the prior holdup. Knocking him over the head with his six-gun, the outlaw growled, "Smithy, the stove racket don't go this time."

While one robber guarded the trainmen, the other ransacked the Wells Fargo car, taking three thousand dollars in U.S. currency and Mexican coin. Then they disappeared in the darkness. A huge manhunt, which included Wells Fargo detectives Jim Hume and John Thacker, and even Virgil Earp, was unsuccessful. Smith and Maier hid out in the Rincon Mountains for several days, then stole a ride back to El Paso on a passing freight train. Emboldened by their success, they began planning yet another train robbery.[2]

Two months later, on the night of October 14, 1887, Windy Smith was at the El Paso depot, aboard the Wells Fargo car on the eastbound Galveston, Harrisburg & San Antonio train. He was accompanied by J. R. Beardsley, a clerk in Wells Fargo's Fort Worth office. Beardsley was "deadheading" a free ride home. Each of them carried a revolver, and Smith kept a double-barreled shotgun inside the car. Windy also had a gift for his sweetheart in San Antonio: a basket of grapes. The train pulled out of El Paso at nine o'clock and proceeded about seven miles. Smith was busy sorting packages and filling out waybills when he heard a loud report and the train groaned to a halt. Thinking that a track torpedo had discharged as warning of an obstruction ahead, the messenger poked his neck outside the door. He spotted a man next to the tracks firing a revolver. "I blew out the lights," Smith said later, "and with Mr. Beardsley . . . retired to the back part of the car."

Unknown to the Wells Fargo man, Kid Smith and Dick Maier, wearing neckerchief masks, had climbed onto the coal tender as the train left the rail yard. A mile out, they dropped into the engine cab, covered the crew with six-guns, and ordered the engineer to stop at a crossing now called Alfafa, midway between El Paso and Ysleta. After forcing the trainmen to walk back to the express car, they opened fire on it with their

Jack "Kid" Smith, *left*, and John "Dick" Maier, slain by Wells Fargo messenger J. Ernest Smith in a train holdup near El Paso in 1887. Both are wearing cheap undertaker's suits. [*Author's collection*]

pistols, plugging half a dozen bullets into the car's walls. The outlaws did not bother ordering Smith to surrender. Instead, they placed a dynamite bomb under the car door and lit the fuse. A huge explosion tore a hole in the front door and shattered the glass windows in both side doors.

As Smith related later, "I told Beardsley we had better get out. So he got out first with his gun on his person. As I dropped down I left my gun in the middle of the door on the floor. My intention was to hit the robber as I landed with my fist and knock him down and then grab my six-shooter, but Beardsley was rather between us and I couldn't reach him. The robber then wanted to get in and strike a light and I volunteered my services and got right back in the car."

As Maier kept his revolver on Beardsley, the messenger climbed up through the doorway. Kid Smith started to follow him. The Wells Fargo man reached across the floor and grabbed his Colt six-gun. Whirling around, he rammed the barrel into the outlaw's chest and exclaimed, "Die, damn you!"

He fired once and the bullet tore into Smith's heart. As the desperado fell, he fired his pistol twice, narrowly missing the expressman, then hit the ground dead. At that, Dick Maier took a quick shot at Messenger Smith, and the bullet passed inches from his head. "I fired back and came near hitting the engineer," recalled Smith. He grabbed his double-barreled shotgun and peered out the car door. Maier was dragging his dead partner toward the engine, hoping to escape in the locomotive, as they had done in the first robbery. When Maier ordered the fireman to hoist Kid Smith into the engine cab, the trainman told him, "He's hurt pretty bad."

All the while, Windy Smith was leaning out the door, sighting down the barrels of his shotgun. "I had been trying to get a shot at the second robber," he said later, "but was prevented on account of the fireman being so near. I noticed the fireman step aside a few feet and my opportunity had arrived." He fired a blast and all the buckshot missed, except one. That lone shot ripped through Dick Maier's left shoulder, ranged downward, and severed the aorta just above the heart. The bandit doubled over and staggered off down the tracks before vanishing in the blackness.[3]

The engineer backed his train into El Paso, with the body of Kid Smith still in the cab. At daybreak, officers rushed to the scene, where they found the body of Dick Maier in the brush, fifty yards from where he had been shot. The dead robbers were photographed and their corpses displayed in an El Paso undertaker's parlor. They were soon identified. Messenger Smith's exploit created a sensation and was featured prominently in newspapers throughout the country. In El Paso, he was presented with a new suit of clothes and a $150 diamond-encrusted gold medal inscribed "Citizens of El Paso, Texas, as a slight memorial of their appreciation of your heroic work on the night of October 14, 1887." The front of the Wells Fargo office in San Antonio was draped with American flags and a portrait of Smith displayed in the window, surrounded by the words "Our Hero." The Southern Pacific Railroad Company, which owned the Galveston, Harrisburg & San Antonio, presented him with two thousand dollars. Wells Fargo gave him two thousand dollars, the state of Texas chipped in another two thousand, El Paso County, four hundred, and the federal government four hundred. These rewards, totaling $6,800, made Smith financially comfortable. He proposed to his sweetheart, Ella Murray, and used some of the money to buy a house in San Antonio. No doubt he considered Ella the biggest prize of all, and six weeks later, on December 5, they were married.[4]

Windy Smith returned to his duties on the San Antonio–El Paso run, and saw no excitement for almost four years. Then, in the morning darkness of September 2, 1891, he was aboard a westbound Galveston, Harrisburg & San Antonio train as it crawled up the steep Horseshoe Cut, a mile east of Samuels Siding (now called Pumpville). This was an extremely isolated spot, 360 miles east of El Paso, at the edge of the Big Bend region. It was 4:00 A.M. when the locomotive's headlight revealed a large pile of rocks on the tracks ahead. The engineer quickly set his air brakes and reversed the engine as it screeched to a halt just in time to avoid a wreck. Four rifle-wielding desperadoes on top of the trackside earth embankments covered the train crew. Windy Smith recalled, "The train stopped suddenly and a masked man appeared on each side of the engine with leveled Winchesters and compelled the engineer and his fireman to get down and walk back to the passenger coach. In the meantime a man appeared on each side of my express coach and two had already taken charge of the passenger coaches. I quickly barred my doors. The robbers made the fireman come back and try to open my door. My idea was to watch and get a shot at them, but they were no novices and remained under the side of my car."

Jack Wellington, leader of the bandits in the Samuels Siding train robbery of 1891. [*Author's collection*]

The brakeman knocked on one door and called to Smith, "Don't come out. They will kill you."

The bandits forced the fireman to break the window in the side door and reach in to unlatch it. When his effort failed, the fireman begged Smith to throw out the keys, saying the robbers were going to kill him. The doughty messenger ignored the plea. "I was ordered to come out," recalled Smith, "but refused and heard the captain of the gang give orders to shoot into my car, and immediately they proceeded to pump lead into my apartments. I started across the car to get behind my safe."

At that, the bandit chief yelled, "Open up and come out of there or I will blow the damned car up!"

"Go to hell," was Smith's simple reply. He said later, "I heard them striking matches and presently a dynamite cartridge thrown at my car exploded so near that I was thrown off my feet."

The outlaw leader called out, "You'd better come out of there, because we've got a whole jackass load of dynamite and if you don't we'll blow you to hell and gone."

Explained Smith, "Finally I heard them climbing up on the car to send off more dynamite cartridges, and seeing that there was no sense in resisting or holding out any longer I called to the captain and asked him what assurance he could give me that the shooting would cease and I not be shot if I come out. 'My word is your assurance,' said he. I told him his word did not amount to much but that I would have to take it. So the shooting was stopped and I opened the door and jumped out."

The bandits, all wearing flour-sack masks, covered Smith with their rifles. "Two of them then placed their guns to my head," he said later, "and I was marched to where the engineer and fireman were by the engine, and they made the engineer hand me his torch and marched me back to my car. As I was returning they said, 'If there is anyone in that car we will kill you.' I replied, 'In that case I shall live a long time.' So I stood near the door in the center of the car holding the torch for them. Two stood on each side of me, pointing their Winchesters at my temples."

Then the robber chief ordered Smith to open the through safe, which was locked by the agent in San Antonio and not opened again until the train reached the agent in El Paso. By Wells Fargo regulations, the messenger was not allowed to know the combination to the through safe. Smith told the outlaws, "You must really excuse me, but I have not got the combination."

"You will have to open the safe or die," one responded.

"I am sorry, but I cannot."

The desperado made one last command: "Open that safe!"

Smith recalled, "I went to the safe and made three attempts before the combination would work. When she opened up they proceeded to help themselves leisurely to all they wanted." The bandit leader spotted Windy's shotgun and asked, "Is that your gun?"

"Yes," Smith replied. "That is the gun the company furnishes us."

"You will never be able to shoot any train robber with it," the outlaw snapped. He slammed the shotgun against the safe so hard, the barrels bent, rendering it useless. Recalled Smith, "They asked the fireman who I was and he said I was a stranger to him and when the mail clerk was asked he gave them a different name, because he thought that they would have killed me if they had known I was the same messenger who had killed the Ysleta robbers."

They relieved Smith of his Colt revolver and seven dollars but then returned the cash, saying they "did not want a working man's money." When the robbers were done with the express car, they entered the mail coach and looted it. Then the bandit chief said to Smith, "You are a damn plucky fellow and if I had a bottle we would drink, but it is too dry out here for even water. We will treat you boys, though, the first time we catch you in San Antonio."[5]

The train had been stopped for two hours when the bandits mounted their horses and rode south toward the Rio Grande, twelve miles distant. Newspapers claimed they had escaped with more than $10,000, but according to Wells Fargo detective Fred Dodge, their haul was $3,600. Windy Smith returned to San Antonio on the morning of September 3. He met with Andrew Christeson, the thirty-year-old

Tom Fields, one of the train robbers who held up J. Ernest Smith in 1891. He was captured by Texas Rangers. [*Author's collection*]

Wells Fargo superintendent for the state of Texas, and made his report about the robbery. Then Smith handed in his resignation, explaining that the work was too dangerous for a married man. Years later, however, an unnamed expressman in El Paso declared that Smith "had no business knowing the combination" to the through safe and "resigned because he knew he had done wrong." Christeson—an office man who had never come within a country mile of an armed robber— nonetheless issued a press report saying that Smith was "so chagrined by his temporary loss of nerve that upon reaching San Antonio he resigned."

Smith was furious at Christeson's statement. He told a reporter, "This is the second time I have been blown up, but the first time I have been robbed. I am tired of it, and since the superintendent has impugned my bravery and since the sum that was paid me for risking my life is so pitiful, I have handed in my resignation." He then published a "card," which ran in all the leading dailies of Texas, and even in the *New York Times*: "As many of my friends wish me to make a statement refuting the charges of cowardice, etc., made by Mr. Christeson, I will say that if he had been there he would have done no better. If anyone thinks I have lost my nerve or showed any timidity, let him ask [the train crew]. I do not claim to be the bravest man in the world, but my former action in a matter of this kind near El Paso, Texas, on which account a fine gold medal was presented me by the citizens of El Paso, is sufficient proof that I am no coward. I do not know whether the article of Mr. Christeson was intended to injure or not, but it seems in no friendly spirit. I had no opportunity to defend myself or would have done so, and all my friends say I did the best thing I could." Christeson's unwarranted criticism had made Windy Smith bitter. He announced that he was "done with the Wells Fargo service, and will have no more of it." It was an unfortunate end to the career of one of the bravest of all express messengers.[6]

Meanwhile, Texas Rangers were busy tracking the train robbers. On October 16, after a long but intermittent manhunt, a posse of Rangers and other officers caught up with them on Live Oak Creek in Crockett

County, about fifty miles due north of the holdup site. The fugitives turned out to be four cowboys: Jack Wellington, John Flynt, Jim Lansford, and Tom Fields. Lansford immediately—and wisely—surrendered, but Wellington, Flynt, and Fields fled on horseback. In a running gunfight, a hundred shots were exchanged. Flynt, wounded in the chest and trapped in an arroyo, wrote out his last will, then put a bullet into his own head. The posse shot Wellington's horse out from under him. He traded gunfire with Capt. Frank Jones before electing to give up. Fields, after his horse was lathered out, also surrendered. A portion of the loot was recovered from the outlaws, along with Wells Fargo money bags. In Wellington's saddlebags Captain Jones found Windy Smith's pistol. The bandit had filed off the serial number, but Smith soon identified it in court. It developed that Wellington was the band's leader and apparently was the robber who had done most of the talking during the holdup. "He is evidently from a good family and is a young man of education," said Captain Jones. "He is a good talker and the coolest-headed young fellow I ever saw." Lansford turned state's evidence and testified against his fellow bandits. He went free, while Jack Wellington and Tom Fields were convicted of mail robbery and sentenced to ten years each in federal prison.[7]

For Windy Smith, there was no shortage of jobs less risky than tangling with train robbers. He got work as a clerk in the post office in San Antonio, a position he held for years. In 1907, he was appointed a deputy collector of customs on the border at Eagle Pass, Texas, but within a few years he transferred to San Antonio, where he served out the rest of his career as a customs officer. J. Ernest Smith died at his home in San Antonio on April 15, 1935, age eighty-two. His hometown newspapers offered very brief obituaries and said nothing about his perilous exploits as a Wells Fargo shotgun messenger. That is exactly how he would have wanted it.[8]

18

SHOTGUNS AND DYNAMITE

Charles F. Charles

Charlie Charles had one of the most memorable careers of any Wells Fargo messenger of the railroad era. He came from fighting stock. His grandfather was Jesse Robinson, pioneer undersheriff of Yuba County, in California's Northern Mines. He was related by marriage to Gold Rush sheriff Mike Gray of Marysville, who later achieved notoriety in Tombstone, Arizona, due to his connections with Curly Bill Brocius and the Cowboys. Charlie's father, Harry A. Charles, was a veteran expressman, having been the agent of the Pacific Express Company in Marysville in the 1850s, then secretary of the California Stage Company in the 1860s. Harry Charles moved his family to San Francisco, where he prospered as a stockbroker. There his son Charles Frank Charles was born on February 16, 1870, the youngest of nine children. The family was well-off until 1878, when the elder Charles was cheated by a business partner and forced to file bankruptcy. His daughter Fannie, who became a popular novelist, wrote a thinly disguised memoir, *Siftings from Poverty Flat*, in which she traced her family's fall from wealth. She recalled how one brother was often in trouble and arrested by the San Francisco police, while Charlie—whom she calls "Chip" in the book—went to work for Wells Fargo as an express messenger.

When Harry Charles died in 1884, he left his family in even more dire straits. The next year Charlie, age fifteen, started with Wells Fargo as a porter in San Francisco. He grew into a tall, slender, and dark-complected young man. Fannie wrote that Charlie was the most handsome of her brothers and "earns his money from Fargo's and more than spends it." In 1891, he was promoted to the position of messenger's helper. His duties were to assist the regular messenger in sorting, delivering, and protecting express packages on the railroad trains between San Francisco and Los Angeles.[1]

While the young expressman was learning Wells Fargo business, train robbers Chris Evans and John Sontag were doing their best to disrupt it. Chris Evans had been a respectable forty-four-year-old farmer who lived with his wife and seven children near Visalia. Like many in the San Joaquin Valley, he despised the Southern Pacific Railroad, which was widely accused of land grabbing, charging exorbitant rates, and controlling state politics. Evans's best friend and hired man was thirty-two-year-old John Sontag, a former Southern Pacific

Charles F. Charles, Wells Fargo's heroic messenger. [*Author's collection*]

brakeman. He had been injured on a train and received inadequate treatment from railroad physicians, igniting an intense hatred of the SP. Though both men were hardworking and neither had a criminal background, they decided to make a big haul by robbing a train. But their rationale was faulty, for the express cars were operated by Wells Fargo, not the Southern Pacific.

On the evening of February 22, 1889, Evans and Sontag held up an SP train in Tulare County. After blowing up the Wells Fargo car with dynamite, they shot dead a train crewman and wounded a deputy sheriff, then fled with the strongbox. The robbery made front-page newspaper headlines. It also set off a determined manhunt, which failed because the bandits simply returned that night to the Evans farm and resumed their quiet lives. Eleven months later, Evans and Sontag struck again. On the night of January 20, 1890, they stopped another SP train near Goshen Junction, nine miles west of Visalia. They compelled Wells Fargo's messenger to turn over the express box, then shot to death a hobo who attempted to flee. The two disappeared, and lawmen would not learn the identities of the robbers for almost two years.

On September 3, 1891, Evans and Sontag struck for the third time. At three o'clock that afternoon, the Los Angeles Express departed the Southern Pacific station in San Francisco. Inside the Wells Fargo car were messenger Wallace Reed and his twenty-one-year-old helper, Charlie Charles. It was a day neither of them would ever forget. The coaches happened to carry two notable passengers. One was Southern Pacific detective Len Harris, a veteran lawman with thirty-five years of experience in California and Arizona. The other was Alfred B. Lawson, a well-known private detective who had received his early training under Harry Morse.

At 8:00 P.M., the train passed through Modesto, proceeded four miles, then stopped at Ceres to let off passengers. Unseen by the crew, two shadowy figures—Evans and Sontag—slipped aboard. They climbed over the coal tender, dropped down into the engine cab, and covered engineer Andy Neff and his fireman with guns. After giving

California's notorious train robber Chris Evans, holding his wounded arm after he was captured in 1892. [*Author's collection*]

the order to stop, they had Neff put out the headlight, then forced the crewmen to grab coal picks and walk back to the express car. As they did so, several tramps jumped down from the baggage car and fled. Sontag opened fire on them but missed.

Messenger Reed later recalled, "When the train stopped I did not think much of it, until I heard some shots. I instantly surmised that it was a case of train robbery. . . . I immediately put out my lights, while Charlie Charles, my helper, got the guns all ready for a fight. In a few moments the engineer and fireman knocked at the door of the car. They said they were in the hands of the robbers, and begged us not to shoot, but to open the door or they would be killed. We kept perfectly quiet."

Engineer Neff then called out, "If you don't open the door, these fellows say they will blow you to pieces."

Reed and Charles clutched their shotguns and stayed deathly still. They crouched on the floor, behind a barricade of freight boxes. One of the robbers affixed a dynamite bomb to the door at one end of the car and lit the fuse. A deafening explosion ripped through the express car, blowing a massive hole in the right-side door. Fortunately for the two Wells Fargo men, they were at the opposite end of the car and were not hit by the flying debris. Now the messengers spotted a head in the shattered door and raised their guns to fire. But the man called out, "Don't shoot, for God's sake!"

They saw that it was the fireman. "These fellows are pushing me in, I can't help myself," he cried.

Reed ordered, "Don't come in any further!"

At that, one of the bandits passed a candle in to the fireman and ordered him to light it. But his hands were shaking so badly, he could not light a match, so the robber took the candle, lit it, and handed it back, saying, "Light the lamps." The fireman did not comply, Reed explained later: "I warned him not to come further, or I would fire at him, and he thought he would be safer with the robbers than with me for he backed out."

The explosion caused pandemonium in the coaches. As one passenger related, "When the bomb went off it was a sight to see the passengers crawl under the seats, and hide their money in all sorts of places. Some of the women screamed, but most of them were braver than the men, and a few of them went right out on the platform to see the row." The conductor and several passengers jumped down from the coaches. As they approached the express car, one of the robbers barked, "Get back there, you sons of bitches, or we will blow you to pieces."

The conductor yanked a small pistol and fired two shots at the outlaws, then scrambled back into the coach. He sought out Detective Len Harris and told him the train was being robbed. Harris, armed with a .32 Smith & Wesson revolver, slipped out of the coach, climbed over a trackside fence, and crawled back toward the Wells Fargo car. Detective Lawson, who was unarmed, borrowed a revolver from a passenger and fired several shots at the bandits. He then ran back along the tracks to Ceres to give the alarm.

Meanwhile, Evans and Sontag readied a second dynamite charge. Said Reed, "In a few minutes they threw another bomb in the hole made by the first, and it rolled along the floor sizzling nastily, and I thought my time had come, but it took a turn and rolled out of the hole down on the ground, where it exploded without doing any harm." Moments later, Reed and Charles spotted one of the robbers trying to climb through the hole in the splintered door. Reed unloosed a blast from his shotgun but missed and the outlaw scrambled to safety.

By this time, Detective Harris had crawled to a point just opposite the express car. He took aim and fired four shots but hit no one. John Sontag stepped forward, raised his rifle, and aimed at the muzzle flashes. Harris was about to squeeze off a fifth round when Sontag fired. The bullet tore into the right side of Harris's neck, paralyzing his right arm. He dropped his pistol, crumpled to the ground, and moments later blacked out. By now, Evans and Sontag realized that the two Wells Fargo messengers would never surrender. They marched Neff and the fireman to a nearby spot, where two saddle horses were tethered. Releasing the crewmen, they swung onto their mounts and escaped into the blackness.

Explained messenger Reed, "The engineer then came along with a lantern and asked us if we were all right. I answered him but would not let him in, because I thought he might still be in the hands of the robbers. A few moments later a number of the passengers brought Harris along in a stretcher, and I then opened the car and took him in. At the next station we took on a doctor, who said he was seriously hurt." Len Harris managed to recover and resume his detective duties, but three years later he was slain in a gun battle with a bandit. Evans and Sontag robbed three more trains and were finally captured after one of the Old West's biggest and bloodiest manhunts. John Sontag died of gunshot wounds inflicted by lawmen, and Chris Evans received a life term in prison.[2]

For their courage in the Ceres holdup, the two Wells Fargo men received high praise from the public and the press. Declared the *San Francisco Call*, "The conduct of Express Messenger Wallace Reed and his assistant, Charles, in refusing to open the doors of this car, is re-

John Sontag, train-robbing partner of Chris Evans. They were unable to best Charlie Charles. [*Author's collection*]

ceiving much favorable comment." The company rewarded each of them with a valuable gold pocket watch, inscribed "For resisting train robbers, September 3, 1891." It was Charlie's most prized possession, and he would carry it for the rest of his life. He was also promoted to messenger. For the next decade, he handled his duties capably and without conflict. Following a spate of train robberies in Arizona in 1894 and 1895, company officials sent him to the Southwest on guard duty. In 1899, he married Maggie Johnson in San Francisco. The same year, Wells Fargo assigned him to trains running out of Portland, Oregon, and he and Maggie moved there in 1900. That year, the couple had a daughter, Hazel. But before long, his abilities as a shotgun messenger would again be severely tested.[3]

Shortly past 2:00 A.M. on October 23, 1901, a California and Oregon express train on the Southern Pacific route pulled out of Cottage Grove, Oregon, headed north for Portland. The first car, behind the coal tender, was the mail coach, then the baggage car, followed by the Wells Fargo car, and finally the passenger coaches. Moments after the train had left the depot, a man wearing a long black mask dropped from the tender into the engine cab. He had a large six-gun in each fist and a Winchester rifle slung across his back. The bandit ordered engineer Burt Lucas and his fireman to throw up their hands. They obeyed. He demanded that the train stop, then ordered the fireman to jump off. The robber then forced engineer Lucas to continue on to a spot five miles north of Cottage Grove, just above Walker station, and to again halt the train. To prevent any passengers from interfering, the desperado raised his Winchester and sent half a dozen shots flying alongside the coaches. He then marched Lucas down to the baggage car, where he was joined by a second robber. Yelling profanities, one bandit demanded that the two baggage men open up. They did so promptly, and the outlaw entered the car and searched it for valuables. Finding none, he jumped down and fired more shots down the train.

Then he forced the engineer to walk in front of him to the next car, the Wells Fargo express. That was a mistake, for inside was Charlie Charles. He had doused the lights and readied his sawed-off shotgun. The bandit ordered Charlie to open up. Just as he had done at Ceres ten years before, the messenger made no response. Lucas yelled to Charles, asking him to hold his fire. Still there was no reply. The robber ripped out a string of oaths, according to the *Portland Oregonian*, "roaring that he had been there before and knew how to deal with blankety-blank messengers who would not respond to his demand." Still no response.

"Open up this car or we will blow you to hell!"

But it was no go. As Charlie explained later, "I made no reply, knowing that the object of the robbers was to locate me in the car and then try to put me out of the way, either with dynamite or bullets."

One of the outlaws produced a sack filled with sticks of dynamite. He handed Lucas a lit cigar, then placed a charge of ten dynamite sticks under the forward side door of the express car. He ordered Lucas to light the fuse, and then the two backed off a car length. A terrific explosion blew out the bottom of the door and the step below it. Charlie recalled that the blast "was so near me and so powerful that it ruined one leg of a pair of overalls, even tearing my trousers and bruising my flesh slightly. This explosion blew my feet from under me and threw me about a dozen feet diagonally across the car."

Again the cursing robber demanded that Charles give up, and again there was only silence. "I never [showed] my head while the robber was shouting for me to open the car and light up and the engineer was urging me not to shoot," said the messenger later. "I knew it might go hard with me if I revealed my exact position. I stood up in the car with my gun ready for action, waiting for an opening."

But the desperadoes were smart enough to stay out of the car. They ordered Lucas to place an even bigger charge of dynamite against the rear side door and to light the fuse. A massive blast completely shattered both the door and the small transom windows along the top of the car. It knocked Lucas to the ground, stunning him. The outlaw shouted and cursed at the engineer to get up. Then the bandits had him toss a stick of dynamite into the express car. This time, Charlie leaped forward, seized the dynamite, and yanked out the sizzling fuse.

Again the robbers yelled, "Come out of there or we will blow you and the car all to hell!"

But again they were met only with silence. They ordered Lucas to light a dynamite stick and throw it in the splintered door. The explosion tore a hole in the floor, but it did not harm the nervy messenger. Again and again sticks of dynamite were thrown into the express car. Charles never once thought of giving up. "All told," he later said, "four sticks of dynamite went off in the car; two failed to explode, and one I prevented exploding by removing the fuse."

At this point, it seemed impossible that anyone could still be alive inside the express car. One bandit ordered the engineer to crawl through the shattered rear door. Lucas called out to Charles that he was coming in. The messenger waited until Lucas got inside the door. Just behind him, on the broken step, was one of the bandits, his guns ready. Lucas spotted the second robber standing behind, on the track bed, but he wasn't sure whether he was a robber or a railroad hand. He raised his shotgun and fired a blast over their heads. The two outlaws leaped for cover.

"Come out of there," one robber yelled to the engineer. "I guess we'll quit this car. To hell with that goddamned expressman. I'd wreck this train if I thought I could kill him."

The outlaws had spent forty minutes trying to enter the Wells Fargo car. Now one bandit marched Lucas back to the mail car. He lit a match and looked at his pocket watch. "Damn it," he growled. "It's getting late. Cut off that mail car and we'll get out of here."

Lucas uncoupled the mail car from the rest of the train; then he and one bandit climbed into the cab. They headed north with just the tender and mail car, leaving the baggage car, the Wells Fargo car, and the passenger coaches behind. As they steamed through the blackness,

Newspaper feature showing Charlie Charles defending his Wells Fargo express car from train robbers near Cottage Grove, Oregon, in 1901. [*Author's collection*]

the desperado bitterly cursed the Wells Fargo messenger. Ten miles down the tracks, he ordered Lucas to stop. The desperado ransacked the mail car and took about three hundred dollars in cash from the registered-mail pouch. He then ordered Lucas to start up again. When they saw the lights of Eugene in the distance, the robber dropped off the cab, calling out, "Good night. You're all right. When they catch me, be easy on me." Then he vanished into the darkness.[4]

Local lawmen and Pinkerton detectives conducted a huge manhunt for the robbers. Though a number of suspects were arrested, the real bandits were never captured. Newspapermen interviewed Charles and asked him if it was true that he had held off train robbers ten years before. He politely declined to say anything about the Ceres train holdup, remarking that "it had nothing to do with this matter." Wells Fargo officials thought otherwise. They issued press releases praising the young messenger and detailing his heroism in both incidents. He was promoted and transferred back to San Francisco so that he could be close to his family. On Thanksgiving Day, company officials called him into San Francisco headquarters. There, before all the officers and directors of Wells Fargo, they presented him with a gold medal, a watch chain with a diamond fob, a check for one thousand dollars, and a letter of gratitude from John J. Valentine, who was then terminally ill and could not attend. The company was about to distribute silver medallions to its five-thousand-plus employees, commemorating Wells Fargo's fifty-year anniversary. Only one was struck in solid gold, and that was the medal presented to Charlie Charles. He thanked them all and said simply that he had only done his duty.[5]

The quiet messenger returned to his work on the Southern Pacific lines in Northern California. By this time, he had become a legendary figure among expressmen and railroaders, who said he was "famous as a man who never knew what fear was." His next six years were uneventful. Then on February 3, 1907, he was aboard the southbound Oregon Express, on the Southern Pacific line in the Sacramento Valley, headed for San Francisco. His messenger's helper was R. J. Smith. It was 6:00 A.M. and Charlie was asleep in his bunk in the Wells Fargo car, while Smith was dozing in a bunk in the baggage car. The train consisted of ten cars: the mail, baggage, express, smoker, chair car, sleeper, diner, two Pullman coaches, and the observation car, in that order.

As the train was two miles north of the water stop at Dunnigan, forty miles northwest of Sacramento, the engineer shut off the steam valve and slowed the train to twenty miles an hour. Suddenly, the locomotive struck a loose rail. The engine and the mail car somehow stayed on the tracks, but with a deafening roar the baggage car, express car, smoker, and chair car careened off the rails and slammed into a ditch. Fortunately for the other passengers, the Pullman coaches and observation car ground to a halt, still on the tracks. The baggage car rolled onto its side in the ditch and the Wells Fargo car flipped upside down. The impact slammed a trunk into helper Smith's head, knocking him unconscious. Passengers, most of them unhurt, scrambled out of the coaches. One dragged Smith from the baggage car, and two nurses worked to revive him. It was a full hour before he regained consciousness.

Charlie Charles was not so fortunate. He was crushed between the side and floor of the express car. Two passengers who escaped from a window in the smoking car heard his groans. They found him pinned under a heavy water tank. As they tried to pull him free, he died. Three hours later, when a relief crew arrived, they cut a hole in the side of the Wells Fargo car and brought his body out. A coroner's jury was assembled at the scene and found that he had been "crushed to death in the express car after it was thrown from the track by a broken rail."

At that time, the Southern Pacific Railroad Company was the most powerful corporation on the West Coast, wielding unparalleled economic and political power. Even though the accident was due to the railroad's obvious negligence in failing to inspect and maintain the tracks, the coroner's jury immediately exonerated it from any fault. The Southern Pacific was never held accountable for the death of one of the bravest men who ever rode the rails.[6]

When railroad workers removed Charlie Charles from the train, they found in his pocket the gold watch presented to him by Wells Fargo in 1891. He had treasured it to the very end.

19

"SEND A COFFIN AND A DOCTOR"

Jeff Milton

On July 30, 1898, the commanding officer at Fort Apache, Arizona Territory, received a handwritten message signed by Jeff Milton, a Wells Fargo special officer and deputy U.S. marshal. It read simply "Send a coffin and a doctor." This terse note marked the sanguinary end to one of Milton's many manhunts for border desperadoes.

Jeff Milton was one of the most noted lawmen of the Old West. For fifty years, he served as a peace officer, first as a Texas Ranger, then deputy sheriff, city marshal of El Paso, mounted customs inspector, and finally U.S. Immigration Service officer. Jeff was extremely handsome and a favorite with the señoritas. At the same time, he was a tough-as-nails border man. His encounters with such deadly gunmen as John Wesley Hardin, John Selman, Martin Mrose, Mannie Clements, "Bronco Bill" Walters, and "Three-Fingered Jack" Dunlap hold a prominent place in the lore of the Old West.

Especially noteworthy was his run-in with John Wesley Hardin, the king of Texas gunfighters, who boasted of killing forty-two men. In 1895, Milton, his good friend George Scarborough, and a third officer killed a wanted outlaw, Martin Mrose, in an El Paso shootout. Hardin, who had been having an affair with Mrose's wife, boasted around town that he had hired Milton to kill Mrose. Jeff, enraged at hearing the false charge, found the gunfighter in an El Paso saloon.

"Hardin," said Milton, "I hear you've been telling around town that you hired me to kill Martin Mrose."

"Well, what of it?" the man-killer replied, shrugging.

"I want you to tell these gentlemen here that when you said that you were a goddamned liar."

"Why, Captain Milton, I don't let any man talk to me that-a-way."

"I'm telling you that in fighting talk. If you don't like it, help yourself. But you are going to do it."

Hardin looked into Jeff's blazing eyes and wilted. He knew he had met his match. "Go on, Milton, I don't want to have any trouble with you. And besides, I am unarmed."

"That's a damn lie," Jeff snapped. "You never go out without your gun. Hardin, I mean what I say. You tell these gentlemen that you were a damn liar when you said you hired me to kill Martin Mrose, or I'm going to count three and when I get to three, you'd better start shooting, because I'm going for my gun."

"All right," the gunfighter answered glumly. "When I said I hired you to kill Martin Mrose, I was a goddamn liar."[1]

Stories of Jeff Milton's iron-fisted dealings with desperadoes are legion. However, what is often forgotten about his long career is that he served Wells Fargo as a shotgun messenger and special officer for five years, from 1895 to 1900, and established a reputation as one of the company's most courageous fighting men.

Jefferson Davis Milton was born into a prominent family in Marianna, Florida, on November 7, 1861. His family lost its fortune in the Civil War, and in 1877, at age sixteen, Jeff headed for Texas, seeking adventure. He enlisted in the Texas Rangers in 1880 and served for three years. In 1884, he drifted west into New Mexico, where he rode the ranges as a deputy sheriff and stock detective. Three years later, he was appointed a mounted U.S. customs inspector on the Arizona-Mexico border. From 1890 to 1894, he worked as a Pullman conductor on railroad lines in Mexico, and then was appointed chief of police of

Jeff Milton, Wells Fargo messenger and special officer, in 1895. [*Author's collection*]

El Paso, the toughest town in Texas. He held the post for eight months and lost it due to political turnover on May 1, 1895.[2]

Soon after, the Wells Fargo agent in El Paso asked Milton to put together a posse of guards to take a multimillion-dollar gold shipment by rail to San Francisco. Jeff refused to do it with anyone else. He told the agent that he "knew what he could do; he was not so sure about other men." Milton collected a few water jugs, a sack of food, and his bedroll, then boarded the express car, armed with a six-gun, a rifle, and a Burgess folding shotgun. He didn't leave the coach until he had safely delivered the gold in San Francisco. After that, Wells Fargo officials offered him a position in Mexico City. Jeff entrained for the Mexican capital but discovered that the job did not pay enough. He turned it down but soon hired on as a Wells Fargo messenger on the railroad between Nogales, Arizona, and the port of Guaymas, Mexico.[3]

Nogales, situated on the border with Mexico, was then home to about fifteen hundred people. The railroad had arrived in 1882 and the town became an important entry point. Milton liked Nogales and made it his home. He spent most of his service with Wells Fargo doing the humdrum work of a messenger: transporting everything from crates of Mexican fruit to bars of silver and gold bullion. Yet even that work could be dangerous to life and limb. Once, he stacked silver bricks, weighing from 50 to 250 pounds each, along the back wall of the express car. He was sleeping on his cot in front of the bars when the train careened off the track into a ditch. The upper bars flew harmlessly over him and crashed through the floor of the coach. "Never touched me," he recalled years later. "Lucky, wa'n't it? But after that I stacked them in the front of the car."[4]

Due to his manhunting experience, Wells Fargo officials called on him from time to time to serve as a special officer. At that time, a new bandit gang, the High Fives, had started raiding in New Mexico and Arizona. Led by William "Black Jack" Christian, it was named after a popular card game. On August 6, 1896, the High Fives held up the International Bank in Nogales. A huge manhunt ensued, and Jeff joined a posse led by deputy U.S. marshal Al Ezekiels, one of several that were hunting the bandits. They trailed part of the gang into Mexico but lost them. Riding back across the border, Milton spotted three of the outlaws in Mulberry Wash, in the San Simon Valley, in southeastern Arizona. "We saw those fellows and we saw them coming out of the mulberry pasture," he recalled.

"Damned if it ain't them," Milton exclaimed to the rest of the posse.

Ezekiels replied, "We'll run them out of the country."

"That is what we want to do," declared Jeff. But Ezekiels lost his nerve and refused to pursue them. Jeff was incensed, saying later of Ezekiels, "But he just quit."

The following morning, Milton, with three of the posse, boarded a train for Tucson to get fresh horses. One of the other possemen was Billy Stiles, an honest cowboy and tracker who was destined to become one of Arizona's noted outlaws. They became friends, something Jeff would later regret. Milton got the spare horses for the posse, but he was unable to capture the High Five gang. As he recalled, only half joking, "I never run on to Black Jack and I'm glad I didn't. I might have got hurt."[5]

On November 20, 1897, Jeff was aboard the Wells Fargo car of a Sonora Railway passenger train in Mexico, northbound from Guaymas to Nogales. Several hours ahead of them was a northbound freight train. That evening, the freight train reached Agua Zarca, eleven miles south of Nogales. On an upgrade, the brakeman cut two boxcars loaded with Mexican oranges from the train and used gravity to roll them back toward a sidetrack. They quickly picked up speed and the brakes would not slow them. The conductor, spotting the brakeman frantically turning the brake wheel, leaped onto one of the boxcars to help. But the brake chains snapped and the two cars careened down the grade at forty miles an hour. For twenty miles, the brakeman and conductor tried to slow or stop the cars, but finally they leaped off and were badly bruised as they landed on the railbed.

In the meantime, Milton's train was steaming north into Imuris, forty miles below Nogales. It was dark, and after stopping at the Imuris depot, the train proceeded another four miles. Suddenly, the engine's lamp revealed the two boxcars racing toward them. The engineer set his air brakes, but it was too late. A massive head-on collision flattened the two boxcars and demolished the locomotive, which careened fifteen feet off the track. The engineer was instantly killed and his fireman badly cut and burned from escaping steam. The glass in every window and lamp on the train shattered. The impact hurled Jeff from one end of his express car to the other, and a wooden beer keg crashed down on him, slamming into his back. A rescue train arrived and he was taken to Nogales with cuts on his face and head and a painful injury to his spine. His life had been saved by a peculiar happenstance: For some reason, a boxcar loaded with oranges had been coupled in front of the express car and had absorbed much of the impact.[6]

Meanwhile, Black Jack Christian had been slain in a gunfight with Arizona lawmen on April 28, 1897, but that did not put an end to his High Five gang. On the night of November 6, 1897, four of the band held up a Santa Fe train near Grant's Station, New Mexico. Wells Fargo messenger Charles C. Lord opened fire and briefly stood them off. But the outlaws uncoupled the express car and forced the engineer to run it down the tracks. Before they dynamited the coach, Lord managed to escape. The bandits looted the car of a hundred pounds worth of gold coins, valued at about thirty thousand dollars, and fled. Creighton Foraker, U.S. marshal of New Mexico, William Griffith, U.S. marshal of Arizona, and Wells Fargo detective John Thacker began organizing posses to track down the robbers.[7]

Within two weeks after the Mexico train wreck, Jeff Milton had recovered from his back injury. Now Thacker wired him in Nogales, asking him to join the manhunt for the High Fives. On December 6, 1897, Milton was commissioned a deputy U.S. marshal, and the next day he left Nogales with two comrades. Their wages and expenses were paid by Wells Fargo. Jeff told friends that they were going "on a prospecting trip to Sonora." Instead, the trio quietly boarded a train for Bowie Station on the Southern Pacific Railroad, twenty miles from the New Mexico line. There they met with sixteen other officers, including Thacker, Marshals Foraker and Griffith, and Milton's best friend, George Scarborough, one of the deadliest and most capable manhunters in the Southwest. On December 9, they procured saddle horses and pack mules and rode eight miles east into the San Simon Valley, where at dusk they made camp. By an extraordinary coincidence, that very night and just a few miles away at Stein's Pass, New Mexico, the gang led by Thomas "Black Jack" Ketchum held up a Southern Pacific train. Three Wells Fargo guards held off the desperadoes and killed gang member Ed Cullen. The rest of the outlaws—Black Jack Ketchum, his brother Sam, Dave Atkins, Leonard Alverson, Walter Hovey, and Bill Warderman—fled south on horseback.[8]

Milton, Scarborough, and about half the posse gathered around their campfire near the railroad tracks while the rest of the lawmen were scouting to the south in the San Simon Valley. Suddenly, a locomotive pulling a lone boxcar steamed in from Bowie Station, the engineer frantically blowing his whistle to alert the lawmen. The rail crew told Jeff they had received a telegraph message that a train had just been robbed at Stein's Pass. The officers nailed together a ramp out of boards and loaded their animals onto the boxcar. The engineer took

George Scarborough, the famous Southwestern lawman who was Jeff Milton's best friend. [*Author's collection*]

them to the Stein's depot just two hours after the holdup. Milton and the rest learned that a gang of six or seven desperadoes had taken part in the attack. Ed Cullen's corpse had been carried from the tracks. Later that night, the rest of the posse rode in from Arizona. At daybreak, Marshals Foraker and Griffith took Ed Cullen's body to Lordsburg, leaving the manhunt in the capable hands of Milton and Scarborough.

The bandits had fled south toward the San Simon Cienega, a stream that ran near the Arizona–New Mexico line. Milton, Scarborough, and their possemen followed the outlaws' tracks to the Cienega ranch, headquarters of the San Simon Cattle Co. Three cowboys were there, and some of the posse wanted to arrest them as suspects. George Scarborough knew the trio and vouched for their honesty. Milton thought that the bandits might have escaped into the Chiricahua Mountains, or across the Mexican border just south. The Chiricahuas, about thirty-five miles long, run north and south, with the San Simon Valley on the east side and the Sulphur Springs Valley on the west. Jeff Milton led half the posse south along the western flank of the Chiricahua Mountains. Scarborough and the rest rode to the east side of the Chiricahuas. Their plan was to circle the Chiricahuas and try to trap the outlaws before they could cross the border into Mexico.

From the Cienega ranch, Milton trailed the robbers south along the western flank of the Chiricahua Mountains, where his men found two saddle horses abandoned by the gang. After two days of riding, the posses met at the southern tip of the Chiricahuas. On the morning of December 12, they trailed the outlaws into nearby Tex Canyon, and then to a ranch owned by a hard case named John Vinnedge, alias John Cush. Vinnedge was not there, but Leonard Alverson, Walter Hovey, and Bill Warderman were. Hovey had a fresh bullet wound in his leg. Inside the ranch house were sticks of dynamite, fuses, and ammunition. The lawmen arrested all three, plus two cowboys, Tom Capehart and Henry Marshall, whom they held for harboring the gang. While several officers took the prisoners to the railroad and on to jail in Tucson, Milton and Scarborough led the rest of the posse after the Ketchum brothers and Dave Atkins. They followed the tracks to a canyon near the crest of the Chiricahuas, where several possemen began to get cold feet.

"Mr. Milton, I've got a wife and children, and I can't afford to go," said one. Several others chimed in. Exclaimed another posseman, "Milt, I'm married too, and I'd hate to get killed."

Scarborough was disgusted. "Milt, you know I'm married and got a wife and a lot of children, and damned if they can't take care of themselves. Let's me and you go."

The two started up the canyon and soon found the camp of the outlaws, but it had been abandoned for several days. From there, Milton and Scarborough led their posse south into Mexico, where they met with Col. Emilio Kosterlitzky, the famous Russian-born chief of the famed Rurales, or rural police. But even with help of the Rurales, they could not locate the Ketchum gang. After spending five weeks in the saddle during the entire holiday season, they gave up the hunt. Jeff returned to Nogales by rail from Mexico on January 8, 1898, and resumed his duties as a Wells Fargo messenger.[9]

Two weeks later, however, Milton again joined up with Scarborough and returned to the Chiricahuas in search of John Vinnedge, alias Cush, who had harbored the gang. As they rode toward Tex Canyon, Scarborough remarked, "Wells Fargo won't mind, so let's just kill old Cush."

"We can't kill him in cold blood," Milton retorted.

"We'd get rid of a good nuisance," insisted Scarborough.

They continued on to the ranch house, but Vinnedge was not there. Leaving Scarborough to watch the house, Jeff rode off to scout the nearby pasture. He soon encountered Vinnedge and a cowboy, both heavily armed. Vinnedge did not know Milton, and greeted him suspiciously. As they rode along, he began to curse Milton and said he "didn't need him there." Jeff was riding a high-strung horse, and when he tried to pull his Winchester from its scabbard the animal began bucking and threw him off. Milton later recalled that his rifle was in his hands when he hit the ground. "I was looking down the sights, right between old Cush's eyes. And I took him right there. But we let the other fellow go, as we had nothing against him."

Vinnedge later said, "Milton came there to kill me. I could see it in his eyes. I never saw such eyes." But Jeff did not kill him. He and Scarborough took their prisoner into Tucson by rail on the morning of January 29, 1898. Vinnedge was arraigned the same day in federal court. He was sent to New Mexico to face charges as an accessory in the Stein's Pass train holdup.[10]

A New Mexico jury acquitted John Vinnedge, Tom Capehart, and Henry Marshall. Leonard Alverson, Walter Hovey, and Bill Warderman were charged with committing the attempted robbery. At trial, members of the train crew identified them. They were convicted and sentenced to ten years each in the territorial prison. With credits for time served in county jail and for good behavior, the three were eligible for release in 1905. Instead, they were pardoned a year early, a common circumstance in that era. Black Jack Ketchum was captured and hanged for another train robbery in 1901. Just before his execution, Ketchum confessed to the Stein's Pass holdup and declared that the other robbers were his brother Sam, Ed Cullen, Dave Atkins, Bronco Bill Walters, and Will Carver. But Black Jack conveniently pinned the holdup on three outlaws who were then dead and another in prison for life. Ketchum, contemptuous of authority to the end, saw little harm in blaming men who could not be punished so as to help release his friends from prison.

Years later, Alverson and Hovey wrote reminiscences claiming that they had been framed by Milton and Scarborough. Based on Ketchum's "confession," the pardons, and the claims of Alverson and Hovey, several modern writers have concluded that the three young cowboys were innocent of the Stein's Pass holdup. However, at their trial it was shown that the trio had been with Ed Cullen just before the crime, they had been tracked from the holdup site, Hovey had a fresh gunshot wound, and they were all identified by the train crew. The evidence of their guilt remains persuasive.[11]

After the manhunt, Jeff Milton returned to Nogales and his messenger's job on the railroad, but he wasn't there long. By this time, three separate outlaw bands were raiding Arizona and New Mexico: the High Five gang, the bunch led by Black Jack Ketchum, and a new gang headed by Bronco Bill. The latter's true name was William Walters; he claimed to have been born in Fort Sill, Indian Territory, in October 1869. Walters had worked as a cowboy in Arizona and New Mexico, but in 1891, he landed in the New Mexico Territorial Penitentiary on a one-year term for shooting up the rail town of Separ. On his release, Bronco Bill punched cattle until 1896, when he was jailed in Socorro for robbery. He soon broke out but was recaptured and served a short jail term.

Bronco Bill hit the big time shortly after midnight on March 29, 1898, when he, Daniel "Red" Pipkin, William "Kid" Johnson, and Ed Colter emulated the High Five gang by holding up a Santa Fe train at Grant's Station, New Mexico. Once again, the Wells Fargo messenger was Charles C. Lord, and this time he was assisted by a special guard,

Charles Fowler. The two Wells Fargo men exchanged gunfire with the bandits and Fowler wounded Colter in the arm.

"I'm shot!" the outlaw yelled. "Get me away from here. We can't finish this job tonight."

The desperadoes picked up their injured comrade and fled on horseback southwest toward Arizona, with New Mexico lawmen in pursuit. Wells Fargo's John Thacker learned that Bronco Bill's gang, on their way from their hideout in eastern Arizona to the train holdup, had stolen horses from the Double Circle ranch on Eagle Creek. The Double Circle was one of the biggest ranches in Arizona. Thacker suspected that the bandits would return to the Eagle Creek country. On April 4, six days after the holdup, Jeff Milton, John Thacker, and five other manhunters arrived by train in Geronimo, Arizona, about fifty miles west of the Double Circle ranch headquarters. They unloaded their horses from a boxcar. Then Thacker sent Milton and the rest to the Double Circle to try to intercept the outlaws. Although the New Mexico lawmen had tracked the robbers into eastern Arizona, about one hundred miles north, the two posses could not find them. Ed Col-

William "Bronco Bill" Walters, one of the Southwest's most notorious train robbers. [*Author's collection*]

ter, harbored by his family, recovered from his wounds and was never captured. Bronco Bill and the rest of his gang vanished. Wells Fargo offered a five-hundred-dollar reward for each of them.[12]

A few weeks later, on May 24, Bronco Bill, Kid Johnson, and Red Pipkin held up another train near Belen, New Mexico, forty miles south of Albuquerque. They blew open the Wells Fargo safe and escaped. Bronco Bill later boasted that they made off with twenty thousand dollars. The next day, Valencia County deputy sheriffs Frank Vigil and Dan Bustamante, with several Navajo trackers, caught up with the gang. In a running gunfight, the outlaws killed both deputies and an Indian trailer. Though Bronco Bill and Kid Johnson were both wounded, a huge manhunt failed to unearth the desperadoes. Bronco Bill and his saddle partners fled back to the Double Circle ranch on Eagle Creek. Even though they had stolen horses from the ranch, its wrangler liked them and nursed the two wounded outlaws back to health. After a month, Bronco Bill and Kid Johnson had recovered enough to attend a Fourth of July dance at a schoolhouse in Geronimo, Arizona. Bronco Bill was drunk, and when several girls refused to dance with him, he drew his pistols and shot up the place.[13]

By this time, Jeff Milton was already back in the saddle, hunting the gang. In June, he had gone to Tucson and made arrangements with John Thacker and Southern Pacific officials to provide money, supplies, and a special train to transport his posse and horses. Jeff then wired George Scarborough to meet him in Tucson. The pair, acting as Wells Fargo special officers and deputy U.S. marshals, slipped out of town at night by rail, their horses in a boxcar, and unloaded in Albuquerque. They were in Albuquerque about July 10, when the Wells Fargo agent received a telegram that Bronco Bill had shot up the dance in Geronimo on the Fourth. The agent promptly notified Milton. John Thacker again thought that the bandits would return to the Double Circle ranch on Eagle Creek. Thacker engaged his twenty-four-year-old son, Eugene, and Bill Martin, a cowboy who knew the outlaws, to join Milton's posse.[14]

On July 13, Milton and Scarborough met with young Thacker and Bill

Martin in Deming, New Mexico. That night, they boarded their special train, which took them west into Arizona, where they unloaded their horses and tack at Buttermilk Point, fifteen miles from Geronimo. Scarborough recalled that "we commenced a ride, the like of which I have not made in many, many days." They skirted the Gila River and rode to the San Carlos Indian Reservation, where they hired several Apache trailers. From there, they rode for two days to Fort Apache, and then south to the Black River country. The Apaches guided the posse until the men had learned the lay of the land, then returned to San Carlos.

The Black River is in the White Mountains just west of Eagle Creek, Bronco Bill's hideout. The posse spent more than a week scouting the mountains, "taking great care that we showed ourselves to no one," said Scarborough. Unable to cut the outlaws' sign, on July 29 they changed tactics. That afternoon they rode into the Double Circle horse camp at McBride Crossing on the Black River and took the wrangler into custody. The manhunters were rightly suspicious that the cowboys in that mountainous region were harboring the gang, either out of friendship or fear. The next morning, as each cowpuncher rode in for breakfast, they arrested him. Soon they had six cowhands and an old bear hunter under guard. Milton's plan was to raid the surrounding cattle camps that night.

At 9:00 A.M., Jeff was fishing for breakfast trout while Martin fed the horses. Scarborough and Thacker were guarding the cowboys. Suddenly, Scarborough spotted three riders cresting a ridge four hundred yards distant. Two of them stopped, drew their pistols, and opened fire on a rattlesnake. Milton, alerted by the gunfire, ran to the camp in time to see the lead horseman ride down toward the corral and dismount. Scarborough turned toward the cowpunchers and asked, "Who is that man?"

"That's Hinton," one of them replied.

In fact, the rider was Bronco Bill. Scarborough, thinking he was just another cowboy to be rounded up, walked toward him, his Winchester in one hand. The outlaw immediately swung back into his saddle.

"Hold on there, Cap," Scarborough called out. "I want to speak with you."

In an instant, Bronco Bill's six-gun was spitting lead. Milton and Scarborough swung their Winchesters up and fired four shots at him, tearing the desperado out of his saddle. He landed heavily, a slug in his right shoulder. Bill's comrades, who turned out to be Kid Johnson and Red Pipkin, took cover behind a boulder on the ridge and opened up. "A bullet sung by my ear and tore up the earth a short distance behind me," Scarborough recalled. Milton yelled at him, "George, did that bullet go through you?"

"No, but goddamn, I heard it!" he shouted back.

Now Milton, Scarborough, and Thacker unleashed a rifle fusillade at the two outlaws behind the rock. The pair fled for their horses, but at long range the manhunters shot the animals dead. Kid Johnson jumped behind a large juniper tree and kept shooting. "All I could see was his hips," Scarborough later said. "I took a dead rest and fired and Johnson fell over and commenced to yell like a panther. I knew that he was bad hit."

Johnson gasped and said to Pipkin, "I'm done for. You get away."

As the three officers kept up a hot fire, Pipkin ran to the top of the ridge and vanished. "The fight was over," Scarborough recalled. "We had expected to stay in that country for three months if necessary, but in less than three weeks we had captured our men." Milton sent a cowboy to Fort Apache with a note asking for a doctor and a coffin. Kid Johnson died in great agony the next day. Then the lawmen took Bronco Bill fifty miles on horseback to Geronimo. His wound healed and he received a life sentence in the New Mexico prison. Red Pipkin was later captured and handed a ten-year term in Yuma prison for horse theft.[15]

Milton returned to his Wells Fargo messenger's run out of Nogales. One day in February 1900, he ran into future outlaw Billy Stiles in Nogales. Stiles, who had accompanied him on the manhunt for the High Five gang in 1896, was a deputy under Constable Burt Alvord of Willcox, Arizona. Jeff, like everyone else who knew Stiles, thought he was an honest lawman. Milton was getting ready to make a run to Guaymas, and Stiles was anxious to know when he would return.

Train robber Daniel "Red" Pipkin.
He shot it out with Jeff Milton's posse
on the Black River in 1898.
[*Author's collection*]

Stiles asked Jeff to go with him to look over some mining claims in the Quijotoa Mountains, northwest of Nogales. Milton answered that he was headed for Mexico but would be back in a few days.

"You're sure of that, are you, Jeff? Dead sure?" asked Stiles. When Milton answered in the affirmative, the deputy said, "Well, now, when you find yourself coming north, will you promise to telegraph to me, so I can meet you in Benson?"

Milton agreed. A few days later, on February 15, Jeff was aboard his express car on a northbound train, which stopped at Imuris, Mexico. There he got a wire from the Wells Fargo agent in Nogales advising that the regular messenger on the run north of town was ill. He instructed Milton to stay aboard all the way to Benson, seventy-five miles northeast of Nogales. Jeff obeyed. It was dusk when his train pulled into the town of Fairbank, sixty miles northwest of Nogales. Milton opened the car door and began handing packages to the Wells Fargo agent on the platform. He noticed that there was quite a crowd of cowboys gathered around the depot. Suddenly, he heard a shout. "Hands up, there, you sons of bitches!"

"What's the matter?" Jeff asked the agent.

"Some of the cowpunchers are trying to have a little fun, I guess," the agent replied.

"That's mighty poor fun," Jeff exclaimed. "Somebody will be getting killed around here if they don't look out."

"Throw up your hands and come out of there!" another voice yelled.

Milton ducked inside the car, grabbed a Winchester Model 1887 lever-action shotgun, and bellowed, "If there's anything here you want, come and get it!"

At that, several bandits, who had mixed in with the crowd, opened fire on him with six-shooters and Winchesters. One slug tore off his hat and grazed his head. Another ripped though his left arm, just above the wrist. Two more bullets slammed into the same arm, one shattering the bone near his shoulder. The impact knocked him to the floor. Despite the shock and pain, Milton still gripped his shotgun in his right hand but held his fire for fear he would hit an innocent person in the crowd.

Then a robber shouted at the cowering bystanders on the platform, "Line up there, boys! Damn you all, line up!"

At the same time, a Winchester-wielding desperado stepped toward the express car door. With a herculean effort, Jeff raised himself up, leveled the shotgun, and fired a blast at the man's midsection. Three buckshot tore into him, and he collapsed, groaning, "Look out for the son of a bitch, he's shooting to kill!"

Bleeding heavily, Milton slammed the door shut, wrapped a tourniquet around his arm, threw away the keys to the safe, and then passed out. The outlaws soon entered the car, but they could not find the keys and were unable to open the safe. Thinking Milton was dead, they stole his six-gun and a packet containing forty-two Mexican dollars. Then they swung into their saddles and, taking their wounded comrade with them, galloped off into the night. While Jeff was taken to a hospital in Tucson, a pursuing posse from Tombstone found the wounded robber on the road six miles from Fairbank. He was a notorious desperado named Jesse "Three-Fingered Jack" Dunlap. His compadres had abandoned him. Before he died, he made a detailed confession. The robbery had been planned by Constable Burt Alvord and his deputy, Billy Stiles. Because they knew Milton was the deadliest messenger on the road, Stiles had tried to ensure that he would not be on board.[16]

Dunlap revealed that the other bandits were Tom "Bravo Juan" Yoas, Robert Brown, and brothers George and Lewis Owings. He said that Stiles and two other desperadoes had pulled a previous train robbery at Cochise, Arizona, in September 1899. All of them were now quickly rounded up and jailed. Burt Alvord and Billy Stiles went on to become two of Arizona's most notorious fugitives, twice breaking out of the Tombstone jail and dodging lawmen along the Mexican border for several years. Meanwhile, Jeff Milton slowly recovered from his wounds. After the gunfight, doctors removed a section of bone from his shattered left arm. He went to the Southern Pacific hospital in San Francisco for further treatment and two more surgeries. It took him two years to regain full use of his arm, which was now two inches shorter. Wells Fargo paid all his medical bills and rewarded him with four thousand dollars, which he invested, and lost, in Texas oil lands.[17]

Milton then spent several years prospecting for oil and gold, and at least once, in 1903, guarded a large Wells Fargo treasure shipment from Mexico. However, his career as a shotgun messenger was over. A lesser man would have quit law enforcement altogether, but in 1904 he became a U.S. Immigration Service officer and served on the border for another twenty-eight years, retiring in 1932, at the age of seventy. A lifelong bachelor, he finally married in 1919, and spent his last years in Tombstone. When he died in Tucson on May 7, 1947, at the age of eighty-five, his wife scattered his ashes in the desert he loved so well. Jeff Milton was the last of the Old West gunfighters who rode for Wells Fargo.[18]

20

FIGHTING WAGES

David Trousdale

David Trousdale led a long life that was almost entirely unremarkable. A gentle, quiet family man and devoted husband, he served for forty-three years as a faithful employee of Wells Fargo and its successors, the American Railway Express Company and the Railway Express Agency. Yet his life and his character were defined by a single incident that took place in a few hours on a dark Texas night in 1912. When it was over, two dangerous outlaws—one a notorious member of Butch Cassidy's Wild Bunch—were stone dead, and overnight the young Wells Fargo messenger became a national hero.

A native of Columbia, Maury County, Tennessee, David Andrew Trousdale was born on September 20, 1876, the fourth of six children of Wilson Trousdale and Sarah Moore. He grew up on his parents' farm and enjoyed hunting, fishing, and playing baseball. Shooting wild game in the Tennessee hills made him an expert marksman. His mother died when he was nine, and his twelve-year-old sister helped raise him. Although the family struggled financially and the children had to work, they all attended grade school. David, quiet and reserved, also had a great sense of humor. According to a childhood companion, "When but a mere lad he was noted for his tricks and jokes that he would play on his friends." He grew into an upright and scrupulously honest youth. One of his schoolteachers said, "He was always a hero when it came to defending the weaker or smaller boys against the impositions of the larger ones; was always an espouser of the cause and right of women and was ever ready to defend them in any way possible."[1]

Young Trousdale had trouble finding work in Columbia. He unsuccessfully sought a railroad job in Memphis, then returned home and engaged in carpentry for a short time. According to one early account, he "worked at almost everything from which he could earn an honest dollar." In November 1899, at age twenty-three, David left for Texas, "a young man looking for a job," as he later recalled. He first hired on as a ranch hand, then worked as a barber in the state hospital in Austin. Trousdale found his calling in November 1902, when he was appointed a Wells Fargo clerk in San Antonio. A year later, he became a porter, loading and unloading packages from trains and express wagons at a salary of thirty dollars a month. Trousdale proved that he could be entrusted with valuable cargo, and in April 1906, he was promoted to messenger's helper. In 1910, he became a regular messenger, with a pay raise to ninety-five dollars a month, assigned to train routes in South Texas and on the Gulf Coast.[2]

David Trousdale was not the only Texan with roots in Maury County, Tennessee. One of them, Ben Kilpatrick, would achieve notoriety as a partner of Butch Cassidy and the Sundance Kid. His father, George Kilpatrick, hailed from Maury County and emigrated to Texas after service as a Confederate soldier in the Civil War. He married Mary Davis in 1869 and sired nine children. His third son, Benjamin Arnold Kilpatrick, was born in Coleman, Texas, on January 5, 1874. The Kilpatricks were a rough bunch. George Kilpatrick was a suspected horse thief, and neighbors considered his wife, Mary, a "she-devil." As their son Ben grew into a handsome, six-foot-tall cowboy, he and three of his brothers became desperadoes. "Ma" Kilpatrick encouraged her sons' criminal behavior. When Ben was in his early twenties, he took to the saddle with outlaw leader Thomas "Black Jack" Ketchum. On the

David Trousdale, Wells Fargo
messenger, about 1910. [*Courtesy of
Chuck Parsons*]

night of April 28, 1898, the Ketchum gang stopped the San Antonio to
El Paso train at Comstock, about thirty miles north of Del Rio, Texas,
and looted the Wells Fargo car. Ben Kilpatrick was later suspected as
one of the four robbers. Two months later, on July 1, Black Jack's gang,
probably including Kilpatrick and his friend Will Carver, held up another train near Stanton, in West Texas.[3]

By the next year, Ben Kilpatrick and Will Carver had gone north,
where they rode with Butch Cassidy's Wild Bunch. Kilpatrick was
later accused of taking part in the great train robbery at Wilcox, Wyoming, on June 2, 1899. In a scene replicated in the film *Butch Cassidy
and the Sundance Kid*, the gang blew the express car to smithereens and
escaped with as much as $50,000. On August 29, 1900, Kilpatrick,
with Butch Cassidy, Harry Longabaugh (the Sundance Kid), and
Harvey Logan, alias Kid Curry, held up a Union Pacific train near
Tipton, Wyoming, taking a reported $55,000 in cash. In Novem-
ber 1900, members of the Wild Bunch gathered in Hell's Half Acre,
the red-light district of Fort Worth, Texas. While there, Kilpatrick,

Cassidy, Logan, Carver, and Longabaugh posed for a group photograph that became one of the most famous in the annals of American crime. A few months later, in March 1901, Ben Kilpatrick returned to his parents' ranch in Concho County, Texas, accompanied by Will Carver and Harvey Logan. The Kilpatrick family had been feuding with a neighboring cattle rancher, Oliver Thornton. On March 27, Thornton's bullet-riddled body was found at a spring near the Kilpatrick ranch house. Kilpatrick and his saddle mates fled, and Ben and his younger brother George were later charged with the murder.[4]

Six days later, on April 2, Ben and George Kilpatrick, with Will Carver and Harvey Logan, rode into Sonora, Texas, a hundred miles southwest, to case the town's bank. A sheriff's posse was on the alert and tried to arrest Carver and George Kilpatrick in a store. The outlaws went for their guns but came out second best. Will Carver died and George Kilpatrick was badly wounded. Ben Kilpatrick and Harvey Logan fled back north, where they rejoined members of the Wild Bunch. Three months later, on July 3, 1901, Kilpatrick, Logan, and O. C. "Deaf Charley" Hanks stopped a train near Wagner, Montana, and escaped with $40,000 in banknotes from the National Bank of Montana. Wanted circulars were issued, describing the stolen bills.[5]

Now Kilpatrick met up with his paramour, Laura Bullion, a Texas prostitute. They traveled to the resort town of Hot Springs, Arkansas, and then to St. Louis, Missouri. In early November, Kilpatrick passed some of the stolen notes, which were recognized by an alert St. Louis banker who had seen the circulars. On November 5, 1901, police detectives captured Kilpatrick in a St. Louis brothel, taking from him two revolvers and $400 in stolen banknotes. The next morning, detectives picked up Laura Bullion at her hotel; her valise held $7,500 in Bank of Montana notes. Newspapers described him as a "Tall Texan," giving rise to his time-honored nickname. When the pair pled guilty to passing the stolen bills, Ben was handed fifteen years in federal prison and Laura five.[6]

In 1907, Kilpatrick befriended a fellow prisoner, Ole Beck, who was

Ben Kilpatrick, the Tall Texan. He was a member of Butch Cassidy's Wild Bunch. [*Author's collection*]

serving his second term for counterfeiting. The two worked together cutting stone at the U.S. Penitentiary in Atlanta, Georgia, until Beck completed his sentence in August 1909. The Tall Texan, with credit for good behavior, was freed in June 1911. The sheriff of Concho County, Texas, met Kilpatrick on his release and took him back to Texas to stand trial for the murder of Oliver Thornton ten years earlier. Although prosecutors subpoenaed numerous witnesses for the trial, in September they dismissed the charges due to lack of evidence. Kilpatrick was free, but he could not leave well enough alone. He joined up with Ole Beck, who was working on the railroad in Memphis, Tennessee.[7]

Two months later, just after midnight on November 1, 1911, a pair of masked bandits crawled over the coal tender on a train just across the Mississippi River from Memphis. They ordered the crew to stop, then were joined by four more robbers, who entered the express car and blew the safe with nitroglycerin. It turned out to be empty. The outlaws escaped with eight hundred dollars from the registered mail. Three months later, on February 6, 1912, the same train was held up at the same spot in exactly the same manner. Two bandits climbed into the engine cab and forced the train to a halt. Three other robbers appeared and used nitroglycerin to blow the through safe. There were no valuables inside and the holdup men fled empty-handed. It was obvious that the same gang had robbed both trains. Detectives, including Wells Fargo's Fred Dodge, would later conclude that two of the bandits were Ben Kilpatrick and Ole Beck. Both were in Memphis at the time, and Beck had quit his railroad job the day before the first holdup.[8]

Three days after the train robbery, Kilpatrick showed up alone in Texarkana, Arkansas. He soon left for Fort Worth, where he rejoined Ole Beck. From there, they drifted southwest 350 miles to the ranch of Berry Ketchum, older brother of Black Jack Ketchum, who had been legally hanged in New Mexico in 1901. Berry Ketchum, a prosperous cattleman, owned a ranch on Independence Creek, a tributary of the Pecos River, about nine miles southwest of Sheffield, in Pecos County. Though he appeared to be an honest rancher, Ketchum was rumored to have benefited financially from the train robberies of the Ketchum gang. At Berry Ketchum's ranch, Kilpatrick and Beck obtained two saddle mounts, a packhorse, and a pair of binoculars. Ketchum later claimed that the horses had been stolen from him.[9]

Kilpatrick and Beck rode sixty miles south to Sanderson, Texas, arriving on March 11, 1912. Sanderson, the seat of Terrell County, was a railroad town of one thousand and a stop on the route from San Antonio to El Paso. It was Saturday night, and a circus was in town. When the westbound evening train stopped, a stranger approached Wells Fargo's messenger W. T. Bledsoe at the depot. The man was Ole Beck, and he asked if the train "was a through express to California." As Bledsoe later explained, "I replied that this was a through express and the cars would go through to California points. Then he asked if it was warm and comfortable in the cars, and I replied that the cars were heated by steam." When Bledsoe inquired the reason for the questions, Beck pretended to be with the circus and replied that he "had a monkey he wished to ship to Los Angeles" and "wanted to be sure that he shipped him on a through express train." As Bledsoe recalled, "He thanked me and turned away. There was another man standing in the dark and did not come close enough to be identified, a tall slim man with a dark slouch hat." That figure was Ben Kilpatrick, the Tall Texan.[10]

From Sanderson, Kilpatrick and Beck rode their horses east about ten miles to Baxter's Curve, a dangerous bend in the railroad, where at least two trainmen had died in previous accidents. Not far from the tracks, they picketed their mounts and the packhorse, draping nose bags over their heads so the animals could be left alone while they fed. Then they walked another ten miles east to the rail stop of Dryden. The next evening, two young sons of the railroad pumpman at Dryden saw them lounging under the water tower. The boys thought they were hoboes. In fact, Kilpatrick and Beck were about to make the biggest mistake of their lives.[11]

At noon that day, March 12, 1912, David Trousdale and his helper, G. K. Reagan, were busy in a Wells Fargo car at the San Antonio depot, loading express packages and filling out waybills. Trousdale had been transferred to the run between San Antonio and El Paso only a month before. He kept his shotgun and revolver on top of his desk in the express car. The passenger train left San Antonio at 2:00 P.M., headed west. It stopped in Del Rio, where a combination baggage and mail car was coupled behind the engine and in front of the Wells Fargo car. The helper, Reagan, climbed into the combination car, and the train proceeded a hundred miles to Dryden, where it stopped about midnight to take on water. As the engine pulled out, Ben Kilpatrick and Ole Beck, wearing masks, swung aboard. They covered the engineer and fireman with guns and ordered them to stop on an iron trestle that crossed a ravine just east of Baxter's Curve. This was the "trestle method," a common technique used by train robbers. Any passengers who left the coaches to interfere with the holdup risked a fall from the bridge.

Ben Kilpatrick was armed with a pair of Colt revolvers and a Winchester Model 1910, a high-powered semiautomatic rifle with a four-round magazine. Ole Beck also carried a rifle and a brace of pistols. As the train came to a halt, the conductor and an African-American porter walked forward to find out what was wrong. Kilpatrick leveled his Winchester at them, then marched the crewmen back to the Wells Fargo car. He ordered the porter to call for David Trousdale to come out. "I recognized his voice," recalled Trousdale. "Just about that time I was finishing up my work before reaching Sanderson. The negro porter said, 'They's some robbers out here. You better git out.'" Trousdale stepped to the car door. "I opened the door and when I looked out there was a man with a mask on standing there, pointing a rifle at me."

"Fall out with your hands up," barked Kilpatrick. Trousdale promptly jumped down and Kilpatrick searched him, but the messenger was unarmed. The outlaw lined Trousdale up with the rest of the crew, then ordered the conductor and the porter to uncouple the Wells Fargo car from the train. Explained Trousdale, "He then asked me if there was anyone else in my car, and I told him that Helper Reagan

David Trousdale, wearing his express
messenger's hat. [*Courtesy of Chuck Parsons*]

was in the head combination car. He marched me up to the combination car and had me call the helper out." After Reagan and the U.S. mail clerk, M. E. Banks, climbed down, Kilpatrick searched them also. He ordered the conductor and porter to go back to the passenger cars. Then Kilpatrick told Trousdale, "We want all that mail and express thrown out of the car, and then we will attend to the passengers."

That comment made no sense to Trousdale, because they were already walking away from the passenger coaches. As a result, he mistakenly thought that the two robbers were novices. The messenger whispered to Banks, "These fellows are green, and we'll watch our chance and get them, sure."

Kilpatrick and Beck, who had been guarding the engine, ordered Trousdale and the rest of the crew to climb into the cab. As one bandit clung to each side of the locomotive, the engineer pulled forward, leaving the passenger coaches behind on the trestle. They proceeded half a mile and forced the engine to stop on the west side of Baxter's Curve. The outlaws had chosen the spot well, because on the south side of the curve was a high bluff near the tracks, which made it unnecessary for them to guard that side of the train. The outlaws addressed each other by aliases: Ben Kilpatrick was "Frank" and Ole Beck was "Pardner." While Beck watched the engineer and fireman, Kilpatrick forced Trousdale, Reagan, and Banks to walk back to the baggage and mail car while Reagan carried a lantern. Then he ordered the expressmen to climb inside the car with their hands up. Kilpatrick picked up five bags of registered mail, cutting one of them open, then tossed them outside onto the railbed.

Next, he forced Trousdale, Reagan, and Banks to leave the baggage car and walk through the vestibule to the Wells Fargo car. He had Trousdale open the safe and remove several money packets. It was the company's policy to keep very little cash in the safe. Trousdale handed over two packets, one holding thirty-seven dollars and another containing only two dollars. Then Kilpatrick announced that he "would go through and see what Uncle Sam had," and he ordered the three expressmen back into the baggage and mail car. There he again went through the registered mail. Trousdale later said that he "told me that he would take me back to the coaches and see what the passengers had, and that he would take me across the river, meaning the Rio Grande, with him. I thought that if there was any chance for me to get the advantage of him, it would be by taking him back through my car, where I could find some means of 'turning the tables' on him."

After Kilpatrick finished rifling through the mail, Trousdale related, "I persuaded the robber to go back into the express car, telling him that he had missed a valuable package." The outlaw agreed. "We passed through the combination car," said the messenger, "and I opened two or three packages of express, and he took his knife and cut one telescope grip open. He took out a Mexican hat and said there was nothing in the baggage that he wanted." Then Kilpatrick, Trousdale, and Reagan went back into the Wells Fargo car.

All the while, Kilpatrick had been threatening and abusing the messenger. "The robber used me very roughly, striking me frequently with his Winchester and poking me about, ordering me to 'get a move on,'" Trousdale recalled. He told Kilpatrick, "I'm not going to scrap with you. I'm not getting fighting wages."

"Oh, all right," the outlaw replied. "Then you fellows will have to help us get this stuff across the Rio Grande."

Trousdale kept up his banter with the robber, later explaining, "In this way I gained his confidence and he quit treating me as roughly as he had been." In the center of the Wells Fargo car was a barrel of oysters packed in ice; a wooden ice mallet rested on top of the barrel. "I decided then and there that if I could get him in the right position I could hit him with the maul. You know you can hit an awful blow with such a maul. Why, I've broken up a box of ice at a blow." As they passed by, Trousdale quickly picked up the mallet and hid it behind his overcoat. Then he pointed to a small box on the floor and said, "There's the most valuable package in this car."

Kilpatrick rested his rifle against his leg and reached down to pick up the package. Trousdale quickly raised the ice mallet. "While he was stooping over I struck him at the base of the skull. The first blow broke the man's neck. As he went down in a heap a slight groan came from

The ice mallet Trousdale used to kill Ben Kilpatrick. It was kept as a souvenir by Wells Fargo Detective Fred Dodge. [*Robert G. McCubbin collection*]

him. He never spoke. I struck him a second and a third time. On the third blow the maul crashed through his skull and the man's brains spattered over the side of the car." Trousdale snatched the dead out-law's six-shooters, giving one to Reagan and the other to Banks. Then he picked up Kilpatrick's Winchester and turned off the gaslights in the car. As he later said, "I decided I would use the first robber's rifle, because I could work that faster than the shotgun I had in the car."

Trousdale took up a position behind some trunks in the center of the car, opposite the open door, which was illuminated by the lights in the baggage car. Reagan and Banks barricaded themselves at the rear of the express car. For an hour—though it seemed like an eternity—they waited for the second bandit to appear. But Ole Beck was in the engine cab, guarding the crew, and oblivious to his partner's fate. "Nothing developed," said Trousdale, "so I decided to fire a shot through the roof of the car to attract attention." Several minutes later, Beck stepped to the express car door, calling, "Frank, Frank."

Getting no response, Beck climbed up through the open door. "I saw his head sticking out from behind a trunk forty feet from me," Trousdale recalled. "The first time he put his head out I did not get a chance to shoot, but the second time he was looking toward the rear of the car. I fired one shot." The bullet struck the bandit near the top of his forehead, tore out the back of his skull, then ripped through the wall of the express car. Ole Beck died instantly.

Trousdale and his companions, however, were not sure if he was dead or if other robbers might be outside. They clutched their weapons and waited cautiously behind the packing trunks. After another hour, the engineer released his brakes and backed the locomotive and two cars back to the passenger coaches. Trousdale related, "The fireman came back to the coaches and called me. I told him to get the conductor and some of the passengers before I could open the car, that I had killed two men. In a few minutes he came back with the conductor, porter, and fifteen or twenty passengers. When I found that there was no one out there to harm me, I opened the door and admitted the train crew."

Once the crewmen had coupled the passenger coaches behind the express car, the train started for Sanderson. On the way, Trousdale searched the desperadoes' bodies. He found a bottle of nitroglycerin in Kilpatrick's pocket, and from Beck he took six sticks of dynamite and a box of dynamite caps. Declared Banks, the mail clerk, "I shudder to think of what our finish might have been had Trousdale shot that dynamite and nitroglycerine on the robber's person instead of tearing the top of his head off."[12]

When the train arrived in Sanderson, word of the sensational shooting raced through town like wildfire. The county sheriff led a posse to Baxter's Curve, where they found the three hobbled horses. The packhorse carried eight hundred rounds of ammunition for rifles and revolvers. A telephone message was sent to Capt. John J. Sanders and his company of Texas Rangers, who rushed by rail from their headquarters in Del Rio. A thorough search failed to produce any accomplices of the two bandits. Meanwhile, their bodies were laid out on a hand truck at the Sanderson depot, where hundreds of people came by to gawk. Several who knew Ben Kilpatrick quickly identified him. A local photographer

Ben Kilpatrick, *left*, and Ole Beck, dead, at the Sanderson, Texas, railroad depot. David Trousdale killed them both when they held up his train in 1912. Trousdale is directly behind Kilpatrick, propping up his head. [*Robert G. McCubbin collection*]

had Trousdale and a few other men pull the two outlaws off the hand truck and stand them upright. Then, with Trousdale behind Kilpatrick, supporting his head, the photographer took a now-famous image of the last member of Butch Cassidy's Wild Bunch to die with his boots on.[13]

The messenger's extraordinary feat immediately hit the wire services

The gold watch and fob presented to David Trousdale by Wells Fargo.
[*Courtesy of Chuck Parsons*]

and was prominently featured in newspapers throughout the country. The photo was widely distributed, and federal prison officials in Atlanta soon identified the second bandit as Ole Beck. The train's passengers passed the hat and bought Trousdale a gold watch fob in the shape of an eagle-top badge, suitably inscribed on the reverse. Trousdale applied for the U.S. Post Office's standing reward for mail robbers but was denied on the grounds that payment was only for "arrest and conviction." The Southern Pacific Railroad, however, did not split hairs and paid him a five-hundred-dollar reward. Wells Fargo presented the doughty messenger with one thousand dollars and a gold pocket watch. He proudly carried the watch and fob for the rest of his life.

Trousdale was not so proud, however, of the instant notoriety he had gained. Motion picture companies badgered him to star in a short film about his exploit, and vaudeville producers offered to put him on the stage. The ever-modest expressman declined. "All I want to do is live as quietly as I can. I could never, nor am I going to consider any offer to go on the stage or have any moving pictures made of myself," he declared. "I did not kill these two robbers for notoriety. I did it because I thought it was in the line of duty. I had to protect property that was entrusted to me by my employers. You can appreciate how I feel in taking a human life. No man ever wants to kill another."[14]

David Trousdale was true to his word. He promptly left for his father's home in Tennessee and spent several weeks with his family until the excitement died down. Then he returned to San Antonio, where Wells Fargo officials promoted him to chief messenger on the route to Houston, with a raise in pay to two thousand dollars annually. Trousdale was besieged with marriage proposals from women across the country. He ignored them all. However, soon after his return from Tennessee, he met young Allie Bell Lester in San Antonio. According to one newspaper, "it was a case of love at first sight." The next year, they married. He was thirty-seven, she twenty-two. They made their home in San Antonio, where they raised two sons.[15]

Trousdale worked for Wells Fargo until it ceased its express business in 1918, then continued with its successors, the American Railway Express Company and finally the Railway Express Agency. He spent the rest of his career on the San Antonio to El Paso run, and was never again bothered by bandits. In 1935, the U.S. Congress finally rewarded his heroism by awarding him one thousand dollars for protecting the mails. Trousdale retired from his messenger's duties on August 1, 1945, after forty-three years on the job. In 1949, he and Allie moved back to his old Tennessee home. Trousdale enjoyed excellent health for four years, but on August 13, 1953, he died of a sudden heart attack at his house in Columbia. The old expressman's wife paid him his finest tribute: "By nature he was always calm and collected. He was a wonderful husband, father, and Christian."[16]

The death of David Trousdale marked the last of the Wells Fargo messengers who killed an Old West train robber in the line of duty.

EPILOGUE

A LEGACY SQUANDERED

On June 30, 1918, as World War I raged, veteran Wells Fargo detective Fred Dodge sat at his desk and scribbled a few words into his journal: "Good-bye, Wells Fargo & Co.—the passing of a good and old friend." The next day, he added a postscript: "Good morning American Railway Express Co." Dodge's notations marked the quiet passing of a great business enterprise. Due to wartime emergency, the federal government merged all express companies, including Wells Fargo, into a single entity, American Railway Express. In 1929, American Railway Express became the Railway Express Agency, which finally went out of business in 1975. But Wells Fargo, although no longer an express company, never ceased business.

From its earliest years, Wells Fargo & Company had provided banking services, with its agents buying gold dust and making simple loans. Its bank grew steadily, and in 1905, the company separated its express and banking operations. After the 1918 merger of express companies, Wells Fargo's banking business was unaffected. Under steady leadership, Wells Fargo Bank survived the Great Depression and prospered during and after World War II. Over the years, Wells Fargo slowly grew into one of the nation's largest and most successful financial institutions. As late as the 1980s, it was primarily a California bank, but in the 1990s, it expanded throughout the country. In 1986, Wells Fargo purchased Crocker National Bank, and ten years later acquired First Interstate Bancorp, making it the ninth-largest bank in the United States.

At the same time, Wells Fargo remained firmly moored to its Wild West heritage. Its logo was a stagecoach; its advertisements in newspapers and magazines emphasized the company's history of safety and stability on the American frontier. In the 1920s, the bank first organized its History Department in San Francisco. Wells Fargo opened a small history museum in its main bank building in 1935. Because many of its records had been lost in the 1906 earthquake and fire, the company began actively soliciting donations of documents, photographs, and artifacts from the families of old expressmen. The result, accumulated over the ensuing decades, was a massive collection of Wells Fargo memorabilia—stagecoaches, signs, firearms, images, strongboxes, and pony safes—and a dizzying array of office equipment—stamps, sealers, reward posters, and gold scales. Eventually, these were exhibited in a dozen museums in Wells Fargo banks around the country.

The bank and its historians delighted in preserving and displaying photos and memorabilia related to its agents, messengers, and detectives. Wells Fargo savored its record as a product of the frontier and as a byword for honesty and integrity. Since 1852, Wells Fargo's principal mission had been to transport and safeguard money and property. The company's men had risked their lives to protect express shipments. Between 1855 and 1915, at least fifty-three Wells Fargo expressmen died in the line of duty. Nineteen were slain by outlaws or bandits, four were accidentally shot, four more died in shipwrecks and steamboat explosions, and many of the others perished in train wrecks. The biggest loss of life took place in 1866, when, incomprehensibly, an unmarked parcel of nitroglycerin was shipped via Wells Fargo. Five expressmen died when the parcel exploded in the company's San Francisco headquarters. The legacy of Wells Fargo's heroes was carefully preserved and publicized by the bank's History Department. The traditions those Wells Fargo men established were no quaint and distant memory. Their privations, their exploits, and their bloodshed were both revered and celebrated by the bank and served as a living, breathing standard for fair, safe, and honest dealings with the public.

In the mid-1930s, Stuart N. Lake, author of the bestselling book *Wyatt Earp: Frontier Marshal* (1931), began working on a history of Wells Fargo. The bank provided him with artifacts and research materials, but Lake soon realized that more money could be made from a motion picture. The result was the 1937 film *Wells Fargo*. Starring Joel McCrea, it depicted the fictional life of a young expressman working to expand Wells Fargo's operations on the frontier. The film became a huge commercial success and helped cement the company's reputation as an iconic American institution. Then, during the heyday of Westerns on television in the 1950s, *Tales of Wells Fargo* became one of the most popular. It ran from 1957 to 1962 and featured Dale Robertson. The series detailed the adventures of a "special agent" (even though Wells Fargo never employed anyone called a special agent) who battles bandits and desperadoes in the Old West.

Wells Fargo continued to embrace its frontier heritage throughout the 1970s and 1980s. The bank's television commercials routinely featured Wells Fargo stagecoaches and voice-overs that reminded the public of its hard-earned reputation for integrity and trustworthiness. But things began to change in 1998, when Wells Fargo merged with Norwest Corporation of Minneapolis. The chief of Norwest, Richard Kovacevich, became CEO of Wells Fargo. Norwest regional presidents took control over Wells Fargo's retail banking and instituted the practice of cross-selling. Bank employees were encouraged to use a "hard sell" approach to get customers to open new accounts. For example, a customer with a savings account would be pressed to open a credit card account or to apply for a home mortgage. Employees were rewarded for opening new accounts. CEO Kovacevich considered bank branches to be stores, its employees to be salespeople rather than bankers, and its consumers to be customers rather than clients. This profound change in bank culture and leadership would prove disastrous for Wells Fargo's image.

During the Great Recession in 2008, Wells Fargo acquired the faltering Wachovia Corporation, thus becoming the nation's largest financial institution. By then, cross-selling and aggressive retail practices were firmly entrenched as bank policy. As Wells Fargo drifted further and further from its traditions of honesty and service, it simultaneously drifted away from the long-standing emphasis on its Wild West origins. In 2010, the bank commissioned its new logo, which showed a six-horse stagecoach racing across the canvas. But in a laughingly inept nod to political correctness, the driver had no whip and the shotgun messenger had no shotgun. The bank officers who commissioned the painting were so ignorant of Wells Fargo history that they thought a whip was used to inflict pain on the stage team. They did not know that the driver controlled his trained horses by the whip's sound, not by its touch. More recently, and in the same vein, bank management indicated their intention to remove all Wells Fargo firearms from display in their museums. The company's officials seem oblivious to the fact that these historic weapons are tangible symbols of Wells Fargo's reputation for security and integrity. The bank's history archives, open to the public for many decades, stopped welcoming researchers and writers. And in late 2017, Wells Fargo's marketing department gutted its ninety-year-old Historical Services department, leaving no one in authority to preserve and utilize the company's vital legacy.

These events coincided with the rise of the biggest banking scandal in modern American history. Just as Wells Fargo's executives forgot the company's story, they forgot that a bank's principal mission is to safeguard wealth. At the very time Wells Fargo was offering a false and sanitized depiction of its own history, its managers were defrauding their own customers. CEO Kovacevich had developed the slogan "eight is great," meaning that bank employees should sell eight bank products—accounts—to every consumer. But simple common sense would indicate that very few people need eight bank accounts. Half that number should be plenty: one home mortgage, one credit card account, one savings account, and one checking account. As a consequence, bank employees struggled to meet the quota and began opening accounts without the knowledge or permission of their customers. In 2007, Kovacevich retired and John Stumpf, also from Norwest, took over as CEO and continued to press the "eight is great" policy. Between 2011 and 2016, some 5,300 Wells Fargo employees opened more than 1.5 million unauthorized bank accounts and created more than 500,000 unauthorized applications for credit cards.

The news first broke in 2011, when the *New York Times* reported on Wells Fargo's "hard sell" approach. The story, however, failed to gain traction until 2013, when the *Los Angeles Times* revealed that the bank's selling culture had resulted in quota requirements that were impossible to meet without employee fraud. The result was a lawsuit brought in 2015 by the city of Los Angeles against Wells Fargo. On September 8, 2016, the bank announced that it was settling the case by paying $185 million in fines to the city and to federal regulators. The bank thought that would resolve the matter, but instead it caught the attention of Congress.

Wells Fargo CEO John Stumpf testified before the Senate Banking Committee. He apologized for the fraud but was urged to resign, and one senator called for a criminal investigation of the CEO. The hearings revealed that banker Carrie Tolstedt headed the retail banking division that was responsible for the two million phony accounts. And it turned out that the $185 million fine was insignificant, for it was less than what Stumpf and Tolstedt had been paid in the previous five years and was only 3 percent of the bank's profits for a single quarter. Although Wells Fargo fired 5,300 employees for creating the fraudulent accounts, incredibly, Stumpf and Tolstedt kept their jobs.

As early as 1855, during the financial panic in San Francisco, Wells Fargo fired incompetent executives and replaced them with tough-minded, honest ones. But in 2016, following the U.S. Senate hearings, Wells Fargo's board of directors did not fire either Stumpf or Tolstedt. It was only due to intense public pressure and media scrutiny that both were soon forced to retire and forfeit a combined $136 million in compensation. Wells Fargo then announced that starting on January 1, 2017, it would eliminate its sales quotas. Yet this did not put an end to Wells Fargo's scandals.

Even though Wells Fargo's express business in the Old West had catered to blacks, Hispanics, and Chinese, between 2004 and 2009, Wells Fargo discriminated against African-Americans and Latinos who applied for home loans. After an investigation by the Department of Housing and Urban Development and the Department of Justice, in 2012 the bank paid $175 million in damages. Then, following the 2016 U.S. Senate hearings, evidence surfaced that the actual number of unauthorized accounts was closer to 3.5 million. In 2017, regulators forced Wells Fargo to pay $3.4 million to brokerage customers who had lost money investing in complex securities that even the company's brokers did not fully understand. Then regulators found that Wells Fargo had engaged in unfair and deceptive business practices by forcing more than 800,000 customers who took out automobile loans to buy car insurance they didn't need. Next the bank was accused of forcing consumers to pay millions of dollars in improper fees connected with home mortgages. At the end of 2017, the Navajo Nation sued Wells Fargo for predatory tactics from 2009 to 2016, including creating unauthorized accounts and telling tribal elders who didn't speak English that they had to open unnecessary savings accounts in order to cash checks. And to close out 2017, Wells Fargo set aside $3.25 billion from its fourth-quarter earnings to pay for litigation arising from the scandals.

Although Wells Fargo generated nearly $22 billion in profits in 2016, there seemed to be no end to the reports of dishonest and unethical behavior by its leadership. In February 2018 the Federal Reserve Board condemned Wells Fargo for "widespread consumer abuses and compliance breakdowns" and "pervasive and persistent misconduct." The Fed issued a cease-and-desist order that the bank must improve its governance and risk management and its oversight by its board of directors. In an unprecedented punishment of an American bank, the Federal Reserve froze Wells Fargo's growth and forced four members of its board of directors to step down. This was first time the Fed ever imposed a limit on the assets of a financial institution. The final blow came in April 2018 when federal regulators levied a billion dollar fine against Wells Fargo.

Just as Wells Fargo lost its historical compass, it also lost its moral compass. That was inexcusable, given the sophistication of its leaders. It is noteworthy that of the twenty Wells Fargo men profiled in these pages, not one had more than an elementary education. They did not need a high school diploma, let alone an MBA, to know the difference between right and wrong. By comparison, the morally bankrupt managers who led Wells Fargo down the road to perdition were highly educated and sophisticated. The principal villains—Kovacevich, Stumpf, and Tolstedt—created and led the unprincipled bank management that encouraged and enabled consumer fraud on a massive scale. They gutted Wells Fargo's core values for unscrupulous profits. Their combined efforts show that nineteenth-century robber barons are not a thing of the past.

No American business enterprise has a history as colorful and as meaningful as Wells Fargo's. Its modern leaders squandered that legacy in the name of pure corporate greed. Until Wells Fargo has regained its once-sterling reputation, Shotgun Jimmy Brown, Andy Hall, and Steve Venard are rolling over in their unmarked graves.

ACKNOWLEDGMENTS

When I was a boy in the early 1960s, my grandmother took me to visit the Wells Fargo History Museum in San Francisco. I was enraptured at first sight. The place was filled with history that seemed to come alive: photographs, strongboxes, gold scales, shotguns, signs, Pony Express documents, express equipment of every kind, even a Concord stagecoach. While still in high school, I became a regular visitor, doing research on many of the Wells Fargo men who are featured in these pages. Irene Simpson Neasham (1916–2006) was the director for three decades. Beginning in the late 1930s, she spearheaded efforts to collect and preserve Wells Fargo's history, because many of the company's records had been destroyed in the 1906 San Francisco earthquake and fire. Irene and her assistants, Merrilee Gwerder Dowty and the late Elaine Gilleran, helped and encouraged a young researcher who has never forgotten their many kindnesses.

This book is dedicated to Dr. Robert J. Chandler for a good reason. I have been fortunate to count Bob as my good friend for more than thirty years. He is the retired historian for Wells Fargo Bank and is the preeminent authority on western express companies, frontier banking, and the Civil War in California. Bob has helped me over the years on countless research projects. For many years, he assisted me in my research visits to the Wells Fargo History Department. He answered myriad questions, dug up a great deal of obscure information, and read an early draft of this manuscript. I cannot thank him enough for his time, his help, and his fellowship.

My great friend William B. Secrest, the leading authority on crime and lawlessness on the California frontier, helped me in countless ways. Some of his many books and articles are cited in the notes for this book.

Oddly enough, England is home to some of the top experts on the Old West. One of them is Chris Penn, an authority on outlaws and lawmen. He has helped me generously with my Wells Fargo research. I also owe a special word of thanks to my fellow Wells Fargo collectors for their help and advice over the years: Tom Martin, Don Gordon, Greg Martin, Dennis Kurlander, Peter Vourakis, John Wilkinson, Bobby McDearmon, Ed daRoza, and the late Bill Frazier.

I am grateful to many others: the staff of the California State Archives in Sacramento, especially Joe Samora, retired archivist; Dan Buck, Harold L. "Lee" Edwards, Kurt House, Randy Lish, the late Robert G. and Lila Martin, Robert G. McCubbin, Terry Ommen, Chuck Parsons, Arthur Soule, and Florence Thacker. Special thanks to Robert Boessenecker and Amy Castañeda Huerta for their help with the images in this book.

I would also like to thank my fellow members of the Wild West History Association for their friendship and support. Its bimonthly journal and annual rendezvous are highly recommended. I encourage anyone interested in the history of the Old West to join this organization.

To my agent, Claire Gerus, and my editor, Stephen Power, many thanks for all their efforts connected with this book. And last, I am always grateful to my wife and chief literary critic, Marta Diaz, for her love, advice, and support.

NOTES

INTRODUCTION

1. Only three books about Wells Fargo special officers have appeared: Richard H. Dillon's *Wells Fargo Detective: A Biography of James B. Hume* (1969), Fred Dodge's posthumous memoir, *Under Cover for Wells Fargo* (1969), and this author's *When Law Was in the Holster: The Frontier Life of Bob Paul* (2012).
2. Robert J. Chandler, "Wells Fargo: 'We Never Forget!'," part 1, *Quarterly of the National Association and Center for Outlaw and Lawman History* 11, no. 3 (Winter 1987): 5.
3. *Sacramento Daily Union*, September 8, 1856; *San Francisco Chronicle*, July 1, 1906; "Father of the Shotgun Messenger Service," *Wells Fargo Messenger* 6, no. 1 (September 1917): 16; William Lewins, *Her Majesty's Mails: An Historical and Descriptive Account of the British Post Office* (London: Sampson Low, Son, and Maston, 1864), p. 83.
4. John Boessenecker, *When Law Was in the Holster: The Frontier Life of Bob Paul* (Norman: University of Oklahoma Press, 2012), p. 97.
5. *San Francisco Call*, February 5, 1885; Chandler, "Wells Fargo: 'We Never Forget!'," part 1, p. 7.
6. Boessenecker, *When Law Was in the Holster*, pp. 96–97.
7. John Boessenecker, "Stage Robbers and Banditry: Myth vs. Fact," *The Californians* 5, no. 2 (March–April 1987): 32–33.
8. John Boessenecker, *Badge and Buckshot: Lawlessness in Old California* (Norman: University of Oklahoma Press, 1988), p. 200.

1. WELLS FARGO'S PIONEER MESSENGER

1. Pilsbury Hodgkins, "Life of Pilsbury Hodgkins, Better Known Throughout California as Chips," unpublished ms., 1890, pp. 16–17, Wells Fargo Bank

History Department. The town of Jacksonville is now covered by Don Pedro Reservoir.

2. *San Francisco Chronicle,* September 6, 1892.

3. Hodgkins, "Life of Pilsbury Hodgkins," pp. 1–3.

4. Ibid., pp. 14–15.

5. Ibid., pp. 19–20.

6. Ibid., p. 20; *San Francisco Daily Alta California,* July 11, 1851; Hubert H. Bancroft, *Popular Tribunals,* vol. 1 (San Francisco: The History Company, 1887), pp. 468–69.

7. *Mariposa Gazette,* June 21, 1884; *Catalogue, Wells Fargo and Company Historical Exhibit, Etc. at the World's Columbian Exposition* (San Francisco: H. S. Crocker Co., 1893), p. 23.

8. Hodgkins, "Life of Pilsbury Hodgkins," pp. 14, 17–19; "Pilsbury Hodgkins, Pony Rider," *Quarterly of the Society of California Pioneers* 11, no. 3 (September 1925): 180–82.

9. Hodgkins, "Life of Pilsbury Hodgkins," p. 23; *San Francisco Chronicle,* September 6, 1893; William F. Strobridge, "Pilsbury 'Chips' Hodgkins, Gold Miner to Gold Boat Messenger," *CHISPA, The Quarterly of the Tuolumne County Historical Society* 34, no. 1 (July–September 1994): 1159.

10. *Sacramento Daily Union,* February 1, 1862; *San Francisco Bulletin,* February 3, 1862; William F. Strobridge, "Chips Hodgkins: Wells Fargo's Messenger on the San Joaquin River," *The San Joaquin Historian* 8, no. 1 (Spring 1994): 9.

11. Hodgkins, "Life of Pilsbury Hodgkins," p. 24; *Sacramento Daily Union,* October 1, 1866; *San Francisco Daily Alta California,* October 3, 1866.

12. Hodgkins, "Life of Pilsbury Hodgkins," pp. 24–25; Strobridge, "Chips Hodgkins," p. 14.

13. *The Expressman's Monthly* 1, no. 7 (July 1876): 199–202. The original silver treasure box is on display in the Wells Fargo History Museum in San Francisco.

14. *San Francisco Call,* September 6, 1892; *San Francisco Chronicle,* September 6, 1892; William F. Strobridge, "Pilsbury 'Chips' Hodgkins: Wells Fargo's Southern California Messenger," *Southern California Quarterly* 77, no. 4 (Winter 1995): 310–11.

2. THE FIRST WELLS FARGO DETECTIVE

1. *San Francisco Daily Alta California,* June 24, 1868.

2. Ibid., August 1, 1875.

3. *San Francisco Bulletin,* August 23, 1860. For Henry Johnson's many cases with Isaiah W. Lees, see William B. Secrest, *Dark and Tangled Threads of Crime: San Francisco's Famous Police Detective Isaiah W. Lees* (Sanger, CA: Word Dancer Press, 2004).

4. Jesse D. Mason, *History of Amador County, California* (Oakland, CA: Thompson & West, 1881), p. 222.

5. *Sacramento Daily Union,* February 13, 1857; Mason, *History of Amador County, California,* pp. 224–25.

6. *Sacramento Daily Union,* February 3 and 13, 1857, and June 8, 1857; *San Francisco Daily Alta California,* February 11, 14, and 20, 1857. Stories that the notorious Gold Rush bandit Richard "Rattlesnake Dick" Barter burglarized this safe are false.

7. *Mokelumne Hill (California) Calaveras Chronicle,* February 22, 1853; Chauncey L. Canfield, ed., *The Diary of a Forty-niner* (Boston: Houghton Mifflin, 1920), pp. 210–11; *The American Historical Review* 26, no. 3 (April 1921): 592–93. On the fictitious nature of *The Diary of a Forty-niner,* see Gary F. Kurutz, *The California Gold Rush: A Descriptive Bibliography of the Books and Pamphlets Covering the Years 1848–1853* (San Francisco: Book Club of California, 1997), pp. 112–13. There is also a false claim that "Reelfoot" Williams was actually the notorious Gold Rush outlaw George Skinner, alias George Williamson. This yarn seems to have originated with writer B. G. Rousseau, who wrote a highly fictionalized series about California outlaws for the *San Jose News* in 1937.

8. *San Francisco Daily Alta California,* September 7, 1853; *Sacramento Daily Union,* September 7, 1853, and August 5 and 13, 1856.

9. *San Francisco Daily Alta California,* July 17, 19, and 22, 1860; *Sacramento Daily Union,* November 27, 1860; William B. Secrest, *Lawmen and Desperadoes* (Spokane: Arthur H. Clark Co., 1994), p. 193; R. Michael Wilson, *Stagecoach Robberies in California: A Complete Record, 1856–1913* (Jefferson, NC: McFarland & Co., 2014), pp. 24–25.

10. *Sacramento Daily Union,* January 16 and March 25, 1864, April 13, 1865, and December 18, 1866; *San Francisco Daily Alta California,* March 2, 1865; *Marysville (California) Daily Appeal,* April 13, 1865; *Red Bluff (California) Independent,* June 1, 1865.

11. *San Francisco Daily Alta California,* September 12, 1866; *San Francisco Bulletin,* September 12, 1866; *Sacramento Daily Union,* September 14 and 19, 1866, and December 4, 1867; *Marysville (California) Daily Appeal,* February 13, 1867; *Ex Parte Peter D. Hedley* (1866) 31 Cal. Reports 107; *Journal of the Assembly* (Sacramento: State Printer, 1868), p. 76.

12. *San Francisco Daily Alta California,* December 8 and 16, 1867, and February 11, 1868; *San Francisco Call,* December 8, 1867; *Sacramento Daily Union,* December 9 and 11, 1867, February 10, 1868, and May 4, 1868; Wilson, *Stagecoach Robberies in California,* pp. 13–14.

13. *San Francisco Bulletin,* July 6, 1868; *San Francisco Daily Alta California,* July 7, 19, 1868, and January 18, 1869; *People v. Edwin Bogart* (1868) 36 Cal. Reports 245.

14. *New York Herald,* July 25, 1868.

15. *San Francisco Bulletin,* June 30, 1868; *San Francisco Daily Alta California,* June 30, 1868.

16. *San Francisco Daily Alta California,* August 4 and 5, 1868.

17. Ibid., December 3 and 5, 1868.

18. Ibid., February 3 and 10, 1874, August 1 and 10, 1875, and December 16, 1875; *San Francisco Chronicle,* August 1, 1875.

3. FROM FIRST STAGE DRIVER
TO SHOTGUN MESSENGER

1. U.S. Census population schedules, San Francisco, California, 1900; *San Francisco Bulletin,* March 5, 1904; Oscar Osborn Winther, "Stage-coach Days in California: Reminiscences of H. C. Ward," *California Historical Society Quarterly* 13, no. 3 (September 1934): 255–61.

2. Henry C. Ward, "Old Pony the Stage Dog," pp. 1–2, typescript, James Otey Bradford Papers, Stanford University Library.

3. Ibid., p. 3.

4. Ibid., p. 4; *Portland Oregonian,* January 8, 1905; Oscar Osborn Winther, *The Old Oregon Country: A History of Frontier Trade, Transportation, and Travel* (Bloomington: Indiana University Press, 1950), pp. 259, 276–77.

5. Henry C. Ward, "Red the Owyhee Stage Dog," handwritten ms., James Otey Bradford Papers, Stanford University Library; Hubert Howe Bancroft, *History of Oregon,* vol. 2, *1848–1888* (San Francisco: The History Company, 1888), pp. 534, 549.

6. *Boise Idaho Statesman,* June 11 and July 9, 1867.

7. *Silver City (Idaho) Owyhee Avalanche,* September 26, 1868; *Boise Idaho Statesman,* September 24, 29, 1868; *Marysville (California) Daily Appeal,* October 7, 1868.

8. Henry C. Ward, "Between Treasure City, Nevada, and Hamilton in 1869," typescript; James Otey Bradford, "Henry C. Ward: His Flight from Treasure City to Hamilton, Nevada," typescript; both in James Otey Bradford Papers, Stanford University Library.

9. *San Francisco Daily Alta California,* December 4, 5, 1869.

10. *Santa Cruz Sentinel,* May 16, 1874; Stephen M. Payne, *A Howling Wilderness: A History of the Summit Road Area of the Santa Cruz Mountains, 1850–1906* (Santa Cruz: Loma Prieta Publishing Co., 1978), pp. 27–36. The stagecoach owned by Ward and Colegrove, and driven by Ward, is now on display in the Wells Fargo History Museum in San Francisco. This coach was built for Wells Fargo in 1867, one of ten ordered from Abbot-Downing for the overland run. Colegrove acquired it in the early 1870s, and Wells Fargo bought it back in 1928. Robert J. Chandler to author, November 21, 2015.

11. S. D. Brastow to Henry C. Ward, April 22, 1878; L. F. Rowell to Henry C. Ward, May 11, 1878; Route Agent L. A. Hall to Henry C. Ward, July 26, 1879; John J. Valentine to H. C. Ward, March 10, 1881; all in Wells Fargo Bank History Department; Roger D. McGrath, *Gunfighters, Highwaymen & Vigilantes: Violence on the Frontier* (Berkeley: University of California Press, 1984), p. 173.

12. *Silver City (Idaho) Owyhee Avalanche,* May 21, 1881; R. Michael Wilson, *Wells, Fargo & Co. Stagecoach and Train Robberies, 1870–1884* (Jefferson, NC: McFarland & Co., 2010), pp. 98–99.

13. *San Francisco Daily Alta California,* May 10, 1885; *San Francisco Bulletin,* May 9, 1885; *Salt Lake City Herald,* May 16, 1885.

14. *Mendocino Beacon,* May 16, 1885.

15. *San Francisco Daily Alta California,* April 25, 1886; *Sacramento Daily Union,* March 8, 30, 1886; *Santa Rosa Press Democrat,* April 24, 1886.

16. *San Francisco Daily Alta California,* December 22, 1885; *Sacramento Daily Union,* August 18, 1886; Wilson, *Stagecoach Robberies in California,* pp. 233–34.

17. *Carson City (Nevada) Morning Appeal,* January 31, 1888; *San Francisco Chronicle,* May 2, 1888; *San Francisco Bulletin,* August 22, 1888.

18. *San Francisco Daily Alta California,* March 8, 1891; *San Francisco Call,* March 8, 1891; *Los Angeles Herald,* March 8, 1891; Mark Dugan, *Knight of the Road: The Life of Highwayman Ham White* (Athens: Ohio University Press, 1990), pp. 85–88, 103.

19. L. F. Rowell to Agents, January 19, 1893; J. N. Thacker to H. C. Ward, July 16, 1895; both in Wells Fargo Bank History Department; *Ukiah (California) Men-*

docino Dispatch Democrat, December 20, 1895; *San Francisco Bulletin,* March 5, 1904; *Catalogue, Wells Fargo and Company Historical Exhibit, etc. at the World's Columbian Exposition,* p. 18.

20. S. D. Brastow to H. C. Ward, January 4, 1904, Wells Fargo Bank History Department; *San Francisco Bulletin,* March 5, 1904.

4. TWELVE-GAUGE JUSTICE

1. Mexican War Widow's Pension Application File, Sarah E. Gay; Mexican War Land Bounty Application No. 5936216047 (Daniel C. Gay), National Archives, Washington, D.C. *The History of Gentry and Worth Counties, Missouri* (St. Joseph, MO: National Historical Co., 1882), pp. 204–205, 207.

2. Mexican War Widow's Pension Application File, Sarah E. Gay; Mexican War Land Bounty Application No. 5936216047; *The History of Gentry and Worth Counties,* p. 289.

3. *Sacramento Daily Union,* December 5, 1854; *San Francisco Bulletin,* December 6, 8, 1858; *San Francisco California Police Gazette,* June 11, 1859; *San Francisco Call,* October 3, 1879: *San Jose Pioneer,* October 17, 1879.

4. *Sacramento Daily Union,* August 3, 1857, March 15, 1858, and May 22, 1858; *Sacramento Daily Bee,* May 22, 1858; *Marysville (California) Daily Appeal,* June 4, 1868.

5. *Sacramento Union,* November 9, 11, 1859.

6. *Nevada City (California) Democrat,* November 16, 1859; *Auburn (California) Placer Herald,* November 12, 1859; *Sacramento Daily Union,* November 9, 11, 1859; *San Francisco California Police Gazette,* November 12, 26, 1859; *Stockton (California) San Joaquin Republican,* November 19, 1859, and January 17, 1860. James H. Latham was the brother of California governor and U.S. senator Milton S. Latham. *Sacramento Daily Union,* June 24, 1876.

7. *San Andreas (California) Independent,* January 21 and 28, 1860; *San Francisco Bulletin,* January 16, 17, 1860; *Stockton (California) San Joaquin Republican,* January 17, 1860; *Sacramento Daily Union,* November 12, 1859, and January 17, 1860. The Cherokee Bob in this holdup was not the notorious desperado Henry J. "Cherokee Bob" Talbot, for he was then in San Quentin. There were at least five "Cherokee Bobs" in California during the 1850s. It is possible, though by no means certain, that Boss was the noted outlaw Boston G. "Boss" Damewood, lynched in Los Angeles in 1864.

8. *San Andreas (California) Independent,* January 21 and 28, 1860; *San Francisco Bulletin,* January 16 and 17, 1860; *Stockton (California) San Joaquin Republican,* January 17, 1860; *Sacramento Daily Union,* November 12, 1859, and January 17, 1860.

9. *San Francisco California Police Gazette,* January 21, 1860.

10. *Sacramento Daily Union,* October 17, 1862, July 16, 1862, February 17, 1863, April 26, 1866, October 14, 1865, April 12, 1867, December 28, 1872, October 6, 1879; *San Jose Pioneer,* October 18, 1879.

11. *Sacramento Daily Union,* October 4, 1879.

12. *San Francisco Bulletin,* June 12, 1879; *San Francisco Daily Alta California,* September 27, 1879; *Sacramento Daily Record-Union,* October 4, 1879; *San Jose Pioneer,* October 18, 1879. All charges were dismissed against the Roddans and the crime was never solved. *Sacramento Daily Union,* October 6, 1879.

5. FROM PONY EXPRESS TO WELLS FARGO

1. 1850 U.S. Census Population Schedules, Nelson County, Kentucky; 1860 U.S. Census Population Schedules, Savannah, Missouri; *Deer Lodge (Montana) New North-west*, March 26, 1880.

2. *Deer Lodge (Montana) New North-west*, March 26, 1880; Raymond W. Settle and Mary Lund Settle, *Saddles and Spurs: The Pony Express Saga* (Lincoln: University of Nebraska Press, 1955), p. 52.

3. J. V. Frederick, *Ben Holladay, the Stagecoach King: A Chapter in the Development of Transcontinental Transportation* (Glendale, CA: Arthur H. Clark Co., 1940), p. 78.

4. *San Francisco Daily Alta California*, May 26, 1862; *Sacramento Daily Union*, May 8 and 24, 1862, and June 7, 1862; R. F. Elwell, "The Story of the Overland Mail," *Outing Magazine* 48, no. 1 (April 1906): 67; LeRoy R. Hafen, *The Overland Mail, 1849–1869* (Norman: University of Oklahoma Press, 2004), pp. 242–46.

5. *Sacramento Daily Union*, June 7, 1862.

6. *Salt Lake City Daily Tribune*, November 20, 1886; *Helena (Montana) Weekly Herald*, June 12, 1873.

7. *Helena (Montana) Weekly Herald*, July 31, 1873, and October 30, 1873; *Deer Lodge (Montana) New North-west*, August 9, 1873, and April 18, 1874; Wilson, *Wells, Fargo & Co. Stagecoach and Train Robberies*, pp. 153–55, 198, 249–51.

8. *New York Sun*, December 12, 1886; *Salt Lake City Herald*, August 13, 1900.

9. Missouri, County Marriage, Naturalization, and Court Records, 1800–1991; *Deer Lodge (Montana) New North-west*, September 13, 1873, and November 22, 1873; *Glendale (Montana) Madisonian*, October 31, 1874; *Helena (Montana) Weekly Herald*, February 18, 1875.

10. Aaron Y. Ross, memoir, February 23, 1916, pp. 10–12, California State Library, Sacramento, CA.

11. *Helena (Montana) Independent*, July 8, 1876; *Deer Lodge (Montana) New North-west*, July 28, 1876; *Sacramento Daily Union*, November 15 and 30, 1877.

12. *Pioche (Nevada) Weekly Record*, February 23, 1878, and March 16, 30, 1878; *Sacramento Daily Union*, June 28, 1878, and July 3, 1878; *Virginia City (Nevada) Evening Chronicle*, March 29, 1878, May 11, 1878, and July 2, 1878. On Frank Clifford's earlier career, see Wilson, *Wells, Fargo & Co. Stagecoach and Train Robberies*, pp. 68–71.

13. Robert K. DeArment, *Assault on the Deadwood Stage: Road Agents and Shotgun Messengers* (Norman: University of Oklahoma Press, 2011), pp. 151–57, 243 n. 21.

14. Census Population Schedules, Deadwood, Dakota Territory, 1880; *Deadwood (South Dakota) Weekly Pioneer*, March 3, 1880; *Deer Lodge (Montana) New North-west*, March 26, 1880; *Helena (Montana) Independent*, February 25, 1880, and March 16, 1880.

15. *Deadwood (South Dakota) Weekly Pioneer*, January 8 and 22, 1881, and March 24, 1881.

16. Wells Fargo General Cash Books, abstract prepared by Dr. Robert J. Chandler, Wells Fargo Bank History Department; *Deadwood (South Dakota) Weekly Pioneer*, March 24, 1881.

17. *Helena (Montana) Independent Record*, December 15, 1883, February 22, 1884, and November 12, 1886; *Deer Lodge (Montana) New North-west*, December 21, 1883, and July 3, 1885; *Salt Lake City Daily Tribune*, November 20, 1886.

18. *Deer Lodge (Montana) New North-west*, November 12, 1886.

6. THE RIFLEMAN

1. Boessenecker, *Badge and Buckshot*, pp. 37–40.

2. *Sacramento Daily Union,* December 25, 1865, and May 18, 1866; Boessenecker, *Badge and Buckshot,* pp. 41–42; R. Michael Wilson, *Great Stagecoach Robberies of the Old West* (Guilford, CT: Two Dot, 2007), p. 50.

3. *San Francisco Bulletin,* February 26 and 27, 1866; *Sacramento Daily Union,* February 26, 1866, and May 18, 1866; Boessenecker, *Badge and Buckshot,* pp. 42–43.

4. *Sacramento Daily Union,* April 21, 1866; *San Francisco Bulletin,* April 25, 1866; Boessenecker, *Badge and Buckshot,* p. 42.

5. *Sacramento Daily Union,* May 9, 10, and 18, 1866. A report that the stage from Washington was also robbed on May 8 proved to be false. *Marysville (California) Daily Appeal,* May 11, 1866.

6. *Nevada City (California) Transcript,* May 16, 1866; *San Francisco Daily Alta California,* May 17, 1866; *Sacramento Daily Union,* May 19, 1866.

7. *Salt Lake City Tribune,* August 6, 1891.

8. *Nevada City (California) Transcript,* May 16 and 17, 1866.

9. Boessenecker, *Badge and Buckshot,* pp. 44–45.

10. *San Francisco Daily Alta California,* March 7, 1868, and April 26, 1869; *Sacramento Daily Union,* March 26, 1869; *San Francisco Bulletin,* July 16, 1869; *Marysville (California) Daily Appeal,* July 31, 1869.

11. U.S. Census Population Schedules, Cloverdale, CA, 1860, 1880; California Great Register, Mendocino County, CA, 1867, at www.familysearch.org; *San Francisco Daily Alta California,* November 13, 1870; *Healdsburg (California) Russian River Flag,* November 24, 1870; William James Pleasants, *Twice Across the Plains, 1849, 1856* (San Francisco: Warner N. Brunt Co., 1906), p. 160.

12. *San Francisco Daily Alta California,* February 17, 1871; *San Francisco Bulletin,* February 18, 1871; *Healdsburg (California) Russian River Flag,* July 13, 20, and 27, 1871; *San Francisco Chronicle,* July 14, 1871.

13. *San Francisco Bulletin,* August 12, 1871; *San Francisco Daily Alta California,* August 18, 1871.

14. *Healdsburg (California) Russian River Flag,* August 24, 1871, and January 4, 1872; *San Francisco Daily Alta California,* August 21, 1871, and November 12, 1871; Boessenecker, *Badge and Buckshot,* pp. 47–48.

15. *San Francisco Bulletin,* October 11, 1871; *Sacramento Daily Union,* October 11, 1871; John Boessenecker, "Steve Venard, Wells Fargo's Ace Troubleshooter," *Golden West* 8, no. 10 (September 1972): 13.

16. *San Francisco Chronicle,* November 19, 1871; *Healdsburg (California) Russian River Flag,* March 13, 1873, and January 15, 1880; Boessenecker, *Badge and Buckshot,* pp. 49–53.

17. *Sacramento Daily Union,* June 30, 1873; Boessenecker, *Badge and Buckshot,* pp. 53–55; John Boessenecker, *Lawman: The Life and Times of Harry Morse, 1835–1912* (Norman: University of Oklahoma Press, 1998), pp. 220–21.

18. Boessenecker, *Badge and Buckshot,* pp. 55–57; *San Francisco Daily Alta California,* November 1, 1885.

19. *San Francisco Daily Alta California,* May 22, 1891; Boessenecker, *Badge and Buckshot,* pp. 57–58. Steve Venard's grave site, like many of those in the Pioneer Cemetery, is long lost.

7. A SHOTGUN MESSENGER IN OLD MONTANA

1. *Helena (Montana) Independent*, April 2, 1903.
2. Census Population Schedules, Middleton, Pennsylvania, 1850; *Helena (Montana) Independent*, April 2, 1903; Helen Fitzgerald Sanders, *X. Beidler: Vigilante* (Norman: University of Oklahoma Press, 1957), pp. 3–21.
3. *Helena (Montana) Weekly Herald*, January 2, 1868.
4. *Pittsburg (Pennsylvania) Dispatch*, January 26, 1890; Frederick Allen, *A Decent, Orderly Lynching: The Montana Vigilantes* (Norman: University of Oklahoma Press, 2004), pp. 349–50.
5. *Lewistown (Montana) Fergus County Argus*, December 8, 1892; Sanders, *X. Beidler*, pp. 132–35.
6. *Fort Benton (Montana) River Press*, May 24, 1882; *Maiden (Montana) Mineral Argus*, June 12, 1884. On some of Beidler's comings and goings as a Wells Fargo messenger, see *Deer Lodge (Montana) New North-west*, December 9, 1870; *Helena (Montana) Weekly Herald*, January 25, 1872, September 16, 1875, and December 16, 1875; *Corinne (Utah) Daily Reporter*, August 31, 1871, and March 27, 1872.
7. *Fort Benton (Montana) River Press*, May 24, 1882; *Butte (Montana) Semi-Weekly Miner*, December 25, 1886.
8. There are several versions of this story: *Helena (Montana) Independent*, January 23, 1890, and April 2, 1903; *Anaconda (Montana) Standard*, March 30, 1919; and *Virginia City Montana Democrat*, March 21, 1868. The latter account, undoubtedly the most accurate, appears in Larry Barsness, *Gold Camp: Alder Gulch and Virginia City, Montana* (New York: Hastings House, 1962), pp. 99–100.
9. *Sacramento Daily Union*, July 30, 1870; *Idaho City World*, August 4, 1870; *Boise (Idaho) Statesman*, August 6 and 11, 1870; *Butte (Montana) Semi-Weekly Miner*, December 25, 1886. On Nick Freyer, see *Helena (Montana) Weekly Herald*, October 31, 1867; *Virginia City Montana Post*, February 22, 1868.
10. *San Francisco Bulletin*, August 12, 1870; *Chicago Tribune*, August 22, 1870. Beidler's account was published in the *Butte (Montana) Semi-Weekly Miner*, December 25, 1886. Another version appears in the *Choteau (Montana) Acantha*, February 4, 1932.
11. *Great Falls (Montana) Tribune*, January 25, 1890.
12. *Helena (Montana) Independent*, January 23, 1890.
13. *Helena (Montana) Weekly Herald*, September 16, 1875.
14. *Helena (Montana) Independent Record*, March 28, 1954; William Edgar Paxson, *E. S. Paxson: Frontier Artist* (Boulder, CO: Pruett Publishing Company, 1984), p. 13.
15. *Butte (Montana) Semi-Weekly Miner*, March 30, 1887; *Helena (Montana) Independent*, June 6, 1889, and September 4, 1889; Paul F. Sharp, *Whoop Up Country: The Canadian American West, 1865–1885* (Minneapolis: University of Minnesota Press, 1955), pp. 123–26. Henry M. Beidler was murdered in Texarkana in 1888; the whole town mourned. *Fort Benton Montana River Press*, December 26, 1888.
16. *Helena (Montana) Independent*, January 23, 1890; Sharp, *Whoop Up Country*, p. 126.

8. "HONEST, FAITHFUL & BRAVE"

1. *New York Sun*, July 28, 1884.
2. Aubrey John Blair to Eugene Blair, April 2, 1866, Richard Frajola collection; bio-

graphical notes on Eugene Blair, Wells Fargo Bank History Department; *Anaconda (Montana) Standard*, February 8, 1912; Chris Penn, "Eugene Blair: A Terror to Road Agents," *Quarterly of the National Association for Outlaw and Lawman History* 30, no. 3 (July–September 2006): 7–8. In the past, several writers, including me, have mistakenly concluded that the noted stage driver Ned Blair was Eugene Blair. They were two different men.

3. *Pioche (Nevada) Weekly Record*, February 14, 1885; Penn, "Eugene Blair," pp. 8–9; Robert K. DeArment, *Deadly Dozen: Forgotten Gunfighters of the Old West*, vol. 3 (Norman: University of Oklahoma Press, 2010), p. 83.

4. *Salt Lake City Herald*, August 13, 1900; *Helena (Montana) Independent*, June 22, 1875, and July 20, 1884; Penn, "Eugene Blair," pp. 8–9.

5. *New York Sun*, July 28, 1884.

6. *Pioche (Nevada) Daily Record*, December 29, 1875, and January 5, 1876.

7. Ibid., January 20 and 21, 1876, and February 10, 1876; *Salt Lake City Tribune*, January 27, 1876; *Virginia City (Nevada) Chronicle*, January 21, 1876; *Sacramento Daily Union*, February 11 and 26, 1876.

8. *New York Sun*, reprinted in *Columbia (Tennessee) Herald*, October 7, 1898.

9. *Salt Lake City Herald*, February 29, 1876, and July 15, 1881; *Sacramento Daily Union*, March 8, 1876; *Pioche (Nevada) Daily Record*, September 27, 1876; Penn, "Eugene Blair," pp. 9–10.

10. Wilson, *Wells, Fargo & Co. Stagecoach and Train Robberies*, pp. 81–86; John Boessenecker, "The Great Train Holdup," *Nevada Highways and Parks* 33, no. 3 (Fall 1973): 30–32, 42.

11. *Pioche (Nevada) Daily Record*, April 15, 1876; *Reno (Nevada) Evening Gazette*, April 17, 1876; Penn, "Eugene Blair," pp. 10–11; Wilson, *Wells, Fargo & Co. Stagecoach and Train Robberies*, pp. 86–88.

12. *Sacramento Daily Union*, June 1 and 9, 1876; *Carson City (Nevada) Daily Appeal*, May 30, 1876; *The Expressman's Monthly* 1, no. 6 (June 1876): 174; Penn, "Eugene Blair," p. 11; Wilson, *Wells, Fargo & Co. Stagecoach and Train Robberies*, pp. 315–16.

13. *Lewiston (Maine) Evening Journal*, December 2, 1876; Penn, "Eugene Blair," p. 11.

14. *Pioche (Nevada) Weekly Record*, March 3 and 10, 1877, and February 23, 1878; *Placerville (California) Mountain Democrat*, March 17, 1877; *San Francisco Daily Alta California*, July 13, 1884; Penn, "Eugene Blair," p. 11–12; Wilson, *Wells, Fargo & Co. Stagecoach and Train Robberies*, pp. 75–76.

15. *New York Sun*, September 17, 1877; *Boise Idaho Statesman*, November 8, 1877; *San Francisco Bulletin*, December 8, 1877; *San Francisco Daily Alta California*, July 13, 1884; *Expressman's Monthly* 2, no. 10 (October 1877): 310–11; Penn, "Eugene Blair," pp. 13–15; Wilson, *Wells, Fargo & Co. Stagecoach and Train Robberies*, pp. 87–88.

16. *Reno Nevada State Journal*, April 18, 1879, and November 20, 1879; *Sacramento Daily Union*, May 29, 1884; Penn, "Eugene Blair," p. 16.

17. *New York Sun*, July 27, 1884.

18. *Pioche (Nevada) Weekly Record*, February 17, 1883, and January 19, 1884; *Sacramento Daily Union*, May 29, 1884; *Reno (Nevada) Evening Gazette*, May 27 and June 3, 1884; Penn, "Eugene Blair," p. 17.

19. *New York Sun*, July 28, 1884.

9. CHIEF SPECIAL OFFICER

1. Richard H. Dillon, *Wells Fargo Detective: A Biography of James B. Hume* (New York: Coward-McCann, 1969), pp. 24–35.
2. John Boessenecker, *Gold Dust and Gunsmoke* (New York: John Wiley & Sons, 1999), pp. 26–28.
3. *Sacramento Daily Union*, April 22, 1863; *San Francisco Daily Alta California*, December 23, 1863.
4. *Sacramento Daily Union*, April 28, May 24, and August 16, 1864.
5. Dillon, *Wells Fargo Detective*, pp. 89–104; Boessenecker, *Badge and Buckshot*, pp. 133–157.
6. *Sacramento Daily Union*, August 5 and 6, 1867.
7. Ibid., May 18, 1872; *San Francisco Daily Alta California*, March 10, 1873; Dillon, *Wells Fargo Detective*, pp. 115–29. Dillon, p. 115, incorrectly has Hume elected sheriff in 1868.
8. John Boessenecker, "The Bride and the Brigand," *The Californians* 5, no. 2 (March–April 1987): 36–42.
9. *Shasta (California) Courier*, September 14, 1878; *Yreka (California) Journal*, September 11 and 18, 1878; Mae Helene Boggs, *My Playhouse Was a Concord Coach* (Oakland, CA: Howell North Press, 1942), pp. 646–48; Wilson, *Stagecoach Robberies in California*, pp. 221–23.
10. *Expressmen's Monthly* 4, no. 3 (March 1879): 75–76; Dillon, *Wells Fargo Detective*, pp. 156–57, 219.
11. *New York Tribune*, December 16 and 29, 1881; *Dallas Daily Herald*, December 22, 1881; *Red Bluff (California) Sentinel*, January 14, 1882; *Tucson Daily Citizen*, October 27, 1882.
12. *Tombstone (Arizona) Daily Epitaph*, January 8, 1882; *San Francisco Daily Report*, January 9 and 13, 1882; *San Francisco Exchange*, quoted in Chuck Hornung, *Wyatt Earp's Cow-boy Campaign: The Bloody Restoration of Law and Order Along the Mexican Border, 1882* (Jefferson, NC: McFarland & Co., 2016), p. 102; Dillon, *Wells Fargo Detective*, p. 209.
13. *San Francisco Examiner*, August 9, 1896; Boessenecker, *When Law Was in the Holster*, pp. 191–92. Wyatt Earp later claimed that Curly Bill was armed with a Wells Fargo shotgun (supposedly taken from the messenger in the first holdup) and also was wearing Jim Hume's fancy six-guns when he died. Both claims were untrue. See Steve Gatto, *Curly Bill: Tombstone's Most Famous Outlaw* (Lansing, MI: Protar House, 2003), pp. 128–30, 163–64.
14. *San Jose (California) Evening News*, October 22 and 31, 1887; *San Francisco Chronicle*, October 24, 1887.
15. A "swedged ball" is known today as a swaged bullet. Swaging is an improved process over the old method of casting bullets. A swaged lead bullet is die-struck by a machine, instead of molten lead cast into a mold, and is generally more accurate than a cast bullet.
16. *Sacramento Daily Union*, August 24 and October 13, 1888; *Fresno Morning Republican*, July 26 and September 16, 1888, and May 3, 1889; Dillon, *Wells Fargo Detective*, pp. 229–34.
17. San Quentin Prison Register, convict nos. 3092, 3642, and 5528, California State Archives, Sacramento, CA; *Sacramento Union*, August 30, 1865, July 25, 1871, March 10, 1873, and October 23, 1882.

18. *Sacramento Daily Record-Union,* October 27, 1890.
19. *San Francisco Bulletin,* August 10, 1882; *Sacramento Daily Union,* October 23, 1882; *Chicago Inter Ocean,* October 16, 1890; William B. Secrest, "Dead Men and Desperadoes," *True West,* May 1989, pp. 14–20; William B. Secrest, *California Desperadoes: Stories of Early California Outlaws in Their Own Words* (Sanger, CA: Word Dancer Press, 2000), pp. 109–15.
20. *Chicago Inter Ocean,* October 16, 1890; *Chicago Times,* October 16, 1890; *Sacramento Daily Record-Union,* October 27, 1890; *San Francisco Chronicle,* October 16, 1890; Secrest, *California Desperadoes,* pp. 118–24.
21. *San Francisco Chronicle,* May 20, 1904.

10. RIVERMAN, EXPRESSMAN

1. *Leavenworth (Kansas) Bulletin,* October 9, 1867; *Florence Arizona Weekly Enterprise,* August 20, 1882; William Culp Darrah, "Three Letters by Andrew Hall," *Utah Historical Society Quarterly* 16 (1948): 505; Chris Penn, "Frontiersman Andy Hall Served Major Powell and Wells Fargo," *Wild West* 22, no. 2 (August 2009): 20; Hugh Jackson Dobbs, *History of Gage County, Nebraska* (Lincoln, NE: Western Publishing & Engraving Co., 1918), p. 574.
2. John Wesley Powell, *Canyons of the Colorado* (Meadville, PA: Flood & Vincent, 1895), p. 123.
3. Darrah, "Three Letters by Andrew Hall," p. 506.
4. John Cooley, ed., *Exploring the Colorado River: Firsthand Accounts by Powell and His Crew* (Mineola, NY: Dover Publications, 1988), pp. 11–12, 28, 31, 49; Penn, "Frontiersman Andy Hall Served Major Powell and Wells Fargo," pp. 20–21.
5. U.S. Census Population Schedules, Ehrenberg, Arizona, 1870, and Florence, Arizona, 1880; *Prescott (Arizona) Weekly Miner,* March 22 and 29, 1873, August 21, 1874, and January 8, 1875; *Florence Arizona Weekly Enterprise,* August 20, 1882.
6. *Phoenix Arizona Republic,* June 3, 1956; Jess G. Hayes, *Boots and Bullets: The Life and Times of John G. Wentworth* (Tucson: University of Arizona Press, 1967), pp. 121–24.
7. *Yuma Arizona Sentinel,* September 24, 1881; *Florence Arizona Weekly Enterprise,* quoted in *Los Angeles Herald,* September 21, 1881; *Globe Arizona Silver Belt,* August 23, 1884.
8. *Florence Arizona Weekly Enterprise,* December 3 and 10, 1881; *San Francisco Chronicle,* September 3, 1893.
9. U.S. Census Population Schedules, Globe, Arizona, 1880; *Salt Lake City Tribune,* October 2, 1875, and September 2, 1882; *Salt Lake City Herald,* August 27, 1882; *Globe Arizona Silver Belt,* March 12, 1881; *San Luis Obispo (California) Tribune,* December 7 and 21, 1878; *Ukiah City (California) Press,* March 21, 1879. Many accounts incorrectly spell the brothers' surname as Grimes.
10. *Florence Arizona Weekly Enterprise,* February 18, 1882, June 3, 1882, and August 26, 1882; *Globe Arizona Silver Belt,* August 26, 1882; James H. McClintock, *Arizona, the Youngest State* (Chicago: S. J. Clarke, 1916), p. 239.
11. *Globe Arizona Silver Belt,* August 26, 1882; *Florence Arizona Weekly Enterprise,* August 26, 1882.
12. *Florence Arizona Weekly Enterprise,* August 26, 1882, September 9, 1882, and October 7, 14, and 21, 1882; *Globe Arizona Silver Belt,* August 26, 1882; *Tucson Weekly*

Citizen, August 27, 1882, and October 22, 1882; *San Francisco Chronicle,* September 3, 1893; John Boessenecker, "Pete Gabriel: Gunfighting Lawman of the Southwestern Frontier," *Journal of Arizona History* 53, no. 1 (Spring 2012): 16–18; Robert J. Chandler, "Wells Fargo: 'We Never Forget!'," part 2, *Quarterly of the National Association and Center for Outlaw and Lawman History* 11, no. 3 (Spring 1988): 8; Wilson, *Wells, Fargo & Co. Stagecoach and Train Robberies,* p. 107. A commonly told but totally false story is that Valentine wired to Vosburgh, "Damn the money. Hang the murderers."

13. *Globe Arizona Record,* August 22, 1963.

11. THE MAN WHO CAPTURED BLACK BART

1. In one of the first press reports of Black Bart's capture, a San Francisco newspaper claimed that Black Bart was arrested by Hume, assisted by Harry Morse and police captain A. W. Stone. *San Francisco Daily Alta California,* November 14, 1883. Despite the fact that this error was promptly corrected in print, the myth lives on.
2. For Morse's story, see Boessenecker, *Lawman.* On Vásquez, see John Boessenecker, *Bandido: The Life and Times of Tiburcio Vasquez* (Norman: University of Oklahoma Press, 2010).
3. William Collins and Bruce Levene, *Black Bart: The True Story of the West's Most Famous Stagecoach Robber* (Mendocino, CA: Pacific Transcriptions, 1992), pp. 19–23, 56–68.
4. Boessenecker, *Lawman,* pp. 247–49.
5. *San Francisco Call,* February 19, 1899; Collins and Levene, *Black Bart,* pp. 136–47.
6. The Ferguson & Biggy laundry was co-owned by William J. Biggy, who became San Francisco's chief of police in 1907 and whose death, under suspicious circumstances the following year, remains one of the city's enduring mysteries.
7. *San Francisco Call,* November 17, 1883; *San Francisco Examiner,* November 19, 1883; Boessenecker, *Lawman,* pp. 249–51.
8. *San Francisco Call,* November 15 and 17, 1883; *San Francisco Bulletin,* December 24, 1905; Boessenecker, *Lawman,* pp. 249–51.
9. Boessenecker, *Lawman,* pp. 244–45, 259–60.

12. TRUE GRIT

1. U.S. Census Population Schedules, Fort Calhoun, Washington County, Nebraska Territory, 1860; Tovey family history notes, at www.rootsweb.ancestry.com; *San Francisco Examiner,* April 30, 1892; *Vinita (Oklahoma) Indian Chieftain,* July 6, 1893.
2. *San Francisco Examiner,* June 18, 1893; *Deer Lodge (Montana) New North-west,* September 5, 1874, and December 4, 1874; *Helena (Montana) Weekly Herald,* September 10, 1874; *Silver City (Idaho) Owyhee Daily Avalanche,* November 26, 1874.
3. *Deer Lodge (Montana) New North-west,* June 15, 1877, and November 22, 1878; *Butte (Montana) Miner,* August 28, 1877; *Helena (Montana) Independent,* August 21, 1877; Doug Brodie and James Watson, *Big Bad Bodie: High Sierra Ghost Town* (San Francisco: Robert D. Reed Publishers, 2002), p. 197. On Bob Paul's

career as a Wells Fargo messenger and detective, see Boessenecker, *When Law Was in the Holster: The Frontier Life of Bob Paul*, pp. 91–129.

4. William B. Secrest, *Perilous Trails, Dangerous Men: Early California Stagecoach Robbers and Their Desperate Careers, 1856–1900* (Clovis, CA: Quill Driver Books, 2002), pp. 180–82; Wilson, *Wells, Fargo & Co. Stagecoach and Train Robberies*, pp. 193–96; Roy O'Dell, "Milton Sharp, Scourge of Wells Fargo," *Quarterly of the National Association for Outlaw and Lawman History* 23, no. 3 (July–September 1999): 1, 45–47.

5. Aaron Y. Ross, memoir, February 23, 1916, p. 15, California State Library, Sacramento, CA.

6. *Carson City (Nevada) Morning Appeal*, September 7, 1880; *Bodie (California) Daily Free Press*, reprinted in the *Tombstone (Arizona) Daily Epitaph*, September 15, 1880; *Sacramento Daily Union*, September 11, 1880; *Reno (Nevada) Evening Gazette*, September 6 and 10, 1880; R. Michael Wilson, *Wells, Fargo & Company's Report of Losses*, (Las Vegas, NV: RaMA PRESS, 2008) pp. 266–68; Roger D. McGrath, *Gunfighters, Highwaymen, & Vigilantes: Violence on the Frontier* (Berkeley: University of California Press, 1984), pp. 168–71.

7. Aaron Y. Ross, memoir, pp. 16–17; *Omaha (Nebraska) Daily Bee*, February 11, 1885.

8. Aaron Y. Ross, memoir, pp. 17–18; *San Francisco Bulletin*, September 13 and 14, 1880; *Sacramento Daily Union*, September 15, 1880; Wilson, *Wells, Fargo & Company's Report of Losses*, pp. 268–69. The account of Milt Sharp in Eugene B. Block, *Great Stagecoach Robbers of the West* (Garden City, NY: Doubleday & Co, 1962), pp. 157–67, is largely fictitious.

9. *Virginia City (Nevada) Enterprise*, reprinted in the *Omaha (Nebraska) Daily Bee*, March 11, 1885; *Denver Rocky Mountain News*, March 7, 1885; *Silver City (Idaho) Owyhee Avalanche*, April 4, 1885.

10. *Deer Lodge (Montana) New North-west*, December 3, 1880; *Reno (Nevada) Weekly Nevada State Journal*, October 11, 1884; *Sacramento Daily Union*, October 17, 1884; *San Francisco Chronicle*, October 17, 1884; Wells Fargo General Cash Books, abstract prepared by Dr. Robert J. Chandler, Wells Fargo Bank History Department; Wilson, *Wells, Fargo & Company's Report of Losses*, pp. 147–49.

11. *Carson City (Nevada) Morning Appeal*, December 23, 1884; *Virginia City (Nevada) Evening Chronicle*, December 22 and 31, 1884, May 23, 1885; *San Francisco Daily Alta California*, December 22, 1884; *Reno (Nevada) Weekly Gazette*, June 4, 1885; *Reno (Nevada) Evening News*, December 23, 1884; *Salt Lake City Tribune*, January 8, 1885; McGrath, *Gunfighters, Highwaymen, & Vigilantes*, pp. 210–12; Wilson, *Wells, Fargo & Company's Report of Losses*, pp. 228–30.

12. *San Francisco Call*, August 17, 1889, and May 1, 1892.

13. *San Francisco Call*, May 1, 2, and 4, 1892; *San Francisco Examiner*, April 30, 1892; *San Francisco Chronicle*, May 1, 1892; *San Andreas (California) Calaveras Prospect*, May 7, 1892. A historical marker, erected in 1963, stands at the scene of the murder.

14. *San Francisco Call*, May 1, 2, 3, and 4, 1892; *Sacramento Daily Union*, May 5, 1892; *San Andreas (California) Calaveras Prospect and Citizen*, May 19, 1934; *Sacramento Bee*, October 4, 1952; *Lodi (California) News-Sentinel*, January 14, 1963.

15. *San Francisco Chronicle*, February 18, 1893; *Sacramento Daily Union*, February 18, 1893.

16. *San Francisco Examiner*, June 16 and 17, 1893; *San Francisco Call*, June 16 and 17, 1893; *San Francisco Chronicle*, June 16, 1893. A marker, erected in 1929, is at the site of the murder.

17. *San Francisco Examiner,* June 17 and 18, 1893.

18. *San Francisco Examiner,* June 18, 1893; *San Francisco Chronicle,* June 16 and 17, 1893, and September 29, 1893; *San Francisco Call,* June 16, 1893; *Sacramento Daily Record-Union,* October 4, 1893; Secrest, *Perilous Trails, Dangerous Men,* pp. 184–85.

19. *San Francisco Call,* August 3, 1893.

20. For a detailed account of the Evans case, see Boessenecker, *Badge and Buckshot,* pp. 79–83.

21. *San Francisco Examiner,* June 18, 1893; *Chicago Tribune,* June 19, 1893.

13. VIGILANTE VENGEANCE

1. U.S. Census Population Schedules, Cottonwood Township, Yolo County, California, 1860; *Ukiah (California) Dispatch Democrat,* May 19, 1905, and September 23, 1910; *Ukiah (California) Daily Journal,* June 25, 1999.

2. *Ukiah (California) Republican Press,* May 20, 1892.

3. *San Francisco Chronicle,* May 16, 1892; Laika Dajani, *Black Bart: Elusive Highwayman-Poet* (Manhattan, KS: Sunflower University Press, 1997), pp. 45–50.

4. *Ukiah (California) Dispatch Democrat,* December 29, 1882; *Sacramento Daily Record-Union,* September 17, 1886; *San Francisco Chronicle,* May 16, 1892; California, County Marriages, 1850–1952, and California Great Registers, 1880, both at www.familysearch.org; genealogical notes about Buck Montgomery, Wells Fargo Bank History Department; Frank Asbill and Argle Shawley, *The Last of the West* (New York: Carlton Press, 1975), p. 203. On the Mendocino Outlaws, see Boessenecker, *Badge and Buckshot,* pp. 90–100.

5. Dajani, *Black Bart,* pp. 122–25.

6. *Ukiah (California) Dispatch Democrat,* June 21 and 28, 1889; *San Diego Union,* June 21, 1889; *San Rafael (California) Marin Journal,* July 4, 1889; *Ukiah (California) Republican Press,* March 5, 1897; Asbill and Shawley, *The Last of the West,* pp. 195–203; Lynwood Carranco and Estle Beard, *Genocide and Vendetta: The Round Valley Wars of Northern California* (Norman: University of Oklahoma Press, 1981), pp. 200–205. Carranco and Beard give an incorrect reason for the stage holdup. Their purported photo of Jim Neafus (pp. 166) is wrongly identified; this is a San Quentin mug shot of another convict.

7. *Ukiah (California) Daily Journal,* July 25, 1890; *Ukiah (California) Dispatch Democrat,* September 5, 1890, and October 17 and 31, 1890.

8. *Ukiah (California) Dispatch Democrat,* January 9, 1891, May 15, 1891, and May 20, 1892; *San Francisco Chronicle,* May 16, 1892.

9. *Winters (California) Advocate,* November 2, 1878; Harold L. Edwards, "The Struggles of the Ruggles," *Wild West,* August 1995, pp. 60–61; Secrest, *Perilous Trails, Dangerous Men,* pp. 163–64.

10. *Woodland (California) Daily Democrat,* June 20, 1892.

11. Ibid.; Secrest, *Perilous Trails, Dangerous Men,* pp. 164–65.

12. *Red Bluff (California) Daily News,* May 12, 1892; Secrest, *Perilous Trails, Dangerous Men,* p. 165.

13. *Sacramento Daily Union,* May 16, 1892; Edwards, "The Struggles of the Ruggles," pp. 58–59.

14. *Sacramento Daily Union,* May 16, 1892; *Ukiah (California) Dispatch Democrat,* May 20, 1892; Edwards, "The Struggles of the Ruggles," p. 59.

15. *Sacramento Daily Union*, May 16, 1892; *Ukiah (California) Dispatch Democrat*, May 20, 1892; Secrest, *Perilous Trails, Dangerous Men*, pp. 167–68.
16. *Sacramento Daily Union*, May 21, 1892; *Woodland (California) Daily Democrat*, June 20, 1892.
17. *Red Bluff (California) Daily News*, June 25, 1892; Secrest, *Perilous Trails, Dangerous Men*, p. 169.
18. *Red Bluff (California) Daily News*, July 9, 1892; *Redding (California) Free Press*, quoted in *Ukiah (California) Dispatch Democrat*, July 29, 1892; *San Francisco Call*, July 25, 1892.
19. *San Francisco Call*, July 25, 1892; *Woodland (California) Daily Democrat*, July 25, 1892, and December 5, 1933.
20. *San Francisco Call*, July 25, 1892; John Boessenecker, "The Ruggles Boys' Death Treasure," *Westerner* 5, no. 3 (May–June 1973), pp. 35–37.
21. Ed Schwartz to Wells Fargo Bank, April 26, 1965, Wells Fargo Bank History Department; *Reno Nevada State Journal*, March 19, 1899, and February 18, 1908; *Ukiah (California) Dispatch Democrat*, May 11, 1894, October 11, 1895, and August 23, 1912; *Ukiah (California) Daily Journal*, January 24, 1896, and February 14, 1944; R. G. Dunn, "Forty-Seven Years at Redding," *Wells Fargo Messenger*, (January 1917), p. 78.

14. DOUBLE-BARRELED DEATH

1. California Death Index, William Nathaniel Hendricks, www.familysearch.org; U.S. Census Population Schedules, Milton, Calaveras County, California, 1880; California Great Registers, Calaveras County, 1871, 1875–1877; *Sacramento Bee*, June 28, 1941.
2. Census Population Schedules, Santa Rita Mountains, Pima, Arizona, 1880; Eugene L. Menefee and Fred A. Dodge, *History of Tulare and Kings Counties, California* (Los Angeles: Historic Record Co., 1913), pp. 622–23; Terry L. Ommen, *Wild Tulare County: Outlaws, Rogues and Rebels* (Charleston, SC: The History Press, 2012), pp. 91–92.
3. *Tucson Weekly Citizen*, June 23, 1883; *Visalia (California) Weekly Delta*, May 24, 1894; *San Francisco Call*, December 11, 1894; *Coconino (Arizona) Weekly Sun*, November 29, 1894; Larry D. Ball, *Ambush at Bloody Run: The Wham Paymaster Robbery of 1889* (Tucson: Arizona Historical Society, 2000), pp. 191–97; R. Michael Wilson, *Encyclopedia of Stagecoach Robbery in Arizona* (Las Vegas, NV: RaMA Press, 2003), pp. 150–51.
4. *Visalia (California) Weekly Delta*, May 24, 1894; *San Francisco Call*, March 21, 1896.
5. *Stockton (California) Daily Mail*, March 8, 10, 1894; John Boessenecker, "John Keener Cashes In," *Old West* 28, no. 2 (Winter 1991): 15–16.
6. *Stockton (California) Daily Mail*, April 17, 1894; Boessenecker, "John Keener Cashes In," pp. 15–16; Wilson, *Stagecoach Robberies in California*, p. 53.
7. Bierer's confession is in the *San Francisco Chronicle*, June 25, 1894. He admitted involvement in the last holdup only.
8. *Stockton (California) Daily Mail*, May 4, 1894; Boessenecker, "John Keener Cashes In," p. 16.
9. *San Francisco Chronicle*, May 8, 1894; *Stockton (California) Daily Mail*, May 8, 1894; Boessenecker, "John Keener Cashes In," pp. 16–17.

10. *San Francisco Chronicle*, May 4 and 20, 1894; *San Francisco Call*, May 20, 1894.

11. *San Francisco Call*, May 20 and 21, 1894; *San Francisco Chronicle*, May 20, 1894; *San Francisco Examiner*, May 20 and 23, 1894; *Visalia (California) Weekly Delta*, May 24, 1894; *Visalia (California) Daily Times*, May 21, 1894; *Stockton (California) Daily Mail*, May 21, 22, 1894; *Sacramento Bee*, June 28, 1941; Boessenecker, "John Keener Cashes In," pp. 17–18.

12. *San Francisco Chronicle*, May 21, 1894; *San Francisco Examiner*, May 21, 1894; *Stockton (California) Daily Mail*, May 31, 1894; *San Francisco Call*, June 13, 1894.

13. *San Francisco Chronicle*, June 25, 1894; *Stockton (California) Daily Mail*, June 25, 1894.

14. *Tucson Citizen*, January 31, 1906; Leland Edwards, "The Story of John Keener and William Dowdle," *Los Tulares: Quarterly Bulletin of the Tulare County Historical Society*, no. 173 (September 1991): 6.

15. Calaveras County Marriage Index, August 18, 1894; *Sacramento Bee*, June 28, 1941.

16. *Stockton (California) Record*, March 15, 1950; *Oakland (California) Tribune*, April 16, 1950; Robert O'Brien, *California Called Them: A Saga of Golden Days and Roaring Camps* (New York: McGraw-Hill, 1951), pp. 64–65.

17. *Fresno (California) Morning Republican*, March 31, 1895; *Los Angeles Herald*, March 28, 1895; *Bakersfield Daily Californian*, March 29, 1895; *San Francisco Chronicle*, March 27 and 31, 1895.

18. *San Francisco Chronicle*, June 29, 1895; *San Francisco Call*, August 1, 1896, and October 8, 1896.

19. Census Population Schedules, Calaveras County, 1900, 1910, 1940; California Death Index, 1940–1997, at www.familysearch.org; *San Andreas Calaveras Californian*, June 27, 1957.

15. "I AIN'T AFRAID OF ANY MAN"

1. *Carson City (Nevada) New Daily Appeal*, October 15, 1872; *Sacramento Daily Union*, October 14 and 15, 1872; *New York Tribune*, reprinted in *San Francisco Bulletin*, February 24, 1882.

2. *New York Sun*, reprinted in *Madison Wisconsin State Journal*, October 24, 1884.

3. Death Certificate of Aaron Y. Ross, at www.familysearch.org; *Ogden (Utah) Standard-Examiner*, April 3, 1922; Noble Warfum, ed., *Utah Since Statehood, Historical and Biographical*, vol. 2 (Chicago: S. J. Clarke Publishing Co., 1919), p. 638. Ross's middle name is also variously spelled Yerx, Yerks, and Yearksey.

4. Ross's account appeared in the *San Francisco Examiner* and was reprinted in the *Cincinnati Enquirer*, August 25, 1888.

5. *Ogden (Utah) Standard-Examiner*, April 3, 1922; *Cincinnati Enquirer*, August 25, 1888.

6. Aaron Y. Ross, memoir, February 23, 1916, pp. 1–2, California State Library, Sacramento, CA.

7. *Cincinnati Enquirer*, August 25, 1888; *Portland Oregon Journal*, September 6, 1914.

8. *San Francisco Chronicle*, September 3, 7, and 11, 1869; *San Francisco Bulletin*, September 6, 10, 14, and 15, 1869; *Helena (Montana) Weekly Herald*, September 9 and 23, 1869; *Boise Idaho Statesman*, September 7, 1869; *Silver City (Idaho) Owyhee Semi-Weekly Tidal Wave*, September 16, 1869.

9. Aaron Y. Ross, memoir, pp. 5–7.

10. Aaron Y. Ross, memoir, p. 5; *Ogden (Utah) Standard-Examiner,* March 26, 1916, and April 3, 1922.

11. Aaron Y. Ross, memoir, pp. 3–4; *Helena (Montana) Daily Herald,* September 16 and 17, 1872; *Pioche (Nevada) Daily Record,* September 25, 1872. On John Featherstone, see *Expressman's Monthly* 2, no. 8 (August 1877): 239. His name is misspelled "Fetherstun" by Montana vigilante writers.

12. *Helena (Montana) Weekly Herald,* January 8, 1874.

13. *Virginia City (Nevada) Territorial Enterprise,* August 26, 1876; *Winnemucca (Nevada) Silver State,* February 7, 1876; *Pioche (Nevada) Weekly Record,* August 18, 1877; "Wells Fargo's Shotgun Era," *Wells Fargo Messenger* 5, no. 6 (February 1917): 94.

14. *Virginia City (Nevada) Territorial Enterprise,* March 17, 1878; *Pioche (Nevada) Weekly Record,* August 27, 1881; *Salt Lake City Herald,* March 17, 1882.

15. *Boise Idaho Statesman,* July 29, 1882; Wilson, *Wells, Fargo & Company's Report of Losses,* pp. 13–14.

16. *Salt Lake City Tribune,* August 5, 1882; Wilson, *Wells, Fargo & Company's Report of Losses,* p. 14.

17. *Pioche (Nevada) Weekly Record,* August 26, 1882; *Boise Idaho Statesman,* August 26, 1882; *White Pine (Nevada) News,* September 2, 1882; *Salt Lake City Herald,* September 10, 1882; Wilson, *Wells, Fargo & Company's Report of Losses,* p. 98.

18. *Roseburg (Oregon) Douglas Independent,* December 30, 1882; *Salt Lake City Herald,* February 18, 1883; *Salt Lake City Tribune,* March 20, 1883.

19. *Roseburg (Oregon) Douglas Independent,* December 30, 1882; *San Francisco Chronicle,* December 21, 1882, and October 14, 1884; *Sacramento Daily Record-Union,* January 22, 1883; *Salt Lake City Tribune,* January 31, 1883. The Swasey Mountains were then known as the Antelope Mountains.

20. *San Francisco Chronicle,* January 23 and 24, 1883; *San Francisco Bulletin,* January 22 and 24, 1883; *Ogden (Utah) Herald,* January 22, 1883; *Salt Lake City Daily Tribune,* January 23, 1883, and March 20, 1883; *Reno (Nevada) Evening Gazette,* January 24, 1883. Most accounts claim that the sum of sixty thousand dollars was in the Wells Fargo safe. That is incorrect.

21. *San Francisco Chronicle,* January 24, 1883; *Salt Lake City Daily Tribune,* January 30 and 31, 1883, February 7, 1883, and March 20, 1883; *San Francisco Bulletin,* January 30, 1883; *Los Angeles Herald,* February 21, 1883; *Salt Lake City Herald,* January 30 and 31, 1883; *Deseret (Utah) News,* April 18, 1883; *Reno (Nevada) Evening Gazette,* March 23, 1883; Walt Mason, "Hold-the-Fort Aaron," *Wells Fargo Messenger* 4, no. 8 (April 1916): 123.

22. *Tonopah (Nevada) Daily Bonanza,* January 19, 1911; *San Francisco Chronicle,* September 20, 1912; *Ogden (Utah) Evening Standard,* September 18, 1912, August 11, 1913, and July 24, 1916; *San Diego Union,* August 16, 1913; *Los Angeles Times,* May 1, 1915; *Salt Lake City Tribune,* January 25, 1918; *Salt Lake City Herald,* May 11, 1919.

23. For Ross's false stories, see Aaron Y. Ross, memoir, pp. 7–8, 18–19, 21–22, 25–26; *Omaha (Nebraska) Herald,* September 8, 1888; *Los Angeles Times,* May 1, 1915; *Ogden (Utah) Standard-Examiner,* April 3, 1922; *New York Times,* July 9, 1922.

24. *Ogden (Utah) Standard-Examiner,* April 3, 1922; *New York Times,* July 9, 1922.

16. TRAIN ROBBERS' NEMESIS

1. *Fresno (California) Morning Republican,* August 11, 1892; *San Francisco Chronicle,* August 10, 1892. Molly Evans's account of this incident appeared in the *San Francisco Examiner,* September 25, 1892.

2. J. C. McCubbin, "Joel Thacker," unpublished ms., July 6, 1927, Florence Thacker collection.

3. *Unionville (Nevada) Humboldt Register,* December 7, 1867, and September 19, 1868.

4. John Boessenecker, "John Thacker, Train Robbers' Nemesis," *Real West* 19, no. 147 (September 1976): 14; Secrest, *Lawmen and Desperadoes,* p. 291.

5. *Silver City (Idaho) Owyhee Daily Avalanche,* May 13, 1876; *The Expressman's Monthly* 1, no. 7 (July 1878): 220–21; Wilson, *Wells, Fargo & Co. Stagecoach and Train Robberies,* pp. 50–51.

6. *Winnemucca (Nevada) Silver State,* May 9, 1881; Boessenecker, *When Law Was in the Holster,* p. 170.

7. U.S. Census Population Schedules, Mantua, Ohio, 1870; "United States Naval Enlistment Rendezvous, 1855–1891," at www.familysearch.org; *Ravenna (Ohio) Democratic Press,* December 19, 1878; *Kansas City Times,* February 16, 1889; *McPherson (Kansas) Republican and Weekly Press,* February 22, 1889.

8. *San Francisco Daily Alta California,* December 6, 1888; *San Francisco Call,* February 15, 1889; *Kansas City Times,* February 26, 1889; *Sacramento Daily Union,* June 1, 1889.

9. *San Francisco Call,* February 15, 1889; *Kansas City Times,* February 26, 1889.

10. *Sacramento Daily Union,* December 25, 26, and 27, 1888; *San Francisco Chronicle,* December 26, 1888; *San Francisco Daily Alta California,* December 26, 1888; *San Francisco Call,* June 3, 1889.

11. *San Francisco Chronicle,* December 26, 1888; *Kansas City Times,* February 26, 1889.

12. *San Francisco Daily Alta California,* December 26, 1888; *Sacramento Daily Union,* December 27, 1888.

13. *Kansas City Times,* February 16 and 17, 1889; Dillon, *Wells Fargo Detective,* pp. 242–43.

14. *Kansas City Times,* February 26, 1889; *Sacramento Daily Union,* June 1, 1889, July 27 and 31, 1889; Edward Hungerford, *Wells Fargo: Advancing the American Frontier* (New York: Random House, 1949), p. 150.

15. *San Francisco Chronicle,* August 20, 1889.

16. *Fresno (California) Morning Republican,* September 9, 1897; *San Francisco Chronicle,* September 9 and 10, 1897; Boessenecker, *Badge and Buckshot,* pp. 123–25.

17. *San Francisco Chronicle;* September 10, 13, and 16, 1897, and October 23, 1897; *San Francisco Call,* December 31, 1897; Boessenecker, *Badge and Buckshot,* pp. 125–28.

18. Andrew Christeson to J. N. Thacker, October 10, 1907, Wells Fargo Bank History Department.

19. *San Francisco Call,* January 4, 1913; *Oakland (California) Tribune,* January 5, 1913.

20. Undated newspaper clipping, Wells Fargo Bank History Department.

17. "DIE, DAMN YOU"

1. U.S. Census Population Schedules, Texarkana, Texas, 1880; *Dallas Morning News,* October 20, 1887; *El Paso Times,* November 27, 1887; *Georgetown (Texas)*

Williamson County Sun, November 3, 1887; *Jefferson (Texas) Jimplecute,* May 22, 1913. Santa Anna's cork leg is on display in the Illinois State Military Museum in Springfield. The identification tag on the leg attributes its capture to three other soldiers. On Smith's nickname, see *Waco (Texas) Daily Examiner,* October 21, 1887; *El Paso Herald,* March 14, 1912, and February 14, 1917.

2. For a full account of the train robberies by Kid Smith and Dick Maier, see Jeffrey Burton, *Western Story* (Portsmouth, England: Palomino Books, 2008), and Boessenecker, *When Law Was in the Holster,* pp. 341–49.

3. *Sacramento Daily Union,* October 17, 1887; *El Paso Times,* October 15, 1887; *Fort Worth Daily Gazette,* October 16, 1887; *Galveston Daily News,* October 17, 1887.

4. *Galveston Daily News,* October 19, 1887; *Tucson Weekly Citizen,* October 22, 1887; *Sacramento Daily Union,* November 23, 1887; *San Antonio Daily Light,* November 25, 1887; *San Antonio Daily Express,* November 29, 1887; *El Paso Times,* October 19, 1887, and November 1, 1887; Burton, *Western Story,* p. 187.

5. *El Paso Daily Times,* September 3, 1891; *Galveston Daily News,* September 3, 4, and 5, 1891; *Fort Worth Gazette,* September 4, 1891.

6. *San Antonio Daily Light,* September 4, 1891; *Galveston Daily News,* September 5, 1891; *Fort Worth Gazette,* September 4 and 7, 1891; *El Paso Daily Times,* September 5 and 9, 1891, and March 4, 1900; *New York Times,* September 6, 1891.

7. *El Paso Daily Times,* October 23 and 24, 1891, and April 21, 22, 23, 28, and 29, 1892; Bob Alexander, *Winchester Warriors: Texas Rangers of Company D, 1874–1901* (Denton: University of North Texas Press, 2009), pp. 245–48.

8. *Official Register of the United States* (Washington, D.C.: Government Printing Office, 1901), p. 692; *Official Register of the United States* (Washington, D.C.: Government Printing Office, 1905), p. 545; *San Antonio Express,* March 13, 1907, April 10, 1915, and April 16, 1935; *Abilene (Texas) Daily Reporter,* March 18, 1912; *San Antonio Daily Light,* April 16, 1935.

18. SHOTGUNS AND DYNAMITE

1. U.S. Census Population Schedules, San Francisco, CA, 1870 and 1880; *Marysville (California) Daily Herald,* December 16, 1856; *Sacramento Daily Union,* January 2, 1865; *San Francisco Call,* March 5, 1893, and February 4 and 6, 1907; *Portland Oregonian,* October 28, 1901; *Langley's San Francisco Directory* (San Francisco: George B. Wilber Publisher, 1891), p. 354; Fannie Asa Charles, *Siftings from Poverty Flat* (San Francisco: Californian Publishing Co., 1893), pp. 28–29.

2. *Los Angeles Herald,* September 5, 1891; *San Francisco Call,* September 4 and 5, 1891; *San Francisco Chronicle,* September 4, 1891; *Sacramento Daily Union,* September 5, 1891; *Portland Oregonian,* October 28, 1901.

3. U.S. Census Population Schedules, Portland, OR, 1900; *San Francisco Call,* September 5, 1891, April 6, 1899, and October 24, 1901.

4. *Portland Oregonian,* October 24 and 25, 1901; *San Francisco Call,* October 24, 1901. Engineer Lucas reported that he saw only one robber. However, Messenger Charles and the brakeman were certain there were two. Lawmen later found two masks and the tracks of two men at the scene.

5. *Roseburg (Oregon) Plaindealer,* October 31, 1901; *San Francisco Call,* November 30,

1901; *Salem (Oregon) Daily Journal,* December 3, 1901; "Some Wells Fargo Celebrations," *Wells Fargo Messenger* 4, no. 6 (February 1916): 84–85.

6. *Woodland (California) Daily Democrat,* February 4, 1907; *San Francisco Call,* February 4, 1907.

19. "SEND A COFFIN AND A DOCTOR"

1. J. Evetts Haley, *Jeff Milton: A Good Man with a Gun* (Norman: University of Oklahoma Press, 1948), pp. 244–46; Robert K. DeArment, *George Scarborough: The Life and Death of a Lawman on the Closing Frontier* (Norman: University of Oklahoma Press, 1992), pp. 123–24.

2. For details of Milton's career, see the standard biography, Haley, *Jeff Milton.*

3. Ibid., pp. 252–53.

4. Ibid., pp. 253–54.

5. Karen Holliday Tanner and John D. Tanner, Jr., *Last of the Old-Time Outlaws: The George West Musgrave Story* (Norman: University of Oklahoma Press, 2002), pp. 49–50.

6. *San Francisco Call,* November 22, 1897.

7. Tanner and Tanner, *Last of the Old-Time Outlaws,* pp. 138–43.

8. *Nogales (Arizona) Border Vidette,* December 11, 1897, and January 20, 1898; Haley, *Jeff Milton,* pp. 280–81; Jeff Burton, *The Deadliest Outlaws: The Ketchum Gang and the Wild Bunch* (Denton: University of North Texas Press, 2009), pp. 110–12, 395 n.1.

9. *Tucson Daily Star,* December 15, 1897; *Albuquerque Daily Citizen,* January 11, 1898; *Nogales (Arizona) Oasis,* January 8, 1898; *Nogales (Arizona) Border Vidette,* January 13, 1898; Haley, *Jeff Milton,* pp. 283–85; Burton, *The Deadliest Outlaws,* pp. 112–15; DeArment, *George Scarborough,* pp. 176–83.

10. Haley, *Jeff Milton,* p. 286. On the arrest of Vinnedge, see the *Tucson Citizen,* January 29, 1898, reprinted in the *Nogales (Arizona) Oasis,* February 5, 1898. Jeff Burton's lengthy discussion of Vinnedge's capture (*The Deadliest Outlaws,* pp. 118, 397 n.36) is wholly incorrect. Unaware of the report in the *Citizen,* he places the date of the arrest in mid-February and concludes, erroneously, that George Scarborough was not present and that Milton gave a false account of the capture to his biographer, J. Evetts Haley.

11. For arguments that Alverson, Hovey, and Warderman were innocent, see Burton, *The Deadliest Outlaws,* pp. 119–32.

12. *Globe (Arizona) Arizona Silver Belt,* April 14, 1898; *Solomonville (Arizona) Bulletin,* August 12, 1898; *Topeka (Kansas) State Journal,* August 11, 1898; Karen Holliday Tanner and John D. Tanner, Jr., *The Bronco Bill Gang* (Norman: University of Oklahoma Press, 2011), pp. 12–22, 81–90.

13. *Phoenix Arizona Republican,* August 4, 1898; *San Francisco Chronicle,* August 7, 1898; *Lordsburg (New Mexico) Western Liberal,* August 5, 1898; *Albuquerque Daily Citizen,* August 6, 1898; Tanner and Tanner, *The Bronco Bill Gang,* pp. 96–111, 118–25.

14. *Albuquerque Daily Citizen,* August 6, 1898; Michael Williams, "Real Men of Arizona," *Pearson's Magazine* 28, no. 3 (September 1912): 121. George Scarborough told a newspaper reporter, "We were undertaking this job on our own hook. We were not in the employ of Wells Fargo or anyone else." *Solomonville (Arizona) Arizona Bulletin,* August 12, 1898; John Boessenecker, ed., "I Shot Bronco Bill," *Real*

West, February 1986, pp. 25–26. Jeff Milton agreed, telling his biographer that he took a leave from Wells Fargo. Haley, *Jeff Milton,* p. 294. However, in two much earlier biographical sketches, Milton told journalists that Wells Fargo detailed him to go after the gang. See Williams, "Real Men of Arizona," p. 120, and *Tombstone (Arizona) Epitaph,* August 26, 1917. The contemporary newspaper accounts cited in note 12 confirm that John Thacker organized the posse and hired its members. Scarborough may have believed that he would not be eligible for the Wells Fargo rewards if he admitted to being on the company payroll. See *Phoenix Weekly Herald,* April 14, 1898.

15. *Solomonville (Arizona) Bulletin,* August 12, 1898; *Albuquerque Daily Citizen,* August 6, 1898; *St. Johns (Arizona) Herald,* August 13, 1898; *Nogales (Arizona) Border Vidette,* August 11, 1898; Williams, "Real Men of Arizona," pp. 122–23; Boessenecker, ed., "I Shot Bronco Bill," pp. 26–27; Tanner and Tanner, *The Bronco Bill Gang,* pp. 127–35. According to J. Evetts Haley, Milton's message to Fort Apache was "Send a coffin and a doctor." In 1917, Milton told a newspaperman that the message read "Send a doctor and one coffin." See Haley, *Jeff Milton,* p. 299, and *Tombstone (Arizona) Epitaph,* August 26, 1917.

16. *Tombstone (Arizona) Daily Epitaph,* February 18 and 25, 1900; *Phoenix Arizona Republican,* October 18, 1900; *Bisbee (Arizona) Daily Review,* July 15, 1903; Williams, "Real Men of Arizona," pp. 123–24; Haley, *Jeff Milton,* pp. 302–307; Don Chaput, *The Odyssey of Burt Alvord: Lawman, Train Robber, Fugitive* (Tucson: Westernlore Press, 2000), pp. 70–77. The railroad route from Nogales to Fairbank has long been abandoned.

17. *Nogales (Arizona) Oasis,* March 3, 1900, May 12, 1900, and June 30, 1900; *Nogales (Arizona) Border Vidette,* October 6, 1900; *Flagstaff (Arizona) Coconino Sun,* February 9, 1901; *Los Angeles Herald,* April 23, 1901.

18. *Phoenix Arizona Republican,* September 25, 1903; Haley, *Jeff Milton,* p. 415.

20. FIGHTING WAGES

1. *Columbia (Tennessee) Daily Herald,* March 29, 1912.

2. G. A. Taft to Burns D. Caldwell, March 13, 1912, Robert G. McCubbin collection; D. A. Trousdale to Mr. Hastings, December 12, 1949, Arthur Soule collection; *San Antonio Express,* March 15, 1912, and August 5, 1945; *Columbia (Tennessee) Daily Herald,* March 29, 1912; Arthur Soule, "The Brave Wells Fargo Man," *Quarterly of the National Association for Outlaw and Lawman History* 29, no. 3 (July–September 2005): 21.

3. Arthur Soule, *The Tall Texan: The Story of Ben Kilpatrick* (Deer Lodge, MT: Trail Dust Publishing, 1995), pp. 1–10; Burton, *The Deadliest Outlaws,* pp. 53–54, 135, 138.

4. Burton, *The Deadliest Outlaws,* pp. 248, 274–75, 285–88; Mark T. Smokov, *He Rode with Butch and Sundance: The Story of Harvey "Kid Curry" Logan* (Denton: University of North Texas Press, 2012), pp. 152–53, 168–70, 176–82.

5. Smokov, *He Rode with Butch and Sundance,* pp. 183–94.

6. Ibid., pp. 218–22.

7. *Abilene (Texas) Daily Reporter,* March 17, 1912; Soule, *The Tall Texan,* pp. 114, 119–21, 128, 143.

8. *Kansas City Star,* November 1, 1911; *Little Rock (Arkansas) Gazette,* February 7,

1912; Soule, *The Tall Texan*, pp. 157–60. Jim Wedding, a local chicken raiser, was charged with the first train robbery. The main witness against him at trial was sixty-nine-year-old Kit Dalton, who claimed that Wedding had asked him to participate in the holdup. Dalton, who lived in Memphis, achieved notoriety by claiming that he rode with Quantrill's guerrillas in the Civil War and had been a member of the Jesse James gang for seventeen years. He even wrote a popular book about his alleged exploits, *Under the Black Flag* (1914). At the time, his stories were widely believed, but modern historians have proved that Dalton was a fraud. Fortunately for Jim Wedding, he established a solid alibi and the trial judge ordered the jury to acquit him. See *Jonesboro (Arkansas) Evening Sun*, November 14, 1912; *Jonesboro (Arkansas) Daily Tribune*, November 14 and 15, 1912.

9. W. C. Rutherford to Wells Fargo superintendent C. N. Campbell, March 16, 1912, Robert G. McCubbin collection; Soule, *The Tall Texan*, pp. 162–63.

10. W. T. Bledsoe to C. N. Campbell, March 15, 1912, Robert G. McCubbin collection; *San Antonio Express*, March 16, 1912; Soule, *The Tall Texan*, pp. 163–64.

11. Burton, *The Deadliest Outlaws*, pp. 331–32. In 1945, the tracks were moved and Baxter's Curve was eliminated. *El Paso Herald Post*, November 10, 1945.

12. Conductor Henry Erkel to T. Fay, March 13, 1912; David A. Trousdale to C. N. Campbell, March 15, 1912; G. K. Reagan to C. N. Campbell, March 15, 1912; and Fred J. Dodge to G. A. Taft, March 19, 1912, all in Robert G. McCubbin collection; *San Antonio Express*, March 15, 1912; *San Antonio Light*, March 14, 1912; *San Francisco Chronicle*, March 14, 1912.

13. *Houston Chronicle*, March 15, 1912; *Abilene (Texas) Daily Reporter*, March 15, 1912.

14. *San Antonio Express*, March 16, 17, and 21, 1912; *San Antonio Light*, March 17, 1912.

15. *Houston Chronicle*, April 25, 1912, and February 27, 1914; *Temple (Texas) Daily Telegram*, March 15, 1914; *Fort Worth Star-Telegram*, April 19, 1912.

16. *San Antonio Express*, August 5, 1945; *Columbia (Tennessee) Daily Herald*, August 13, 1953; *Nashville Daily Tennessean*, August 15, 1953; Soule, "The Brave Wells Fargo Man," pp. 23–24.

INDEX